IPSWICH TOWN

IPSWICH TOWN

Peter Waring

breedon **books**
PUBLISHING

First published in Great Britain in 2005 by
The Breedon Books Publishing Company Limited
Breedon House, 3 The Parker Centre, Derby, DE21 4SZ.

ISBN 1 85983 461 2

Printed and bound by Biddles Ltd, Kings Lynn, Norfolk

Introduction

This book contains the results of all matches played by Ipswich to the end of the 2004-05 season in the following competitions:

Premiership and Football League

FA Cup

League Cup

Football League play-offs and test matches

European Cup, Cup-Winners' Cup and UEFA Cup

Some clubs have changed their name over the course of their history. Where this has happened, the results are nonetheless included under the club's current name, unless there have been no matches since the name change. Some of the more significant name changes are as follows:

Arsenal (known as Royal Arsenal until 1893, then Woolwich Arsenal until 1914)

Birmingham (known as Small Heath until 1905)

Gateshead (known as South Shields until 1930)

Leyton Orient (known as Clapton Orient until 1946, and Orient between 1967 and 1987)

Manchester City (known as Ardwick until 1894)

Manchester United (known as Newton Heath until 1902)

Milton Keynes Dons (known as Wimbledon until 2004)

Notes on cups

FA Cup ties have always been straight knockout affairs, except in 1945-46, when all ties up to and including the quarter-finals were played over two legs. Between 1970 and 1974, the losing semi-finalists participated in third place play-offs. Penalty shoot-outs were introduced in 1991 to replace multiple replays.

League Cup ties have been decided over one leg, with the following exceptions (played over two legs):

First round ties (1975-76 to 2000-01)

Second round ties (1979-80 to 2000-01)

Semi-finals (every season)

The final (1960-61 to 1965-66)

An asterisk after a cup result denotes extra-time was played.

Two final points

The letters appearing after some final league positions denote the following:

P club was promoted

R club was relegated

F club failed to retain league membership for the following season.

In the lists of top scorers against each club, David Johnson (I) refers to the man who played for Ipswich between 1972 and 1976, while David Johnson (II) refers to the man who played for Ipswich between 1997 and 2001.

v. Aldershot

Season	League	Date	Result	Ipswich	Aldershot	Date	Result	Ipswich	Aldershot	Ipswich	Aldershot
			Home					**Away**		*Final Positions*	
1938-39	Division 3S	27 January	Won	7	2	16 April	Lost	1	3	7th	10th
1946-47	Division 3S	27 May	Drew	1	1	3 November	Lost	1	4	6th	20th
1947-48	Division 3S	18 April	Won	2	0	11 January	Won	1	0	4th	19th
1948-49	Division 3S	31 April	Won	4	1	7 April	Lost	0	2	7th	21st
1949-50	Division 3S	12 February	Won	1	0	30 April	Lost	0	5	17th	20th
1950-51	Division 3S	11 March	Won	5	2	22 October	Won	1	0	8th	18th
1951-52	Division 3S	24 April	Lost	2	3	13 April	Drew	1	1	17th	12th
1952-53	Division 3S	2 May	Won	2	1	14 December	Drew	1	1	16th	19th
1953-54	Division 3S	18 October	Won	4	0	7 March	Lost	0	3	1stP	17th
1955-56	Division 3S	5 February	Won	2	1	25 September	Won	3	0	3rd	15th
1956-57	Division 3S	10 February	Won	4	1	30 September	Lost	1	3	1stP	19th

FA Cup										Division	
1948-49	Round 1	5 December	Lost	0	3					Div 3S	Div 3S

Summary	P	W	D	L	F	A
Ipswich's home league record	11	9	1	1	34	12
Ipswich's away league record	11	3	2	6	10	22
Ipswich's cup record	1	0	0	1	0	3
TOTAL	**23**	**12**	**3**	**8**	**44**	**37**

Ipswich's top scorers vs Aldershot
Tom Garneys 4
Jackie Little, Tommy Parker, Jackie Brown, Billy Reed 3

Played for both clubs
James Gaynor	Ipswich 1951-52 to 1952-53	Aldershot 1953-54 to 1957-58
Joe Ball	Ipswich 1951-52 to 1952-53	Aldershot 1954-55 to 1955-56
Terry Shanahan	Ipswich 1970-71	Aldershot 1978-79 to 1979-80
Brian Talbot	Ipswich 1973-74 to 1978-79	Aldershot 1990-91
David Barnes	Ipswich 1982-83 to 1983-84	Aldershot 1987-88 to 1988-89
Mark Stein	Aldershot 1985-86	Ipswich 1997-98

FACT FILE

- The FA Cup tie had originally kicked off seven days earlier, but was abandonded after an hour due to fog with Ipswich 1-0 up.
- Ipswich won nine of their 11 league games at home to Aldershot, including their biggest win of the 1938-39 season (their first season in league football).
- Only once (1952) did Aldershot outdo Ipswich in terms of league positions.

v. Arsenal

Season	League	Date	Result	Ipswich	Arsenal	Date	Result	Ipswich	Arsenal	Ipswich	Arsenal
			Home				**Away**			*Final Positions*	
1961-62	Division 1	20 April	Drew	2	2	23 April	Won	3	0	1st	10th
1962-63	Division 1	30 March	Drew	1	1	24 November	Lost	1	3	17th	7th
1963-64	Division 1	18 February	Lost	1	2	5 October	Lost	0	6	22ndR	8th
1968-69	Division 1	24 August	Lost	1	2	18 February	Won	2	0	12th	4th
1969-70	Division 1	31 March	Won	2	1	25 October	Drew	0	0	18th	12th
1970-71	Division 1	21 November	Lost	0	1	20 February	Lost	2	3	19th	1st
1971-72	Division 1	19 February	Lost	0	1	30 October	Lost	1	2	13th	5th
1972-73	Division 1	10 March	Lost	1	2	14 October	Lost	0	1	4th	2nd
1973-74	Division 1	16 March	Drew	2	2	20 October	Drew	1	1	4th	10th
1974-75	Division 1	27 August	Won	3	0	20 August	Won	1	0	3rd	16th
1975-76	Division 1	26 December	Won	2	0	17 April	Won	2	1	6th	17th
1976-77	Division 1	25 September	Won	3	1	5 March	Won	4	1	3rd	8th
1977-78	Division 1	20 August	Won	1	0	2 January	Lost	0	1	18th	5th
1978-79	Division 1	17 March	Won	2	0	4 November	Lost	1	4	6th	7th
1979-80	Division 1	9 October	Lost	1	2	21 August	Won	2	0	3rd	4th
1980-81	Division 1	18 April	Lost	0	2	27 December	Drew	1	1	2nd	3rd
1981-82	Division 1	24 October	Won	2	1	13 March	Lost	0	1	2nd	5th
1982-83	Division 1	9 October	Lost	0	1	22 March	Drew	2	2	9th	10th
1983-84	Division 1	12 November	Won	1	0	10 March	Lost	1	4	12th	6th
1984-85	Division 1	15 September	Won	2	1	19 March	Drew	1	1	17th	7th
1985-86	Division 1	11 March	Lost	1	2	19 October	Lost	0	1	20thR	7th
1992-93	Premiership	10 April	Lost	1	2	26 December	Drew	0	0	16th	10th
1993-94	Premiership	5 March	Lost	1	5	11 September	Lost	0	4	19th	4th
1994-95	Premiership	28 December	Lost	0	2	15 April	Lost	1	4	22ndR	12th
2000-01	Premiership	23 September	Drew	1	1	10 February	Lost	0	1	5th	2nd
2001-02	Premiership	1 December	Lost	0	2	21 April	Lost	0	2	18thR	1st

FA Cup

Season		Date	Result	Ipswich	Arsenal		Result	Ipswich	Arsenal	Division	
1977-78	Final	6 May	Wembley				Won	1	0	Div 1	Div 1
1992-93	Q'ter-Final	6 March	Lost	2	4					Prem	Prem

League Cup

Season		Date	Result	Ipswich	Arsenal	Date	Result	Ipswich	Arsenal	Division	
1970-71	Round 2	8 September	Drew	0	0	28 September	Lost	0	4	Div 1	Div 1
2000-01	Round 3					1 November	Won	2	1	Prem	Prem

Summary

	P	W	D	L	F	A
Ipswich's home league record	26	9	4	13	31	36
Ipswich's away league record	26	6	6	14	26	44
Ipswich's cup record	5	2	1	2	5	9
TOTAL	**57**	**17**	**11**	**29**	**62**	**89**

FACT FILE

- On 6 May 1978, the great Ipswich team of that era finally secured a trophy when they beat Arsenal in a very one-sided cup final. On an incredibly energy-sapping pitch, Ipswich dominated the game and hit the woodwork three times, but anxiety grew as they had to wait until the 77th minute before Roger Osborne slotted home a loose ball. He was so exhausted and overcome with emotion that he had to be substituted straight after, but Ipswich held on and the biggest day in the club's history ended happily. Incidentally, those who assume that this was Town's first visit to Wembley might be interested to know that an away match against Ealing in 1928 was played at Wembley as Ealing's own ground was waterlogged. Ipswich won 4-0.
- At one point in the mid-1970s, Ipswich beat Arsenal seven times in succession.
- Ipswich have only won once in the last 15 games with Arsenal. This was in a League Cup tie, when Arsenal rested virtually their entire first team.

Ipswich's top scorers vs Arsenal
John Wark 5
Ray Crawford, Mick Lambert 4
Ted Phillips, Eric Gates, Paul Mariner 3

Played for both clubs

Jimmy Robertson	Arsenal 1968-69 to 1969-70	Ipswich 1969-70 to 1970-72
Brian Talbot	Ipswich 1973-74 to 1978-79	Arsenal 1978-79 to 1984-85
Paul Mariner	Ipswich 1976-77 to 1983-84	Arsenal 1983-84 to 1985-86
Alan Sunderland	Arsenal 1977-78 to 1983-84	Ipswich 1983-84 to 1985-86
Raphael Meade	Arsenal 1981-82 to 1984-85	Ipswich 1989-90
Lee Chapman	Arsenal 1982-83 to 1983-84	Ipswich 1994-95 to 1995-96
Chris Kiwomya	Ipswich 1988-89 to 1994-95	Arsenal 1994-95
Richard Wright	Ipswich 1994-95 to 2000-01	Arsenal 2001-02
Paolo Vernazza	Arsenal 1997-98 to 2000-01	Ipswich 1998-99

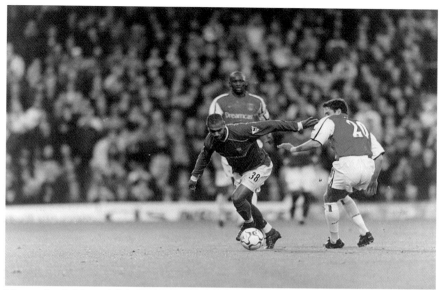

Marcus Bent drives at Edu in the Arsenal defence during the 2-0 defeat in the Premiership game at Portman Road in December 2001. Patrick Vieira is an interested bystander.

The 1978 FA Cup Final at Wembley. Roger Osborne celebrates his goal as Talbot and John Wark prepare to engulf him.

v. Aston Villa

		Home				Away				Final Positions	
Season	League	Date	Result	Ipswich	Blackpool	Date	Result	Ipswich	Blackpool	Ipswich	Blackpool
1959-60	Division 2	23 January	Won	2	1	12 September	Lost	1	3	11th	1stP
1961-62	Division 1	28 April	Won	2	0	9 December	Lost	0	3	1st	7th
1962-63	Division 1	21 May	Drew	1	1	29 September	Lost	2	4	17th	15th
1963-64	Division 1	11 April	Won	4	3	30 November	Drew	0	0	22ndR	19th
1967-68	Division 2	11 November	Won	2	1	6 April	Drew	2	2	1stP	16th
1975-76	Division 1	1 November	Won	3	0	6 March	Drew	0	0	6th	16th
1976-77	Division 1	12 February	Won	1	0	4 September	Lost	2	5	3rd	4th
1977-78	Division 1	3 December	Won	2	0	29 April	Lost	1	6	18th	8th
1978-79	Division 1	9 September	Lost	0	2	2 May	Drew	2	2	6th	8th
1979-80	Division 1	10 November	Drew	0	0	22 March	Drew	1	1	3rd	7th
1980-81	Division 1	6 September	Won	1	0	14 April	Won	2	1	2nd	1st
1981-82	Division 1	20 March	Won	3	1	31 October	Won	1	0	2nd	11th
1982-83	Division 1	2 April	Lost	1	2	29 December	Drew	1	1	9th	6th
1983-84	Division 1	12 May	Won	2	1	17 December	Lost	0	4	12th	10th
1984-85	Division 1	29 September	Won	3	0	2 February	Lost	1	2	17th	10th
1985-86	Division 1	21 September	Lost	0	3	16 April	Lost	0	1	20thR	16th
1987-88	Division 2	15 August	Drew	1	1	16 January	Lost	0	1	8th	2ndP
1992-93	Premiership	15 August	Drew	1	1	6 February	Lost	0	2	16th	2nd
1993-94	Premiership	18 September	Lost	1	2	12 March	Won	1	0	19th	10th
1994-95	Premiership	1 April	Lost	0	1	10 September	Lost	0	2	22ndR	18th
2000-01	Premiership	9 September	Lost	1	2	10 March	Lost	1	2	5th	8th
2001-02	Premiership	23 March	Drew	0	0	17 December	Lost	1	2	18thR	8th

FA Cup

										Division	
1938-39	Round 3	11 January	Lost	1	2	7 January	Drew	1	1	Div 3S	Div 1
1974-75	Round 5	15 February	Won	3	2					Div 1	Div 2
1980-81	Round 3					3 January	Won	1	0	Div 1	Div 1
1995-96	Round 5	17 February	Lost	1	3					Div 1	Prem

League Cup

1961-62	Round 3					21 November	Won	3	2	Div 1	Div 1
1988-89	Round 4					30 November	Lost	2	6	Div 2	Div 1
1992-93	Round 4	15 December	Won	1	0	2 December	Drew	2	2	Prem	Prem

Summary

Summary	P	W	D	L	F	A
Ipswich's home league record	22	11	5	6	31	22
Ipswich's away league record	22	3	6	13	19	44
Ipswich's cup record	9	4	2	3	15	18
TOTAL	**53**	**18**	**13**	**22**	**65**	**84**

FACT FILE

- On 28 April 1962, Ipswich defeated Villa 2-0 at Portman Road, thanks to two goals (on 72 and 76 minutes) by Ray Crawford. On the same day, second-place Burnley were held to a draw by Chelsea, and Ipswich Town were champions of England. Their achievement of winning the Second and First Divisions in successive seasons has not been matched since. They had picked up just one point from their first few games, and for almost all observers this merely confirmed their status as relegation certainties. After all, they had been in Division Three South just five years earlier. Now Alf Ramsey's men had won the ultimate prize in English football. Their record as being the only team to win the First Division in their first ever season there will surely never be matched.
- Villa inflicted upon Ipswich their heaviest ever League Cup defeat, 6-2, in 1988.
- Ipswich beat Villa three times in the 1980-81 season, yet Villa nonetheless pipped Ipswich to the league title.
- Ipswich have lost six and drawn one of their last seven meetings with Villa.
- From 1960 to 1977, Villa lost eight and drew one on their nine trips to Suffolk.

Ipswich's top scorers vs Aston Villa
Ray Crawford 7
Eric Gates 5
John Wark 4
Trevor Whymark, Bryan Hamilton, Russell Osman, Chris Kiwomya 3

Played for both clubs

Jimmy McLuckie	Villa 1934-35 to 1935-36	Ipswich 1938-39 to 1939-40
Jackie Williams	Villa 1935-36	Ipswich 1938-39
Jock Mulraney	Ipswich 1938-39 to 1939-40	Villa 1948-49
John Deehan	Villa 1975-76 to 1979-80	Ipswich 1986-87 to 1987-88
David Geddis	Ipswich 1976-77 to 1978-79	Villa 1979-80 to 1982-83
Dalian Atkinson	Ipswich 1985-86 to 1988-89	Villa 1991-92 to 1994-95

James Scowcroft challenges Aston Villa's David James for the ball as Dion Dublin and Ugo Ehiogu look on.

v. Barnsley

Season	League	Date	Home Result	Ipswich	Barnsley	Date	Away Result	Ipswich	Barnsley	Final Positions Ipswich	Barnsley
1957-58	Division 2	28 August	Won	3	0	4 September	Lost	1	5	8th	14th
1958-59	Division 2	14 March	Won	3	1	25 October	Lost	0	3	16th	22ndR
1986-87	Division 2	22 November	Won	1	0	25 April	Lost	1	2	5th	11th
1987-88	Division 2	3 October	Won	1	0	27 February	Won	3	2	8th	14th
1988-89	Division 2	21 February	Won	2	0	22 October	Lost	0	2	8th	7th
1989-90	Division 2	19 August	Won	3	1	2 December	Won	1	0	9th	19th
1990-91	Division 2	25 April	Won	2	0	2 October	Lost	1	5	14th	8th
1991-92	Division 2	31 March	Won	2	0	14 September	Lost	0	1	1stP	16th
1995-96	Division 1	23 December	Drew	2	2	9 March	Drew	3	3	7th	10th
1996-97	Division 1	1 October	Drew	1	1	18 January	Won	2	1	4th	2ndP
1998-99	Division 1	12 December	Lost	0	2	14 November	Won	1	0	3rd	13th
1999-00	Division 1	30 August	Won	6	1	5 February	Won	2	0	3rdP	4th

Division One play-offs

| 1999-00 | Final | 29 May | Wembley | | | | Won | 4 | 2 | 3rdP | 4th |

FA Cup

| | | | | | | | | | | Division | |
| 1989-90 | Round 4 | | | | | 27 January | Lost | 0 | 2 | Div 2 | Div 2 |

League Cup

| 1960-61 | Round 1 | 11 October | Lost | 0 | 2 | | | | | Div 2 | Div 3 |

Richard Wright's eventful game at Wembley in the 2000 play-off final ultimately ended in triumph for Ipswich. Wright's career seemed to promise so much, especially when he won a full England cap and signed for Arsenal, but the move turned sour when he failed to hold down the No.1 spot at Highbury, making only 12 Premiership appearances. A transfer to Everton seemed to rekindle his career, but an injury let in Nigel Martyn, who has kept Wright on the sidelines ever since.

FACT FILE

- Ipswich's long-awaited return to Premiership football arrived at Wembley in 2000 in a marvellous game. It started badly as Richard Wright scored an own goal, but Ipswich then scored twice. Wright's afternoon got worse as he conceded a penalty, but he then made amends by saving it, and in the end Ipswich held on comfortably and Martijn Reuser's late goal sealed the victory. It brought the goals aggregate between the sides that season to 12-3 in Ipswich's favour.
- Barnsley provided the opposition in Ipswich's first tie in the new League Cup competition.
- In March 1996, Ipswich trailed Barnsley 3-0 at Oakwell with just five minutes left, yet recovered to claim a draw.
- Ipswich won their first eight home league games against the Yorkshiremen.

Summary	P	W	D	L	F	A
Ipswich's home league record	12	9	2	1	26	8
Ipswich's away league record	12	5	1	6	15	24
Ipswich's cup record	3	1	0	2	4	6
TOTAL	**27**	**15**	**3**	**9**	**45**	**38**

Ipswich's top scorers vs Barnsley

Chris Kiwomya, Ian Marshall, David Johnson (II) 3

Ray Crawford, Tony Humes, Dalian Atkinson, David Lowe, Simon Milton, Alex Mathie, James Scowcroft, Richard Naylor, Marcus Stewart 2

Played for both clubs

Billy Houghton	Barnsley 1957-58 to 1963-64	Ipswich 1966-67 to 1968-69
Ron Wigg	Ipswich 1967-68 to 1969-70	Barnsley 1976-77 to 1977-78
David Johnson	Ipswich 1972-73 to 1975-76	Barnsley 1983-84
David Geddis	Ipswich 1976-77 to 1978-79	Barnsley 1983-84 to 1984-85
Clive Baker	Barnsley 1984-85 to 1990-91	Ipswich 1992-93 to 1994-95
John Deehan	Ipswich 1986-87 to 1987-88	Barnsley 1990-91
Neil Thompson	Ipswich 1989-90 to 1995-96	Barnsley 1996-97 to 1997-98
Tony Vaughan	Ipswich 1994-95 to 1996-97	Barnsley 2004-05
Richard Naylor	Ipswich 1996-97 to 2004-05	Barnsley 2001-02

v. Birmingham City

Season	League	Date	Result	Ipswich	Birmingham	Date	Result	Ipswich	Birmingham	Ipswich	Birmingham
		Home					**Away**			**Final Positions**	
1954-55	Division 2	15 September	Lost	1	2	8 September	Lost	0	4	21stR	1stP
1961-62	Division 1	9 September	Won	4	1	20 January	Lost	1	3	1st	17th
1962-63	Division 1	17 November	Lost	1	5	6 April	Won	1	0	17th	20th
1963-64	Division 1	1 February	Won	3	2	21 September	Lost	0	1	22ndR	20th
1965-66	Division 2	26 March	Lost	0	1	3 May	Lost	1	4	15th	10th
1966-67	Division 2	8 October	Won	3	2	25 February	Drew	2	2	5th	10th
1967-68	Division 2	6 January	Won	2	1	2 September	Drew	0	0	1stP	4th
1972-73	Division 1	19 August	Won	2	0	30 December	Won	2	1	4th	10th
1973-74	Division 1	22 December	Won	3	0	29 September	Won	3	0	4th	19th
1974-75	Division 1	1 April	Won	3	2	28 December	Won	1	0	3rd	17th
1975-76	Division 1	30 August	Won	4	2	13 April	Lost	0	3	6th	19th
1976-77	Division 1	11 April	Won	1	0	7 December	Won	4	2	3rd	13th
1977-78	Division 1	15 October	Won	5	2	11 April	Drew	0	0	18th	11th
1978-79	Division 1	17 April	Won	3	0	3 April	Drew	1	1	6th	21stR
1980-81	Division 1	13 January	Won	5	1	20 December	Won	3	1	2nd	13th
1981-82	Division 1	5 January	Won	3	2	1 September	Drew	1	1	2nd	16th
1982-83	Division 1	5 March	Won	3	1	23 October	Drew	0	0	9th	17th
1983-84	Division 1	21 January	Lost	1	2	17 September	Lost	0	1	12th	20thR
1985-86	Division 1	14 September	Lost	0	1	11 January	Won	1	0	20thR	21stR
1986-87	Division 2	21 February	Won	3	0	27 September	Drew	2	2	5th	19th
1987-88	Division 2	2 May	Won	1	0	28 November	Lost	0	1	8th	19th
1988-89	Division 2	29 April	Won	4	0	26 November	Lost	0	1	8th	23rdR
1995-96	Division 1	20 January	Won	2	0	12 August	Lost	1	3	7th	15th
1996-97	Division 1	4 May	Drew	1	1	15 October	Lost	0	1	4th	10th
1997-98	Division 1	26 December	Lost	0	1	28 October	Drew	1	1	5th	7th
1998-99	Division 1	5 December	Won	1	0	2 May	Lost	0	1	3rd	4th
1999-00	Division 1	18 September	Lost	0	1	27 February	Drew	1	1	3rdP	5th

FA Cup *Division*

Season	League	Date	Result	Ipswich	Birmingham	Date	Result	Ipswich	Birmingham	Division	
1953-54	Round 4	30 January	Won	1	0					Div 3S	Div 2
1971-72	Round 4					5 February	Lost	0	1	Div 1	Div 2
1981-82	Round 3					2 January	Won	3	2	Div 1	Div 1
1986-87	Round 3	10 January	Lost	0	1					Div 2	Div 2

League Cup

Season	League	Date	Result	Ipswich	Birmingham	Date	Result	Ipswich	Birmingham	Division	
1966-67	Round 3					4 October	Lost	1	2	Div 2	Div 2
1973-74	Round 4	21 November	Lost	1	3					Div 1	Div 1
1980-81	Round 4					28 October	Lost	1	2	Div 1	Div 1
2000-01	Semi-Final	9 January	Won	1	0	31 January	Lost*	1	4	Prem	Div 1

Summary	P	W	D	L	F	A
Ipswich's home league record	27	19	1	7	59	30
Ipswich's away league record	27	7	9	11	26	35
Ipswich's cup record	9	3	0	6	9	15
TOTAL	**63**	**29**	**10**	**24**	**94**	**80**

FACT FILE

- Ipswich won 12 successive league games against Birmingham at Portman Road between 1966 and 1983, although Birmingham won their only cup match there in that time.
- Ipswich have not won in their last nine visits to St Andrews. The last of these was a surprising defeat that cost high-flying Ipswich the chance of appearing in their first League Cup final.

Ipswich's top scorers vs Birmingham City
Alan Brazil 8
Ray Crawford, Paul Mariner, John Wark 6
Trevor Whymark 5
Mick Lambert 4

Played for both clubs

Tom Fillingham	Birmingham 1929-30 to 1937-38	Ipswich 1938-39
Jackie Brown	Birmingham 1938-39	Ipswich 1948-49 to 1950-51
Jock Mulraney	Ipswich 1938-39 to 1939-40	Birmingham 1946-47
Willie Havenga	Birmingham 1949-50	Ipswich 1951-52 to 1952-53
Tommy Carroll	Ipswich 1966-67 to 1971-72	Birmingham 1971-72 to 1972-73
Paul Cooper	Birmingham 1971-72 to 1973-74	Ipswich 1973-74 to 1986-87
Keith Bertschin	Ipswich 1975-76 to 1976-77	Birmingham 1977-78 to 1980-81
David Geddis	Ipswich 1976-77 to 1978-79	Birmingham 1984-85 to 1986-87
Ian Atkins	Ipswich 1985-86 to 1987-88	Birmingham 1987-88 to 1991-92
Nigel Gleghorn	Ipswich 1985-86 to 1987-88	Birmingham 1989-90 to 1992-93
Steve Whitton	Birmingham 1985-86 to 1988-89	Ipswich 1990-91 to 1993-94
Louie Donowa	Ipswich 1989-90	Birmingham 1991-92 to 1992-93
Jonathan Hunt	Birmingham 1994-95 to 1996-97	Ipswich 1998-99
Frederick Barber	Ipswich 1995-96	Birmingham 1995-96
Andrew Legg	Birmingham 1995-96 to 1996-97	Ipswich 1997-98
Danny Sonner	Ipswich 1996-97 to 1998-99	Birmingham 2000-01 to 2001-02
Jamie Clapham	Ipswich 1997-98 to 2002-03	Birmingham 2002-03 to 2004-05
Mark Burchill	Ipswich 2000-01	Birmingham 2000-01

Martijn Reuser in action against Birmingham at Portman Road.

v. Bishop Auckland

FA Cup		Home					Away			Division	
	Date	Result	Ipswich	Bishop A	Date	Result	Ipswich	Bishop A	Ipswich	Bishop A
1954-55 Round 3	8 January	Drew	2	2	12 January	Lost	0	3	Div 2	Non L

Summary	P	W	D	L	F	A
Ipswich's cup record	2	0	1	1	2	5
TOTAL	2	0	1	1	2	5

FACT FILE

- The lowest point of a season that ended in relegation came as Ipswich were comprehensively beaten by the non-leaguers from the North-East.

Billy Reed (left) & Tom Garneys (right), seen here in the 1953 line up either side of Jim Feeney, scored the goals in the 2–2 draw at home, but Bishop Auckland capitalised on Ipswich's poor season by trouncing them 3–0 four days later.

v. Blackburn Rovers

Season	League	Date	Result		Home Ipswich Blackburn	Date	Result		Away Ipswich Blackpool	Final Positions Ipswich	Blackburn
1954-55	Division 2	26 February	Drew	1	1	9 October	Lost	1	4	21stR	6th
1957-58	Division 2	21 December	Won	2	1	24 August	Drew	0	0	8th	2ndP
1961-62	Division 1	5 September	Won	2	1	18 September	Drew	2	2	1st	16th
1962-63	Division 1	18 August	Drew	3	3	15 December	Won	1	0	17th	11th
1963-64	Division 1	7 December	Drew	0	0	18 April	Lost	1	3	22ndR	7th
1966-67	Division 2	4 February	Drew	1	1	24 September	Won	2	1	5th	4th
1967-68	Division 2	11 May	Drew	1	1	6 September	Lost	1	2	1stP	8th
1986-87	Division 2	2 May	Won	3	1	29 November	Drew	0	0	5th	12th
1987-88	Division 2	30 January	Lost	0	2	1 September	Lost	0	1	8th	5th
1988-89	Division 2	13 May	Won	2	0	10 December	Lost	0	1	8th	5th
1989-90	Division 2	28 April	Won	3	1	11 November	Drew	2	2	9th	5th
1990-91	Division 2	8 September	Won	2	1	19 January	Won	1	0	14th	19th
1991-92	Division 2	28 December	Won	2	1	31 August	Won	2	1	1stP	6thP
1992-93	Premiership	28 December	Won	2	1	12 April	Lost	1	2	16th	4th
1993-94	Premiership	27 November	Won	1	0	7 May	Drew	0	0	19th	2nd
1994-95	Premiership	19 November	Lost	1	3	28 January	Lost	1	4	22ndR	1st
1999-00	Division 1	7 March	Drew	0	0	6 November	Drew	2	2	3rdP	11th
2001-02	Premiership	16 September	Drew	1	1	13 March	Lost	1	2	18thR	10th

FA Cup

										Division	
1995-96	Round 3	6 January	Drew	0	0	16 January	Won*	1	0	Div 1	Prem

League Cup

1961-62	Round 4					11 December	Lost	1	4	Div 1	Div 1
1983-84	Round 2	5 October	Won	4	3	26 November	Won	2	1	Div 1	Div 2

Summary

	P	W	D	L	F	A
Ipswich's home league record	18	9	7	2	27	19
Ipswich's away league record	18	4	6	8	18	27
Ipswich's cup record	5	3	1	1	8	8
TOTAL	**41**	**16**	**14**	**11**	**53**	**54**

Ipswich's top scorers vs Rovers

John Wark 8
Ray Crawford 5
Ted Phillips 4
Kevin Wilson 3

Ipswich hat-tricks vs Rovers

5 October 1983 John Wark (cup)
2 May 1987 Kevin Wilson

FACT FILE

- The last time Ipswich won an FA Cup tie against a team in a higher division than themselves was in 1996, when they beat champions Blackburn Rovers at Ewood Park. The previous season, Rovers striker Alan Shearer had claimed 'There are no easy games in the Premiership, except perhaps Ipswich at home.' He was slightly quieter after this result.
- A 1-1 draw with Blackburn in May 1968 ensured the Second Division title, and with it promotion back to the First Division. The glory years were now just around the corner.
- Ipswich have not won in their last seven league games against Blackburn.
- Ipswich lost only once in their first 16 home games in the series.

Played for both clubs

George McLuckie	Blackburn 1952-53	Ipswich 1953-54 to 1957-58
Roy Stephenson	Blackburn 1957-58 to 1958-59	Ipswich 1960-61 to 1964-65
Bobby Bell	Ipswich 1968-69 to 1971-72	Blackburn 1971-72
Allan Hunter	Blackburn 1969-70 to 1971-72	Ipswich 1971-72 to 1980-81
Terry Shanahan	Ipswich 1970-71	Blackburn 1971-72
Glenn Keeley	Ipswich 1972-73 to 1973-74	Blackburn 1976-77 to 1986-87
Mark Grew	Ipswich 1984-85	Blackburn 1990-91
Niklas Gudmundsson	Blackburn 1995-96 to 1996-97	Ipswich 1996-97
Gary Croft	Blackburn 1995-96 to 1998-99	Ipswich 1999-00 to 2000-01
Marcus Bent	Blackburn 2000-01 to 2001-02	Ipswich 2001-02 to 2003-04
Alan Mahon	Blackburn 2000-01 to 2003-04	Ipswich 2003-04

Uruguayan Adrian Paz fends off Graeme Le Saux at Portman Road in Ipswich's 3–1 defeat to Blackburn on 19 November 1994. It was a season of contrasts for the two sides as Blackburn ended the season as Premiership champions, while Ipswich were relegated to Division One. Paz was the first Uruguyan international to play in the Premiership when he was signed from Penarol, but his career in English football lasted for just one year before he was transferred to American side Columbus Crew.

v. Blackpool

Season	League	Date	Result	Ipswich	Blackpool	Date	Result	Ipswich	Blackpool	Ipswich	Blackpool
			Home				Away			Final Positions	
1961-62	Division 1	17 March	Drew	1	1	28 October	Drew	1	1	1st	13th
1962-63	Division 1	28 August	Won	5	2	20 August	Lost	0	1	17th	13th
1963-64	Division 1	25 April	Won	4	3	19 October	Drew	2	2	22ndR	18th
1967-68	Division 2	29 August	Drew	1	1	21 August	Drew	0	0	1stP	3rd
1970-71	Division 1	30 January	Won	2	1	28 November	Won	2	0	19th	22ndR

League Cup

1978-79	Round 2					30 August	Lost	0	2	Div 1	Div 3

Summary	P	W	D	L	F	A
Ipswich's home league record	5	3	2	0	13	8
Ipswich's away league record	5	1	3	1	5	4
Ipswich's cup record	1	0	0	1	0	2
TOTAL	**11**	**4**	**5**	**2**	**18**	**14**

FACT FILE

● **Blackpool still await their first win at Portman Road.**

Ipswich's top scorers vs Blackpool
Ray Crawford, Gerry Baker 3
Ted Phillips, Doug Moran 2

Played for both clubs

Frank Yallop	Ipswich 1983-84 to 1995-96	Blackpool 1995-96
David Linighan	Ipswich 1988-89 to 1995-96	Blackpool 1995-96 to 1997-98
Frederick Barber	Blackpool 1990-91 & 1995-96	Ipswich 1995-96
Ian Marshall	Ipswich 1993-94 to 1996-97	Blackpool 2001-02
James Pullen	Blackpool 2001-02	Ipswich 2002-03
Tony Dinning	Blackpool 2003-04	Ipswich 2004-05

There have only been six players to have played for both sides, one of which, James Pullen (pictured) had a spell on loan in the North-West while at Ipswich. Incredibly, all of the six players moved clubs after the teams last met, in the 1978 League Cup match.

v. Bolton Wanderers

Season	League	Date	Result	Home Ipswich	Home Bolton	Date	Result	Away Ipswich	Away Bolton	Final Positions Ipswich	Final Positions Bolton
1961-62	Division 1	16 December	Won	2	1	19 August	Drew	0	0	1st	11th
1962-63	Division 1	17 May	Won	4	1	8 September	Won	3	1	17th	18th
1963-64	Division 1	1 October	Lost	1	3	18 September	Lost	0	6	22ndR	21stR
1964-65	Division 2	19 September	Lost	1	4	23 January	Drew	0	0	5th	3rd
1965-66	Division 2	18 September	Won	2	0	12 March	Lost	1	3	15th	9th
1966-67	Division 2	1 October	Drew	2	2	11 February	Drew	1	1	5th	9th
1967-68	Division 2	9 September	Drew	1	1	9 March	Won	2	1	1stP	12th
1978-79	Division 1	16 December	Won	3	0	21 April	Won	3	2	6th	17th
1979-80	Division 1	26 April	Won	1	0	15 December	Won	1	0	3rd	22ndR
1996-97	Division 1	15 March	Lost	0	1	14 December	Won	2	1	4th	1stP
1998-99	Division 1	21 November	Lost	0	1	17 April	Lost	0	2	3rd	6th
1999-00	Division 1	21 August	Won	1	0	22 January	Drew	1	1	3rdP	6th
2001-02	Premiership	18 November	Lost	1	2	6 April	Lost	1	4	18thR	16th

Division One play-offs

Season	League	Date	Result	Ipswich	Bolton	Date	Result	Ipswich	Bolton	Final Positions Ipswich	Final Positions Bolton
1998-99	Semi-Final	19 May	Won*	4	3	16 May	Lost	0	1	3rd	6th
1999-00	Semi-Final	17 May	Won*	5	3	14 May	Drew	2	2	3rdP	6th

FA Cup

Season	Round	Date	Result							Division	
2004-05	Round 3	8 January	Lost	1	3					Champ	Prem

League Cup

Season	Round	Date	Result			Date	Result			Division	
1994-95	Round 2	21 September	Lost	0	3	5 October	Lost	0	1	Prem	Div 1

Summary

	P	W	D	L	F	A
Ipswich's home league record	13	6	2	5	19	16
Ipswich's away league record	13	5	4	4	15	22
Ipswich's cup record	7	2	1	4	12	16
TOTAL	**33**	**13**	**7**	**13**	**46**	**54**

Jim Magilton cemented his place in Ipswich fans' hearts with a hat-trick against Bolton in their 5–3 win in the 2000 play-off semi-final second leg. Ipswich went on to record their only play-off success in the final when they beat Barnsley 4–2.

FACT FILE

- Town's two successive play-off ties with Bolton provided some of the club's biggest drama of recent years. In 1999, a late first-leg goal proved crucial, as Bolton progressed on away goals. It was Ipswich's third defeat in a row in play-off semi-finals; two of them on away goals.
- The following year, it looked like heartache for a fourth time as Bolton took an early two-goal lead. But two goals from recent signing Marcus Stewart salvaged a draw, and set up the second leg nicely for what was to prove one of the best games of Ipswich's history. Bolton took the lead three times, but three times Jim Magilton equalised – the third equaliser arrived in the 90th minute. Against a team eventually reduced to nine men, extra-time goals from Clapham and Reuser finally got Ipswich to Wembley.
- Unfortunately, the Blues have lost all three games against Bolton since, conceding nine goals in the process.

Ipswich's top scorers vs Bolton Wanderers
Ray Crawford 7
Matt Holland 4
Frank Brogan, Alan Brazil, Jim Magilton 3

Ipswich hat-tricks vs Bolton Wanderers
17 May 2000 Jim Magilton (play-offs)

Played for both clubs

Glenn Keeley	Ipswich 1972-73 to 1973-74	Bolton 1988-89
Keith Branagan	Bolton 1992-93 to 1999-00	Ipswich 2000-01 to 2001-02
Ian Marshall	Ipswich 1993-94 to 1996-97	Bolton 2000-01 to 2001-02

v. AFC Bournemouth

			Home				**Away**			*Final Positions*	
Season	*League*	*Date*	*Result*	Ipswich	Bournemouth	*Date*	*Result*	Ipswich	Bournemouth	Ipswich	Bournemouth
1938-39	Division 3S	7 September	Lost	0	2	6 May	Drew	0	0	7th	15th
1946-47	Division 3S	19 April	Won	2	1	1 January	Drew	1	1	6th	7th
1947-48	Division 3S	6 September	Drew	1	1	17 January	Lost	0	4	4th	2nd
1948-49	Division 3S	26 February	Won	1	0	2 October	Lost	2	4	7th	3rd
1949-50	Division 3S	20 August	Lost	1	2	17 December	Lost	0	4	17th	12th
1950-51	Division 3S	23 September	Won	1	0	3 February	Lost	1	2	8th	9th
1951-52	Division 3S	2 February	Won	3	1	23 February	Drew	2	2	17th	14th
1952-53	Division 3S	17 January	Won	2	1	6 September	Lost	1	2	16th	9th
1953-54	Division 3S	23 September	Won	2	1	30 September	Won	3	2	1stP	19th=
1955-56	Division 3S	8 October	Won	1	0	18 February	Drew	1	1	3rd	9th
1956-57	Division 3S	29 August	Won	1	0	22 August	Lost	0	1	1stP	5th
1987-88	Division 2	19 March	Lost	1	2	31 October	Drew	1	1	8th	17th
1988-89	Division 2	14 March	Won	3	1	29 October	Lost	0	1	8th	12th
1989-90	Division 2	2 September	Drew	1	1	20 January	Lost	1	3	9th	22ndR

FA Cup
Division

1952-53	Round 1	22 November	Drew	2	2	26 November	Drew*	2	2	Div 3S	Div 3S
		1 December	Highbury (2nd replay)				Won	2	0		
1991-92	Round 4	5 February	Won	3	0					Div 2	Div 3

League Cup

1996-97	Round 1	20 August	Won	2	1	3 September	Won	3	0	Div 1	Div 2

Summary

	P	W	D	L	F	A
Ipswich's home league record	14	9	2	3	20	13
Ipswich's away league record	14	1	5	8	13	28
Ipswich's cup record	6	4	2	0	15	7
TOTAL	**34**	**14**	**9**	**11**	**48**	**48**

Ipswich's top scorers vs Bournemouth
Tom Garneys 10
John Elsworthy 5
Tommy Parker, Ted Pole, Thomas Brown, Jason Dozzell, Dalian Atkinson 2

FACT FILE

- The last meeting between the sides, in 1996, produced Ipswich's first away win for 40 years.
- Ipswich and Bournemouth have not played out a 0-0 draw since 1939.

Played for both clubs

Brian Siddall	Bournemouth 1953-54 to 1956-57	Ipswich 1957-58 to 1960-61
Ron Bolton	Bournemouth 1958-59 to 1965-66	Ipswich 1965-66 to 1967-68
	& 1967-68 to 1968-69	
John Compton	Ipswich 1960-61 to 1963-64	Bournemouth 1964-65
David Best	Bournemouth 1960-61 to 1966-67	Ipswich 1968-69 to 1973-74
	& 1975-76	
Charlie Woods	Bournemouth 1962-63 to 1964-65	Ipswich 1966-67 to 1969-70
John O'Rourke	Ipswich 1967-68 to 1969-70	Bournemouth 1973-74 to 1974-75
Alec Bugg	Ipswich 1968-69 to 1969-70	Bournemouth 1969-70
Terry Shanahan	Ipswich 1970-71	Bournemouth 1977-78
Leo Cotterell	Ipswich 1994-95	Bournemouth 1996-97
Matt Holland	Bournemouth 1994-95 to 1996-97	Ipswich 1997-98 to 2002-03
Andy Marshall	Bournemouth 1996-97	Ipswich 2001-02 to 2002-03
Mark Stein	Ipswich 1997-98	Bournemouth 1997-98 to 1999-00

Matt Holland signed from Bournemouth in 1997 and became one of George Burley's best signings. The former captain is pictured in action against his Republic of Ireland teammate, Manchester United's Roy Keane. Ipswich's relegation from the Premiership in 2002 and subsequent failure to return at the first attempt signalled Holland's departure to Charlton in 2003, a great loss to the Suffolk club.

v. Bradford City

Season	League	Date	Result	Ipswich	Bradford	Date	Result	Ipswich	Bradford	Ipswich	Bradford
				Home			**Away**			*Final Positions*	
1986-87	Division 2	14 March	Won	1	0	18 October	Won	4	3	5th	10th
1987-88	Division 2	5 December	Won	4	0	7 May	Won	3	2	8th	4th
1988-89	Division 2	24 September	Drew	1	1	15 April	Drew	2	2	8th	14th
1989-90	Division 2	24 March	Won	1	0	18 October	Lost	0	1	9th	23rdR
1996-97	Division 1	4 March	Won	3	2	16 November	Lost	1	2	4th	21st
1997-98	Division 1	31 January	Won	2	1	23 August	Lost	1	2	5th	13th
1998-99	Division 1	8 September	Won	3	0	13 February	Drew	0	0	3rd	2ndP
2000-01	Premiership	4 March	Won	3	1	21 October	Won	2	0	5th	20thR
2002-03	Division 1	26 August	Lost	1	2	1 February	Lost	0	2	7th	19th
2003-04	Division 1	14 February	Won	3	1	11 October	Won	1	0	5th	23rdR

FA Cup

										Division	
1952-53	Round 2	10 December	Won	5	1	6 December	Drew	1	1	Div 3S	Div 3N
1985-86	Round 3	4 January	Drew	4	4	13 January	Won	1	0	Div 1	Div 2
						(replay at Elland Road)					

League Cup

1981-82	Round 3	10 November	Drew	1	1	2 December	Won*	3	2	Div 1	Div 4

Summary	P	W	D	L	F	A
Ipswich's home league record	10	8	1	1	22	8
Ipswich's away league record	10	4	2	4	14	14
Ipswich's cup record	6	3	3	0	15	9
TOTAL	**26**	**15**	**6**	**5**	**51**	**31**

FACT FILE

- **Ipswich were unbeaten in their first 12 meetings with Bradford.**
- **Ipswich have lost just once in their 13 home matches in the series.**

Ipswich's top scorers vs Bradford City
Nigel Gleghorn 4
John Elsworthy, Mich D'Avray, Romeo Zondervan 3

Ipswich hat-tricks vs Bradford City
18 October 1986 Nigel Gleghorn

Played for both clubs

Frank Shufflebottom	Ipswich 1938-39	Bradford 1946-47 to 1947-48
Pat Curran	Ipswich 1938-39	Bradford 1947-48
Jack Connor	Ipswich 1946-47	Bradford 1950-51 to 1951-52
Kevin Wilson	Ipswich 1984-85 to 1986-87	Bradford 1993-94
Neil Woods	Ipswich 1987-88 to 1989-90	Bradford 1989-90
Mark Stuart	Ipswich 1989-90	Bradford 1990-91 to 1991-92
Eddie Youds	Ipswich 1991-92 to 1994-95	Bradford 1994-95 to 1997-98
Andrew Petterson	Ipswich 1992-93 & 1995-96	Bradford 1994-95
Gus Uhlenbeek	Ipswich 1995-96 to 1997-98	Bradford 2002-03
Alun Armstrong	Ipswich 2000-01 to 2003-04	Bradford 2003-04

Liverpool-born defender Eddie Youds moved from Ipswich to Bradford City in 1994-95.

v. Brentford

				Home				Away		Final Positions	
Season	League	Date	Result	Ipswich	Brentford	Date	Result	Ipswich	Brentford	Ipswich	Brentford
1955-56	Division 3S	24 March	Drew	1	1	12 November	Lost	2	3	3rd	6th
1956-57	Division 3S	22 September	Won	4	0	2 February	Drew	1	1	1stP	8th

League Cup

1966-67	Round 2					13 September	Won	4	2	Div 2	Div 4
1999-00	Round 1	24 August	Won	2	0	11 August	Won	2	0	Div 1	Div 2
2004-05	Round 1	24 August	Won	2	0					Champ	Lg 1

Summary	P	W	D	L	F	A
Ipswich's home league record	2	1	1	0	5	1
Ipswich's away league record	2	0	1	1	3	4
Ipswich's cup record	4	4	0	0	10	2
TOTAL	8	5	2	1	18	7

FACT FILE

- **Brentford have not beaten Ipswich since the sides' very first match, in 1955.**

Ipswich's top scorers vs Brentford
Wilf Grant, Jamie Clapham 2

Played for both clubs

Charlie Fletcher	Brentford 1933-34 to 1935-36	Ipswich 1938-39 to 1939-40
George Smith	Brentford 1946-47	Ipswich 1949-50
Tom Garneys	Brentford 1949-50 to 1950-51	Ipswich 1951-52 to 1958-59
Jim Belcher	Ipswich 1958-59 to 1959-60	Brentford 1961-62
Gerard Baker	Ipswich 1963-64 to 1967-68	Brentford 1969-70
David Geddis	Ipswich 1976-77 to 1978-79	Brentford 1986-87
Nigel Gleghorn	Ipswich 1985-86 to 1987-88	Brentford 1997-98
John Moncur	Brentford 1989-90	Ipswich 1991-92
Keith Branagan	Brentford 1989-90	Ipswich 2000-01 to 2001-02
Marcus Bent	Brentford 1995-96 to 1997-98	Ipswich 2001-02 to 2003-04
Hermann Hreidarsson	Brentford 1998-99 to 1999-00	Ipswich 2000-01 to 2002-03

Brentford have proved a fruitful breeding ground for Ipswich in recent years, with both Marcus Bent and Hermann Hreidarsson (pictured against Chelsea's Gianfranco Zola) playing for the Bees before furthering their career at Portman Road.

v. Brighton & Hove Albion

Season	League	Date	Result			Date	Result			Final Positions	
				Ipswich	Brighton			Ipswich	Brighton	Ipswich	Brighton
1938-39	Division 3S	11 February	Drew	0	0	8 October	Lost	0	2	7th	3rd
1946-47	Division 3S	9 November	Lost	1	2	15 March	Drew	0	0	6th	17th
1947-48	Division 3S	11 October	Won	4	0	24 January	Lost	1	4	4th	22nd
1948-49	Division 3S	12 February	Drew	2	2	7 May	Lost	1	6	7th	6th
1949-50	Division 3S	25 March	Drew	2	2	5 November	Lost	1	2	17th	8th
1950-51	Division 3S	10 February	Won	3	0	14 April	Lost	0	4	8th	13th
1951-52	Division 3S	5 September	Won	5	0	12 September	Lost	1	5	17th	5th
1952-53	Division 3S	27 September	Won	1	0	14 February	Won	4	1	16th	7th
1953-54	Division 3S	13 February	Lost	2	3	26 September	Won	2	1	1stP	2nd
1955-56	Division 3S	25 April	Won	2	1	28 September	Lost	0	3	3rd	2nd
1956-57	Division 3S	29 December	Won	4	0	1 September	Lost	2	3	1stP	6th
1958-59	Division 2	15 November	Won	5	3	4 April	Lost	1	4	16th	12th
1959-60	Division 2	26 December	Won	3	0	28 December	Won	4	1	11th	14th
1960-61	Division 2	13 September	Won	4	0	7 September	Won	4	2	1stP	16th
1979-80	Division 1	1 February	Drew	1	1	15 September	Lost	0	2	3rd	16th
1980-81	Division 1	19 August	Won	2	0	11 November	Lost	0	1	2nd	19th
1981-82	Division 1	30 March	Won	3	1	8 May	Won	1	0	2nd	13th
1982-83	Division 1	15 January	Won	2	0	28 August	Drew	1	1	9th	22ndR
1986-87	Division 2	11 October	Won	1	0	21 March	Won	2	1	5th	22ndR
1988-89	Division 2	19 November	Lost	2	3	6 May	Won	1	0	8th	19th
1989-90	Division 2	10 March	Won	2	1	27 September	Lost	0	1	9th	18th
1990-91	Division 2	3 November	Lost	1	3	11 May	Lost	1	2	14th	6th
1991-92	Division 2	1 May	Won	3	1	12 October	Drew	2	2	1stP	23rdR
2002-03	Division 1	22 March	Drew	2	2	10 December	Drew	1	1	7th	23rdR
2004-05	Champ'ship	27 November	Won	1	0	8 May	Drew	1	1	3rd	20th

FA Cup

										Division	
1949-50	Round 1	26 November	Won	2	1					Div 3S	Div 3S
1950-51	Round 2					9 December	Lost	0	2	Div 3S	Div 3S

League Cup

1965-66	Round 2					21 September	Won	2	1	Div 2	Div 3
1976-77	Round 2	31 August	Drew	0	0	7 September	Lost	1	2	Div 1	Div 3
2002-03	Round 2	24 September	Won	3	1					Div 1	Div 1

Summary

	P	W	D	L	F	A
Ipswich's home league record	25	16	5	4	58	25
Ipswich's away league record	25	7	5	13	31	50
Ipswich's cup record	6	3	1	2	8	7
TOTAL	**56**	**26**	**11**	**19**	**97**	**82**

- The last 0-0 draw in league football between the sides was in 1947.
- Ipswich won eight out of nine home games in the 50's and 60's.

Ipswich's top scorers vs Brighton & Hove Albion

Ted Phillips, Ray Crawford 11
Tom Garneys, John Wark 5
Stan Parker 4
Jackie Brown, Sam McCrory, Alan Brazil, Mich D'Avray 3

Ipswich hat-tricks vs Brighton & Hove

15 November 1958 Ray Crawford
7 September 1960 Ray Crawford

Played for both clubs

Billy Reed	Brighton 1948-49 to 1952-53	Ipswich 1953-54 to 1957-58
Jimmy Leadbetter	Brighton 1952-53 to 1954-55	Ipswich 1955-56 to 1964-65
Eddie Spearritt	Ipswich 1965-66 to 1968-69	Brighton 1968-69 to 1973-74
Russell Osman	Ipswich 1977-78 to 1984-85	Brighton 1995-96
Ron Fearon	Ipswich 1987-88 to 1988-89	Brighton 1988-89
Raphael Meade	Ipswich 1989-90	Brighton 1991-92 1994-95
Andrew Petterson	Ipswich 1992-93	Brighton 2002-03 1995-96
Darren Currie	Ipswich 2004-05	Brighton 2004-05

This fixture has proved very entertaining over the years, with 179 goals being scored in only 56 matches, over three per game. Surprisingly, Ipswich goal legend Paul Mariner (seen here being chased by Brighton's defenders) does not feature in the top-scorers list. The top-scorer honours against the Seagulls are shared by Ted Phillips and Ray Crawford.

v. Bristol City

Season	League	Date	Result (Home)	Ipswich	Bristol	Date	Result (Away)	Ipswich	Bristol	Ipswich	Bristol
			Home				**Away**			**Final Positions**	
1938-39	Division 3S	8 April	Won	4	0	3 December	Lost	2	3	7th	8th
1946-47	Division 3S	5 April	Won	3	2	11 January	Won	2	1	6th	3rd
1947-48	Division 3S	7 February	Won	1	0	20 September	Lost	0	4	4th	7th
1948-49	Division 3S	29 January	Won	2	0	23 April	Lost	0	2	7th	16th
1949-50	Division 3S	29 October	Drew	0	0	18 March	Lost	2	4	17th	15th
1950-51	Division 3S	5 May	Won	2	0	18 April	Lost	1	2	8th	10th
1951-52	Division 3S	26 January	Drew	1	1	22 September	Won	2	0	17th	15th
1952-53	Division 3S	17 September	Won	1	0	9 September	Lost	2	4	16th	5th
1953-54	Division 3S	27 February	Won	2	1	10 October	Won	3	2	1stP	3rd
1957-58	Division 2	1 November	Won	4	2	15 March	Lost	0	1	8th	17th
1958-59	Division 2	30 March	Drew	1	1	27 March	Lost	0	3	16th	10th
1959-60	Division 2	15 April	Lost	1	3	18 April	Lost	1	5	11th	22ndR
1965-66	Division 2	20 November	Drew	0	0	10 May	Lost	1	4	15th	5th
1966-67	Division 2	14 January	Drew	0	0	10 September	Drew	1	1	5th	15th
1967-68	Division 2	26 August	Won	5	0	22 December	Drew	1	1	1stP	19th
1976-77	Division 1	12 March	Won	1	0	1 October	Won	2	1	3rd	18th
1977-78	Division 1	22 April	Won	1	0	10 December	Lost	0	2	18th	17th
1978-79	Division 1	23 September	Lost	0	1	3 February	Lost	1	3	6th	13th
1979-80	Division 1	8 September	Won	1	0	19 January	Won	3	0	3rd	20thR
1990-91	Division 2	24 November	Drew	1	1	9 March	Lost	2	4	14th	9th
1991-92	Division 2	21 September	Won	4	2	18 April	Lost	1	2	1stP	17th
1998-99	Division 1	19 September	Won	3	1	27 February	Won	1	0	3rd	24thR

FA Cup

Season	Round	Date	Result	Ipswich	Bristol	Date	Result	Ipswich	Bristol	Division	
1976-77	Round 3	8 January	Won	4	1					Div 1	Div 1
1979-80	Round 4					26 January	Won	2	1	Div 1	Div 1

Summary

	P	W	D	L	F	A
Ipswich's home league record	22	14	6	2	38	15
Ipswich's away league record	22	6	2	14	28	49
Ipswich's cup record	2	2	0	0	6	2
TOTAL	**46**	**22**	**8**	**16**	**72**	**66**

FACT FILE

- Bristol City have won only twice in 23 visits to Portman Road.
- Ipswich have kept clean sheets in over half of these matches.

Ipswich's top scorers vs Bristol City

Tom Garneys 7
Paul Mariner 5
Ted Phillips 4
Ambrose Mulraney, Frank Brogan 3

Ipswich hat-tricks vs Bristol City

8 April 1939 Ambrose Mulraney
2 November 1957 Ted Phillips
26 August 1967 Frank Brogan

Played for both clubs

Jack Hick	Bristol C 1934-35 to 1938-39	Ipswich 1939-40
Dermot Curtis	Bristol C 1956-57 to 1957-58	Ipswich 1958-59 to 1962-63
Bobby Kellard	Ipswich 1965-66	Bristol C 1968-69 to 1969-70
Steve Stacey	Ipswich 1968-69	Bristol C 1970-71
Russell Osman	Ipswich 1977-78 to 1984-85	Bristol C 1991-92 to 1993-94
Louie Donowa	Ipswich 1989-90	Bristol C 1990-91
Glenn Pennyfather	Ipswich 1989-90 to 1992-93	Bristol C 1992-93 to 1993-94
Jason Cundy	Bristol C 1996-97	Ipswich 1996-97 to 1998-99
Tony Dinning	Ipswich 2004-05	Bristol C 2004-05

Essex boy Glenn Pennyfather (pictured) made his Southend United debut in 1980 at the tender age of 17. He went on to play over 230 games for the Blues before joining Ipswich in 1992 via Crystal Palace. His career at Portman Road was short-lived, making just 15 appearances and scoring one goal, against Oxford on 13 March 1990. He later went on to play for Bristol City before returning to Southend as coach.

v. Bristol Rovers

		Home				Away		Final Positions	
Season	League	Date	Result	Ipswich Bristol R	Date	Result	Ipswich Bristol R	Ipswich	Bristol R
1938-39	Division 3S	1 October	Drew	0 0	4 February	Drew	3 3	7th	22nd
1939-40	Division 3S	30 August	Won	2 0					
1946-47	Division 3S	4 September	Lost	0 2	10 May	Drew	1 1	6th	14th
1947-48	Division 3S	1 May	Lost	0 4	28 April	Lost	0 2	4th	20th
1948-49	Division 3S	18 December	Lost	0 1	21 August	Won	6 1	7th	5th
1949-50	Division 3S	31 August	Won	3 1	22 August	Lost	0 2	17th	9th
1950-51	Division 3S	11 November	Lost	2 3	31 March	Drew	1 1	8th	6th
1951-52	Division 3S	8 December	Lost	1 2	26 April	Lost	0 1	17th	7th
1952-53	Division 3S	25 October	Lost	1 5	14 March	Lost	0 3	16th	1stP
1954-55	Division 2	9 April	Won	1 0	20 November	Lost	0 4	21stR	9th
1957-58	Division 2	21 September	Won	3 2	1 February	Lost	1 3	8th	10th
1958-59	Division 2	26 December	Lost	0 2	27 December	Drew	1 1	16th	6th
1959-60	Division 2	16 September	Won	3 0	7 September	Lost	1 2	11th	9th
1960-61	Division 2	14 January	Won	3 2	3 September	Drew	1 1	1stP	17th
1990-91	Division 2	22 September	Won	2 1	10 April	Lost	0 1	14th	13th
1991-92	Division 2	18 January	Won	1 0	17 August	Drew	3 3	1stP	13th

FA Cup								Division	
1977-78	Round 5	28 February	Won	3 0	18 February	Drew	2 2	Div 1	Div 2
1978-79	Round 5	26 February	Won	6 1				Div 1	Div 2
1984-85	Round 3				5 January	Won	2 1	Div 1	Div 3
1997-98	Round 3	13 January	Won	1 0	3 January	Drew	1 1	Div 1	Div 2

Summary	P	W	D	L	F	A
Ipswich's home league record	16	8	1	7	22	25
Ipswich's away league record	15	1	6	8	18	29
Ipswich's cup record	6	4	2	0	15	5
TOTAL	37	13	9	15	55	59

FACT FILE

- Ipswich have won their last seven home matches against Bristol Rovers.
- They have, however, won only twice in 18 visits to Bristol Rovers and their various grounds.

Ipswich's top scorers vs Bristol Rovers
Ted Phillips 4
Bill Jennings 3

Played for both clubs

Matt O'Mahoney	Bristol R 1936-37 to 1938-39	Ipswich 1939-40 to 1948-49
Fred Chadwick	Ipswich 1938-39 to 1946-47	Bristol R 1947-48
Geoff Fox	Ipswich 1946-47	Bristol R 1947-48 to 1954-55
Ken Wookey	Bristol R 1946-47 to 1948-49	Ipswich 1950-51
Geraint Williams	Bristol R 1980-81 to 1984-85	Ipswich 1992-93 to 1997-98
John Hallworth	Bristol R 1984-85	Ipswich 1985-86 to 1987-88
John Scales	Bristol R 1985-86 to 1986-87	Ipswich 2000-01
Brian Gayle	Ipswich 1989-90 to 1991-92	Bristol R 1996-97 to 1997-98
Marcus Stewart	Bristol R 1991-92 to 1995-96	Ipswich 1999-00 to 2002-03
Jamie Clapham	Bristol R 1996-97	Ipswich 1997-98 to 2002-03
David Whyte	Ipswich 1997-98	Bristol R 1997-98
Lee Hodges	Ipswich 1998-99	Bristol R 2003-04

Ex-Bristol Rovers striker Marcus Stewart (seen here celebrating with Richard Naylor and Jim Magilton), was seen as a bit of a gamble by George Burley when he was signed from Huddersfield in 1999. Stewart more than repaid Burley's faith with 27 goals in 75 appearances before joining Sunderland. In the 2000–01 season, Ipswich were everybody's tip to be relegated straight back down to the First Division following their promotion the previous season. Stewart's 19 goals in just 33 (+1) appearances helped Ipswich to fifth in the Premiership and brought a Manager of the Year award for Burley.

v. Burnley

Season	League	Date	Result	Ipswich	Burnley	Date	Result	Ipswich	Burnley	Ipswich	Burnley
			Home				**Away**			*Final Positions*	
1961-62	Division 1	29 August	Won	6	2	22 August	Lost	3	4	1st	2nd
1962-63	Division 1	27 April	Won	2	1	8 December	Lost	1	3	17th	3rd
1963-64	Division 1	24 August	Won	3	1	14 December	Lost	1	3	22ndR	9th
1968-69	Division 1	11 January	Won	2	0	1 November	Lost	0	1	12th	14th
1969-70	Division 1	17 January	Lost	0	1	27 September	Won	1	0	18th	14th
1970-71	Division 1	5 September	Won	3	0	27 March	Drew	2	2	19th	21stR
1973-74	Division 1	22 September	Won	3	2	9 February	Won	1	0	4th	6th
1974-75	Division 1	24 August	Won	2	0	15 October	Lost	0	1	3rd	10th
1975-76	Division 1	26 August	Drew	0	0	7 February	Won	1	0	6th	21stR
2002-03	Division 1	22 October	Drew	2	2	11 January	Drew	1	1	7th	16th
2003-04	Division 1	14 October	Won	6	1	21 February	Lost	2	4	5th	19th
2004-05	Champ'ship	16 October	Drew	1	1	6 November	Won	2	0	3rd	13th

League Cup										Division	
1977-78	Round 3					25 October	Won	2	1	Div 1	Div 2

Summary	P	W	D	L	F	A
Ipswich's home league record	12	8	3	1	30	11
Ipswich's away league record	12	4	2	6	15	19
Ipswich's cup record	1	1	0	0	2	1
TOTAL	25	13	5	7	47	31

FACT FILE

- Ipswich's first win in top flight football came at the fourth attempt, a 6-2 win over Burnley in 1961.
- Burnley's only win at Portman Road came in 1970.

Ipswich's top scorers vs Burnley
Ray Crawford 7
Ted Phillips 5
Trevor Whymark, Pablo Counago 3
Doug Moran, Peter Morris, Bryan Hamilton, Darren Bent 2

Played for both clubs

Charlie Fletcher	Burnley 1935-36 to 1937-38	Ipswich 1938-39 to 1939-40
Roy Stephenson	Burnley 1949-50 to 1955-56	Ipswich 1960-61 to 1964-65
Nigel Gleghorn	Ipswich 1985-86 to 1987-88	Burnley 1996-97 to 1997-98
Louie Donowa	Ipswich 1989-90	Burnley 1992-93
Danny Sonner	Burnley 1990-91 to 1992-93	Ipswich 1996-97 to 1998-99
Gerry Creaney	Ipswich 1996-97	Burnley 1997-98
David Johnson	Ipswich 1997-98 to 2000-01	Burnley 2001-02
John McGreal	Ipswich 1999-00 to 2004-05	Burnley 2004-05
Drissa Diallo	Burnley 2002-03	Ipswich 2003-04 to 2004-05
Dean Bowditch	Ipswich 2002-03 to 2004-05	Burnley 2004-05

v. Bury

Season	League	Date	Result	Ipswich	Bury	Date	Result	Ipswich	Bury	Ipswich	Bury
			Home					**Away**		*Final Positions*	
1954-55	Division 2	5 February	Lost	2	3	18 September	Lost	1	2	21stR	13th
1964-65	Division 2	5 December	Won	1	0	5 March	Won	1	0	5th	16th
1965-66	Division 2	9 October	Lost	3	4	1 January	Drew	1	1	15th	19th
1966-67	Division 2	3 December	Won	2	0	28 April	Won	2	1	5th	22ndR
1997-98	Division 1	25 October	Won	2	0	25 April	Won	1	0	5th	17th
1998-99	Division 1	15 August	Drew	0	0	6 February	Won	3	0	3rd	22ndR

Summary	P	W	D	L	F	A
Ipswich's home league record	6	3	1	2	10	7
Ipswich's away league record	6	4	1	1	9	4
TOTAL	**12**	**7**	**2**	**3**	**19**	**11**

FACT FILE

- Bury have only scored in five of their 12 matches against Ipswich; Ipswich have scored in 11 of them.
- Bury's three wins all came in the first five matches.

Ipswich's top scorers vs Bury
Gerry Baker 3
Tom Garneys, Ray Crawford, Frank Brogan 2

Played for both clubs

Jack Cope	Bury 1933-34 to 1937-38	Ipswich 1938-39
Ken Hancock	Ipswich 1964-65 to 1968-69	Bury 1971-72 to 1972-73
Danny Sonner	Bury 1992-93	Ipswich 1996-97 to 1998-99
Chris Swailes	Ipswich 1994-95 to 1997-98	Bury 1997-98 to 2000-01
David Johnson	Bury 1995-96 to 1997-98	Ipswich 2000-01

David Johnson (pictured v Manchester United) started his career at Burnley but made his name at north-west rivals Bury. When Johnson was signed from Bury in 1997 he became a big hit at Portman Road, scoring 55 goals in 133 appearances. Qualified to play for all four home nations, plus his native Jamaica, he was widely courted. His sale to Nottingham Forest for £3 million in January 2001 proved good value. Johnson struggled to find any consistency at Forest, except in the 2002–03 season, where he netted 27 goals in just 42 appearances.

v. Cambridge Town

FA Cup		Date	Result	Home Ipswich Cambridge		Date	Result	Away Ipswich Cambridge		Division Ipswich	Cambridge
1932-33	Prelim	21 September	Lost	1	2	17 September	Drew	2	2	Non L	Non L
1936-37	4th Qual	14 November	Won	2	1					Non L	Non L

Summary	P	W	D	L	F	A
Ipswich's cup record	3	1	1	1	5	5
TOTAL	3	1	1	1	5	5

FACT FILE

● In 1951, Cambridge Town became Cambridge City, and still play in the non-league pyramid today.

v. Cambridge United

Season	League	Home Date	Result	Ipswich Cambridge	Away Date	Result	Ipswich Cambridge	Final Positions Ipswich	Cambridge
1991-92	Division 2	9 November	Lost	1 2	21 March	Drew	1 1	1stP	5th

League Cup

								Division	
1986-87	Round 3				28 October	Lost	0 1	Div 2	Div 4
1993-94	Round 2	21 September	Won	2 1	5 October	Won	2 0	Prem	Div 2

Summary

	P	W	D	L	F	A
Ipswich's home league record	1	0	0	1	1	2
Ipswich's away league record	1	0	1	0	1	1
Ipswich's cup record	3	2	0	1	4	2
TOTAL	**5**	**2**	**1**	**2**	**6**	**5**

FACT FILE

● When Cambridge won at Portman Road in 1991, it was Ipswich's seventh match in a row without a league win, but a superb run after Christmas helped them on their way to promotion.

Ipswich's top scorers vs Cambridge
Simon Milton 2

Played for both clubs

Colin Harper	Ipswich 1965-66 to 1974-75	Cambridge 1976-77
Keith Branagan	Cambridge 1983-84 to 1987-88	Ipswich 2000-01 to 2001-02
Ian Atkins	Ipswich 1985-86 to 1987-88	Cambridge 1992-93
John Moncur	Cambridge 1986-87	Ipswich 1991-92
Michael Cheetham	Ipswich 1988-89 to 1989-90	Cambridge 1989-90 to 1993-94
Mark Venus	Ipswich 1997-98 to 2002-03	Cambridge 2003-04
Jonathan Hunt	Ipswich 1998-99	Cambridge 1999-00
Richard Logan	Ipswich 1998-99 to 1999-00	Cambridge 2000-01
Jonas Axeldal	Ipswich 1999-00	Cambridge 2000-01
Lewis Price	Ipswich 2003-04 to 2004-05	Cambridge 2004-05

Starting as an apprentice at his home town club Hartlepool, Mark Venus had two seasons for Leicester City, then spent eight years at Wolves before signing for Ipswich. In his six years at Portman Road, he made 148 appearances and scored 16 goals. He moved from Ipswich in 2003 to Cambridge United. He has now joined former teammate Tony Mowbray at Hibernian, where he has been appointed first-team coach.

v. Cardiff City

Season	League	Date	Result	Home Ipswich	Blackpool	Date	Result	Away Ipswich	Blackpool	Final Positions Ipswich	Blackpool
1938-39	Division 3S	10 September	Lost	1	2	14 January	Lost	1	2	7th	13th
1946-47	Division 3S	21 December	Lost	0	1	26 April	Lost	2	3	6th	1stP
1957-58	Division 2	22 March	Won	3	1	9 November	Drew	1	1	8th	15th
1958-59	Division 2	28 March	Drew	3	3	11 October	Won	2	1	16th	9th
1959-60	Division 2	12 March	Drew	1	1	24 October	Lost	2	3	11th	2ndP
1961-62	Division 1	14 April	Won	1	0	25 November	Won	3	0	1st	21stR
1964-65	Division 2	12 December	Drew	1	1	22 August	Drew	0	0	5th	13th
1965-66	Division 2	9 April	Won	2	1	30 October	Lost	0	1	15th	20th
1966-67	Division 2	17 December	Drew	0	0	20 August	Won	2	0	5th	20th
1967-68	Division 2	24 February	Won	4	2	7 October	Drew	1	1	1stP	13th
2003-04	Division 1	9 May	Drew	1	1	29 November	Won	3	2	5th	13th
2004-05	Champ'ship	21 August	Won	3	1	15 March	Won	1	0	3rd	16th

FA Cup

										Division	
1977-78	Round 3					7 January	Won	2	0	Div 1	Div 2
1983-84	Round 3					7 January	Won	3	0	Div 1	Div 2

League Cup

1965-66	Q'ter-Final					17 November	Lost	1	2	Div 2	Div 2

Summary

	P	W	D	L	F	A
Ipswich's home league record	12	5	5	2	20	14
Ipswich's away league record	12	5	3	4	18	14
Ipswich's cup record	3	2	0	1	6	2
TOTAL	**27**	**12**	**8**	**7**	**44**	**30**

Defender Eddie Youds, seen here attacking a corner against Jamie Redknapp of Liverpool, had a spell on loan at Cardiff City while he was at Everton. He signed for Ipswich from the Toffees for £250,000 in November 1991. His Ipswich career yielded just one goal in 44 games, but it was a match-winner. He scored the only goal at home to Blackburn on 27 November 1993.

- Ipswich lost their first four matches against Cardiff, but have lost only three times in 24 matches since.
- Ipswich have not lost in their last 11 matches against Cardiff.

Ipswich's top scorers vs Cardiff
Ted Phillips, Ray Crawford 4
Frank Brogan, Eric Gates, Tommy Miller 3

Ipswich hat-tricks vs Cardiff
7 January 1984 Eric Gates (cup)

Played for both clubs

Bryn Davies	Cardiff 1935-36 to 1937-38	Ipswich 1938-39
Billy Baker	Cardiff 1938-39 to 1954-55	Ipswich 1955-56
Wilf Grant	Cardiff 1949-50 to 1954-55	Ipswich 1954-55 to 1956-57
Russell Osman	Ipswich 1977-78 to 1984-85	Cardiff 1995-96
Mark Grew	Ipswich 1984-85	Cardiff 1992-93 to 1993-94
Jon Hallworth	Ipswich 1985-86 to 1987-88	Cardiff 1997-98 to 1999-00
Eddie Youds	Cardiff 1989-90	Ipswich 1991-92 to 1994-95
Tony Vaughan	Ipswich 1994-95 to 1996-97	Cardiff 1999-00
Andrew Legg	Ipswich 1997-98	Cardiff 1998-99 to 2002-03
Gary Croft	Ipswich 1999-00 to 2000-01	Cardiff 2001-02 to 2004-05
Alan Mahon	Cardiff 2002-03	Ipswich 2003-04

v. Carlisle United

Season	League	Date	Result	Home Ipswich Carlisle		Date	Result	Away Ipswich Carlisle		Final Positions Ipswich Carlisle	
1965-66	Division 2	6 November	Won	1	0	1 April	Lost	1	3	15th	14th
1966-67	Division 2	17 September	Lost	1	2	21 January	Lost	1	2	5th	3rd
1967-68	Division 2	30 September	Won	3	1	10 February	Lost	1	4	1stP	10th
1974-75	Division 1	30 November	Won	3	1	18 January	Lost	1	2	3rd	22ndR

FA Cup

										Division	
1966-67	Round 4	18 February	Won	2	0					Div 2	Div 2
1978-79	Round 3	10 January	Won	3	2					Div 1	Div 3

Summary	P	W	D	L	F	A
Ipswich's home league record	4	3	0	1	8	4
Ipswich's away league record	4	0	0	4	4	11
Ipswich's cup record	2	2	0	0	5	2
TOTAL	**10**	**5**	**0**	**5**	**17**	**17**

FACT FILE

- Ipswich have not had a chance in over 30 years to improve their dismal record at Brunton Park.
- Nine of the 10 matches in this series have resulted in away wins.

Ipswich's top scorers vs Carlisle
Ray Crawford 3
Eddie Spearritt, Ron Wigg 2

Played for both clubs

Jack Connor	Ipswich 1946-47	Carlisle 1946-47 to 1947-48
Eddie Spearritt	Ipswich 1965-66 to 1968-69	Carlisle 1974-75 to 1975-76
Frank Clarke	Ipswich 1969-70 to 1972-73	Carlisle 1973-74 to 1977-78
Eric Gates	Ipswich 1973-74 to 1984-85	Carlisle 1990-91
Steve McCall	Ipswich 1979-80 to 1986-87	Carlisle 1989-90
Sean Friars	Ipswich 1999-00	Carlisle 2001-02

Eric Gates joined Ipswich in 1972 and stayed at the club for 13 seasons. He didn't establish himself in the first team until the 1977-78 season, but for the next eight years he formed a key part of the midfield, eventually notching up 345 (+36) appearances and 95 goals. Gates was capped twice for England under Ron Greenwood. It was a measure of Ipswich's success that he was one of five players to be given caps in the 1980-81 season by Greenwood (Russell Osman, Terry Butcher, Mick Mills and Paul Mariner being the other four). After a move to Sunderland, Gates finished his career for Carlisle.

v. Charlton Athletic

			Home					Away		Final Positions	
Season	League	Date	Result	Ipswich	Charlton	Date	Result	Ipswich	Charlton	Ipswich	Charlton
1957-58	Division 2	19 April	Lost	1	4	7 December	Lost	1	4	8th	3rd
1958-59	Division 2	1 November	Won	3	1	21 March	Lost	1	5	16th	8th
1959-60	Division 2	12 December	Drew	1	1	16 April	Won	3	1	11th	7th
1960-61	Division 2	25 February	Won	2	1	8 October	Won	2	0	1stP	10th
1964-65	Division 2	21 November	Drew	1	1	3 April	Lost	0	4	5th	18th
1965-66	Division 2	5 February	Lost	1	4	28 August	Lost	0	2	15th	16th
1966-67	Division 2	26 December	Drew	0	0	20 December	Lost	1	2	5th	19th
1967-68	Division 2	28 October	Won	3	2	23 March	Won	1	0	1stP	15th
1990-91	Division 2	29 December	Drew	4	4	6 April	Drew	1	1	14th	16th
1991-92	Division 2	26 December	Won	2	0	30 October	Drew	1	1	1stP	7th
1995-96	Division 1	23 September	Lost	1	5	9 December	Won	2	0	7th	6th
1996-97	Division 1	20 September	Won	2	1	1 January	Drew	1	1	4th	15th
1997-98	Division 1	7 March	Won	3	1	1 November	Lost	0	3	5th	4thP
1999-00	Division 1	19 October	Won	4	2	29 April	Won	3	1	3rdP	1stP
2000-01	Premiership	11 November	Won	2	0	30 April	Lost	1	2	5th	9th
2001-02	Premiership	25 August	Lost	0	1	1 January	Lost	2	3	18thR	14th

Play-offs

										Final Positions	
1986-87	Semi-Final	14 May	Drew	0	0	17 May	Lost	1	2	5th(D2)	19th(D1)
1997-98	Semi-Final	10 May	Lost	0	1	13 May	Lost	0	1	5th	4thP

FA Cup

										Division	
1980-81	Round 5	14 February	Won	2	0					Div 1	Div 3
1982-83	Round 3	8 January	Won	3	2					Div 1	Div 2

League Cup

1997-98	Round 1	26 August	Won	3	1	13 August	Won	1	0	Div 1	Div 1

Summary	P	W	D	L	F	A
Ipswich's home league record	16	8	4	4	30	28
Ipswich's away league record	16	5	3	8	20	30
Ipswich's cup record	8	4	1	3	10	7
TOTAL	**40**	**17**	**8**	**15**	**60**	**65**

Ipswich's top scorers vs Charlton Athletic
Ray Crawford, Micky Stockwell 4
Ted Phillips, John Wark, David Johnson (II) 3

- Ipswich's highest scoring draw has been 4-4. This has occurred on four occasions, most recently against Charlton in 1990.
- Charlton have twice been Ipswich's bête noire in play-off ties. The first was under a format whereby one team from Division One and three teams from Division Two would play off to see which team would play in Division One the following season. Charlton won the competition and thus avoided relegation. The second was in the Division One play-offs and was the second of Ipswich's three semi-final defeats in successive seasons.
- Ipswich have won four out of four in FA Cup and League Cup matches.

Played for both clubs

George Smith	Charlton 1938-39	Ipswich 1949-50
Jimmy Walls	Charlton 1949-50 to 1952-53	Ipswich 1954-55
Ray Crawford	Ipswich 1958-59 to 1963-64 & 1965-66 to 1968-69	Charlton 1968-69 to 1969-70
Chris Barnard	Ipswich 1966-67 to 1970-71	Charlton 1971-72
Bobby Hunt	Ipswich 1967-68 to 1970-71	Charlton 1970-71 to 1972-73
Steve Stacey	Ipswich 1968-69	Charlton 1969-70
Geoff Hammond	Ipswich 1970-71 to 1973-74	Charlton 1976-77
Mark Stuart	Ipswich 1990-91	Charlton 1992-93
David Whyte	Charlton 1991-92 & 1994-95 to 1996-97	Ipswich 1997-98
Eddie Youds	Ipswich 1991-92 to 1994-95	Charlton 1997-98 to 1999-00
Andrew Petterson	Ipswich 1992-93 & 1995-96	Charlton 1994-95 to 1998-99
Matt Holland	Ipswich 1997-98 to 2002-03	Charlton 2003-04 to 2004-05
Hermann Hreidarsson	Ipswich 2000-01 to 2002-03	Charlton 2003-04 to 2004-05
Chris Bart-Williams	Charlton 2001-02 to 2002-03	Ipswich 2003-04

Dutch midfielder Bobby Petta, seen here being challenged by Danny Mills of Charlton, signed from Feyenoord in June 1996. He hardly featured in his first season at the club, making just one league appearance with five as sub. The following two years were more fruitful though, with over 25 league appearances in each one. His final appearance for Ipswich came in the play-off semi-final against Bolton in 1999. Petta moved to Celtic, where he spent five years with little success before moving to Fulham on loan. He is now in the North-East, having signed for Darlington in February 2005.

v. Chelmsford City

FA Cup		Date	Result	Home Ipswich Chelmsford	Date	Result	Away Ipswich Chelmsford	Division Ipswich Chelmsford
1949-50	Round 2	14 December	Won*	1 0	10 December	Drew	1 1	Div 3S Non L
1972-73	Round 3				13 January	Won	3 1	Div 1 Non L

Summary	P	W	D	L	F	A
Ipswich's cup record	3	2	1	0	5	2
TOTAL	3	2	1	0	5	2

Ipswich nearly slipped up against non-league Chelmsford in 1973, but goals from Colin Harper, Bryan Hamilton and David Johnson (seen here against Liverpool) saw Ipswich safely through to round four.

v. Chelsea

Season	League	Date	Result	Ipswich	Chelsea	Date	Result	Ipswich	Chelsea	Ipswich	Chelsea
			Home				**Away**			**Final Positions**	
1961-62	Division 1	1 December	Won	5	2	21 April	Drew	2	2	1st	22ndR
1963-64	Division 1	12 October	Lost	1	3	22 February	Lost	0	4	22ndR	5th
1968-69	Division 1	26 December	Lost	1	3	5 October	Lost	1	3	12th	5th
1969-70	Division 1	18 November	Lost	1	4	16 August	Lost	0	1	18th	3rd
1970-71	Division 1	1 May	Drew	0	0	26 September	Lost	1	2	19th	6th
1971-72	Division 1	1 April	Lost	1	2	27 December	Lost	0	2	13th	7th
1972-73	Division 1	26 December	Won	3	0	23 September	Lost	0	2	4th	12th
1973-74	Division 1	26 February	Drew	1	1	13 October	Won	3	2	4th	17th
1974-75	Division 1	21 September	Won	2	0	31 March	Drew	0	0	3rd	21stR
1977-78	Division 1	3 September	Won	1	0	21 January	Lost	3	5	18th	16th
1978-79	Division 1	30 December	Won	5	1	5 May	Won	3	2	6th	22ndR
1984-85	Division 1	1 March	Won	2	0	27 October	Lost	0	2	17th	6th
1985-86	Division 1	1 November	Lost	0	2	5 April	Drew	1	1	20thR	6th
1988-89	Division 2	28 March	Lost	0	1	26 December	Lost	0	3	8th	1stP
1992-93	Premiership	6 April	Drew	1	1	17 October	Lost	1	2	16th	11th
1993-94	Premiership	21 August	Won	1	0	11 December	Drew	1	1	19th	14th
1994-95	Premiership	21 January	Drew	2	2	23 October	Lost	0	2	22ndR	11th
2000-01	Premiership	26 December	Drew	2	2	20 January	Lost	1	4	5th	6th
2001-02	Premiership	1 April	Drew	0	0	4 November	Lost	1	2	18thR	6th

FA Cup

										Division	
1967-68	Round 3					27 January	Lost	0	3	Div 2	Div 1
1972-73	Round 4					3 February	Lost	0	2	Div 1	Div 1

League Cup

										Division	
1997-98	Q'ter-Final	7 January	Drew*	2	2					Div 1	Prem
		(lost 1-4 pens)									

Summary

	P	W	D	L	F	A
Ipswich's home league record	19	7	6	6	29	24
Ipswich's away league record	19	2	4	13	18	42
Ipswich's cup record	3	0	1	2	2	7
TOTAL	**41**	**9**	**11**	**21**	**49**	**73**

(+ one penalty shoot-out defeat)

Ipswich's top scorers vs Chelsea
Ray Crawford 5
David Johnson (I), John Wark, Marcus Stewart 3

Ipswich hat-tricks vs Chelsea
2 Dec 1961 Ray Crawford

FACT FILE

- In September 1970, Chelsea's second goal in their 2-1 win was awarded despite, as TV pictures later confirmed, the ball clearly hitting the stanchion on the outside of the goal rather than going in. The referee and linesman both believed the ball had gone in.
- Ipswich's last seven meetings with Chelsea have produced four home draws and three away defeats.
- Between 1963 and 1970, Chelsea beat Ipswich eight times in succession.
- Ipswich's last win at Stamford Bridge came in 1979, when Alan Brazil scored twice against already relegated Chelsea.

Played for both clubs

Jimmy Leadbetter	Chelsea 1951-52	Ipswich 1955-56 to 1964-65
John Compton	Chelsea 1955-56 to 1959-60	Ipswich 1960-61 to 1963-64
Roger Wosahlo	Chelsea 1966-67	Ipswich 1967-68 1969-70
Colin Viljoen	Ipswich 1966-67 to 1977-78	Chelsea 1979-80 to 1981-82
Kevin Wilson	Ipswich 1984-85 to 1986-87	Chelsea 1987-88 to 1991-92
Craig Forrest	Ipswich 1988-89 to 1996-97	Chelsea 1996-97
Jason Cundy	Chelsea 1990-91 to 1991-92	Ipswich 1996-97 to 1998-99
Mark Stein	Chelsea 1993-94 to 1995-96	Ipswich 1997-98

Danish midfielder Claus Thomsen, seen here against Chelsea, scored just seven goals for the club in 81 appearances before signing for Everton for £900,000 in January 1997.

v. Chester City

Ipswich Chester

FA Cup		Date	Result	Home			Division	
				Ipswich	Chester		Ipswich	Chester
1979-80	Round 5	16 February	Won	2	1		Div 1	Div 3

Summary	P	W	D	L	F	A
Ipswich's cup record	1	1	0	0	2	1
TOTAL	1	1	0	0	2	1

FACT FILE

● **John Wark and George Burley scored the goals as Ipswich progressed to the quarter-finals, where they lost to Everton.**

Played for both clubs

Steve Stacey	Ipswich 1968-69	Chester 1969-70
Keith Bertschin	Ipswich 1975-76 to 1976-77	Chester 1990-91
Frederick Barber	Chester 1990-91	Ipswich 1995-96

Ipswich legend George Burley, seen here in action against Liverpool, scored just 11 goals in exactly 500 appearances for Ipswich. One of them came in the match against Chester. Burley never made a substitute appearance for Ipswich in his 13-season playing career at the club.

v. Colchester United

Season	League	Date	Result	Home Ipswich	Colchester	Date	Result	Away Ipswich	Colchester	Final Positions Ipswich	Colchester
1950-51	Division 3S	24 March	Won	3	0	4 November	Won	3	2	8th	16th
1951-52	Division 3S	13 October	Lost	0	2	1 March	Lost	0	1	17th	10th
1952-53	Division 3S	20 December	Drew	2	2	23 August	Drew	0	0	16th	22nd
1953-54	Division 3S	22 August	Won	3	0	19 December	Won	2	1	1stP	23rd
1955-56	Division 3S	27 December	Won	3	1	26 December	Drew	3	3	3rd	12th
1956-57	Division 3S	6 October	Won	3	1	16 February	Drew	0	0	1stP	3rd

League Cup						Division
1969-70	Round 2	3 September	Won	4	0	Div 1 Div 4

Summary	P	W	D	L	F	A
Ipswich's home league record	6	4	1	1	14	6
Ipswich's away league record	6	2	3	1	8	7
Ipswich's cup record	1	1	0	0	4	0
TOTAL	13	7	4	2	26	13

FACT FILE

- Ipswich have not lost in their last nine meetings against Colchester.
- Despite being geographically closer to Ipswich than any other league club, the sides have not met competitively since 1969.

Ipswich's top scorers vs Colchester
Allenby Driver, Billy Reed, George McLuckie, Ted Phillips 3

Ipswich hat-tricks vs Colchester
6 October 1956 Ted Phillips

Titus Bramble had a spell on loan at Colchester before cementing his place in the Ipswich first team, where he went on to make only 40 league starts before his £5 million transfer to Newcastle United.

Played for both clubs

Ted Phillips	Ipswich 1953-54 to 1963-64	Colchester 1965-66
Colin Lundstrum	Ipswich 1957-58 to 1959-60	Colchester 1961-62
Ray Crawford	Ipswich 1958-59 to 1963-64 & 1965-66 to 1968-69	Colchester 1970-71
Bobby Blackwood	Ipswich 1962-63 to 1964-65	Colchester 1965-66 to 1967-68
Charlie Woods	Ipswich 1966-67 to 1969-70	Colchester 1971-72
Bobby Hunt	Colchester 1959-60 to 1963-64	Ipswich 1967-68 to 1970-71
Trevor Whymark	Ipswich 1969-70 to 1978-79	Colchester 1985-86
Allan Hunter	Ipswich 1971-72 to 1980-81	Colchester 1981-82 to 1982-83
Glenn Keeley	Ipswich 1972-73 to 1973-74	Colchester 1987-88
Kevin Beattie	Ipswich 1972-73 to 1980-81	Colchester 1982-83
Roger Osborne	Ipswich 1973-74 to 1980-81	Colchester 1980-81 to 1985-86
George Burley	Ipswich 1973-74 to 1985-86	Colchester 1994-95
Pat Sharkey	Ipswich 1975-76 to 1976-77	Colchester 1978-79
Robin Turner	Ipswich 1975-76 to 1983-84	Colchester 1985-86
David Barnes	Ipswich 1982-83 to 1983-84	Colchester 1996-97
Trevor Putney	Ipswich 1982-83 to 1985-86	Colchester 1994-95
Jason Dozzell	Ipswich 1983-84 to 1992-93} & 1997-98	Colchester 1998-99 to 2000
Mick Stockwell	Ipswich 1985-86 to 1999-00	Colchester 2000-01 to 2002-03
Michael Cheetham	Ipswich 1988-89 to 1989-90	Colchester 1994-95 to 1995-96
David Gregory	Ipswich 1988-89 to 1994-95	Colchester 1995-96 to 2001-02
Gavin Johnson	Ipswich 1988-89 to 1994-95	Colchester 1999-00 to 2004-05
Craig Forrest	Colchester 1987-88	Ipswich 1988-89 to 1996-97
Steve Whitton	Ipswich 1990-91 to 1993-94	Colchester 1993-94 to 1997-98
Andrew Petterson	Ipswich 1992-93 & 1995-96	Colchester 1995-96
Geraint Williams	Ipswich 1992-93 to 1997-98	Colchester 1998-99 to 1999-00
Neil Gregory	Ipswich 1994-95 to 1997-98	Colchester 1997-98 to 1998-99
Adam Tanner	Ipswich 1994-95 to 1998-99	Colchester 2000-01
Frederick Barber	Colchester 1992-93	Ipswich 1995-96
Chris Keeble	Ipswich 1997-98	Colchester 1999-00 to 2002-03
Titus Bramble	Ipswich 1998-99 to 2001-02	Colchester 1999-00

v. Coventry City

		Home					**Away**			**Final Positions**	
Season	League	Date	Result	Ipswich	Coventry	Date	Result	Ipswich	Coventry	Ipswich	Coventry
1952-53	Division 3S	11 October	Won	3	0	28 February	Lost	0	2	16th	6th
1953-54	Division 3S	26 December	Won	4	1	25 December	Won	3	1	1stP	14th
1955-56	Division 3S	7 January	Won	1	0	31 March	Lost	1	3	3rd	8th
1956-57	Division 3S	19 September	Won	4	0	24 September	Drew	1	1	1stP	16th
1964-65	Division 2	25 August	Lost	1	3	1 September	Lost	3	5	5th	10th
1965-66	Division 2	8 January	Won	1	0	13 November	Lost	1	3	15th	3rd
1966-67	Division 2	6 May	Drew	1	1	9 December	Lost	0	5	5th	1stP
1968-69	Division 1	25 March	Drew	0	0	30 November	Won	2	0	12th	20th
1969-70	Division 1	23 August	Lost	0	1	26 December	Lost	1	3	18th	6th
1970-71	Division 1	18 August	Lost	0	2	9 January	Lost	0	1	19th	10th
1971-72	Division 1	17 August	Won	3	1	22 January	Drew	1	1	13th	18th
1972-73	Division 1	5 December	Won	2	0	31 March	Lost	1	2	4th	19th
1973-74	Division 1	30 March	Won	3	0	3 November	Won	1	0	4th	16th
1974-75	Division 1	16 November	Won	4	0	22 February	Lost	1	3	3rd	14th
1975-76	Division 1	17 January	Drew	1	1	6 September	Drew	0	0	6th	14th
1976-77	Division 1	5 April	Won	2	1	27 December	Drew	1	1	3rd	19th
1977-78	Division 1	18 March	Drew	1	1	22 October	Drew	1	1	18th	7th
1978-79	Division 1	13 March	Drew	1	1	7 October	Drew	2	2	6th	10th
1979-80	Division 1	12 April	Won	3	0	1 December	Lost	1	4	3rd	15th
1980-81	Division 1	20 September	Won	2	0	28 February	Won	4	0	2nd	16th
1981-82	Division 1	3 April	Won	1	0	16 January	Won	4	2	2nd	14th
1982-83	Division 1	4 September	Drew	1	1	23 November	Drew	1	1	9th	19th
1983-84	Division 1	4 February	Won	3	1	1 October	Won	2	1	12th	19th
1984-85	Division 1	14 May	Drew	0	0	10 November	Lost	0	1	17th	18th
1985-86	Division 1	31 March	Won	1	0	26 December	Won	1	0	20thR	17th
1992-93	Premiership	20 March	Drew	0	0	5 December	Drew	2	2	16th	15th
1993-94	Premiership	4 April	Lost	0	2	1 February	Lost	0	1	19th	11th
1994-95	Premiership	6 May	Won	2	0	10 October	Lost	0	2	22ndR	16th
2000-01	Premiership	21 April	Won	2	0	20 November	Won	1	0	5th	19thR
2002-03	Division 1	23 November	Won	2	1	12 April	Won	4	2	7th	20th
2003-04	Division 1	23 August	Drew	1	1	31 January	Drew	1	1	5th	12th
2004-05	Champ'ship	15 January	Won	3	2	3 October	Won	2	1	3rd	19th

League Cup

										Division	
1964-65	Round 2					23 September	Lost	1	4	Div 2	Div 2
1974-75	Round 2					10 September	Won	2	1	Div 1	Div 1
1979-80	Round 2	29 August	Lost	0	1	4 September	Drew	0	0	Div 1	Div 1
2000-01	Round 4	28 November	Won	2	1					Prem	Prem

FACT FILE

- On 4 February 1984, Jason Dozzell came on as a substitute to become Ipswich's youngest ever player at the age of 16 years and 56 days. In scoring their third goal that day, he became the youngest scorer for any club in top-flight history.
- Ipswich have lost one of their last 22 home league matches against Coventry.
- Ipswich are unbeaten in nine games against Coventry this century.
- Somewhat surprisingly for two teams who have met with such regularity in the league, there has never been an FA Cup tie between the two.

Summary	P	W	D	L	F	A
Ipswich's home league record	32	19	9	4	53	21
Ipswich's away league record	32	10	9	13	43	52
Ipswich's cup record	5	2	1	2	5	7
TOTAL	**69**	**31**	**19**	**19**	**101**	**80**

Ipswich's top scorers vs Coventry City
Paul Mariner 7
Tom Garneys, David Johnson (I), John Wark 5
John Elsworthy, Alan Brazil 4

Ipswich hat-tricks vs Coventry City
26 December 1953 John Elsworthy
16 November 1974 David Johnson (I)

Played for both clubs

Gilbert Alsop	Coventry 1929-30 to 1930-31	Ipswich 1938-39
Jackie Brown	Coventry 1936-37 to 1937-38	Ipswich 1948-49 to 1950-51
Charlie Ashcroft	Ipswich 1955-56	Coventry 1957-58
Gerard Baker	Ipswich 1963-64 to 1967-68	Coventry 1967-68 to 1969-70
John O'Rourke	Ipswich 1967-68 to 1969-70	Coventry 1969-70 to 1971-72
Alan Brazil	Ipswich 1977-78 to 1982-83	Coventry 1985-86
Terry Butcher	Ipswich 1977-78 to 1985-86	Coventry 1990-91
David Barnes	Coventry 1979-80 to 1981-82	Ipswich 1982-83 to 1983-84
Steve Whitton	Coventry 1979-80 to 1982-83	Ipswich 1990-91 to 1993-94
Steve Sedgley	Coventry 1986-87 to 1988-89	Ipswich 1994-95 to 1996-97

Ipswich signed a truly great talent when Arnold Muhren joined them from FC Twente in 1978. Muhren (seen here bamboozling the Coventry defence) formed part of a formidable midfield trio alongside fellow countryman Frans Thijssen and John Wark. Muhren received the Player of the Year award in his first season at the club, and during his four-year spell, Ipswich won the UEFA Cup in 1981, were runners-up in Division 1 in 1981 and 1982, were FA Cup semi-finalists in 1981 and League Cup semi-finalists in 1982.

v. Crewe Alexandra

Season	League	Date	Result	Home Ipswich	Home Crewe	Date	Result	Away Ipswich	Away Crewe	Final Positions Ipswich	Final Positions Crewe
1997-98	Division 1	3 May	Won	3	2	21 October	Drew	0	0	5th	11th
1998-99	Division 1	24 April	Lost	1	2	28 November	Won	3	0	3rd	18th
1999-00	Division 1	27 November	Won	2	1	19 February	Won	2	1	3rdP	19th
2003-04	Division 1	17 January	Won	6	4	16 August	Lost	0	1	5th	18th
2004-05	Champ'ship	30 April	Won	5	1	4 December	Drew	2	2	3rd	21st

League Cup

Season	Round	Date	Result	Ipswich	Crewe	Date	Result	Ipswich	Crewe	Division Ipswich	Division Crewe
1999-00	Round 2	21 September	Drew	1	1	14 September	Lost	1	2	Div 1	Div 1
2001-02	Round 3					9 October	Won	3	2	Prem	Div 1

Summary

	P	W	D	L	F	A
Ipswich's home league record	5	4	0	1	17	10
Ipswich's away league record	5	2	2	1	7	4
Ipswich's cup record	3	1	1	1	5	5
TOTAL	**13**	**7**	**3**	**3**	**29**	**19**

FACT FILE

- **Ipswich have scored 11 goals in their last two home matches with Crewe – an extraordinary total in modern day football.**

Ipswich's top scorers vs Crewe
James Scowcroft, Tommy Miller 4
David Johnson (II), Martijn Reuser, Shefki Kuqi 3

Ipswich hat-tricks vs Crewe
28 November 1998 James Scowcroft

Played for both clubs

Jack Connor	Ipswich 1946-47	Crewe 1956-57
Jimmy Robertson	Ipswich 1969-70 to 1971-72	Crewe 1978-79
Jermaine Wright	Crewe 1997-98 to 1998-99	Ipswich 1999-00 to 2003-04

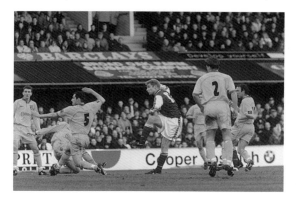

Jamie Scowcroft (seen here getting a shot away while surrounded by Norwich defenders) scored Ipswich's only hat-trick against Crewe, in a 3-0 win at Gresty Road in 1998. This statistic is even more remarkable as this fixture has recently sparked a glut of goals, with 21 being scored in the last four fixtures.

v. Crittals Athletic

FA Cup	Date	Result	Home Ipswich	Crittals				Division Ipswich	Chester
1930-31 2nd Qual	18 October	Lost	2	3				Non L	Non L

Summary	P	W	D	L	F	A
Ipswich's cup record	1	0	0	1	2	3
TOTAL	1	0	0	1	2	3

FACT FILE

- After big wins against Harwich, Leiston and Severalls, Town's interest in the 1930-31 FA Cup came to a disappointing end against a team that have never got beyond the qualifying rounds. Birtchenall and Watson scored for Ipswich.

v. Cromer

		Home					Division	
FA Cup	*Date*	*Result*	Ipswich	Cromer			Ipswich	Cromer
1936-37 3rd Qual	31 October	Won	**11**	**0**			Non L	Non L

Summary	P	W	D	L	F	A
Ipswich's cup record	1	1	0	0	11	0
TOTAL	**1**	**1**	**0**	**0**	**11**	**0**

FACT FILE

- This was Ipswich's biggest win in the FA Cup, and five different players scored a brace of goals.
- The Norfolk outfit have never got beyond the qualifying rounds of the FA Cup.

Ipswich's top scorers vs Cromer
Jack Blackwell, Robert Bruce, George Dobson, Jimmy McLuckie, Jackie Williams 2

Norwich's biggest win in the FA Cup, against their Norfolk rivals Cromer, came in Town's first year in the Southern League after being unaminously elected at the start of the season. Ossie Parry became Ipswich's first professional player following his signing from Crystal Palace. This team line up from the start of the following season includes Parry, but also Robert Bruce, Jimmy McLuckie and Jackie Williams, all scorers of two goals against Cromer. Back row, left to right: D.F. Read (assistant secretary), F. Shufflebottom, F. Houldsworth, R. Thomson, H. Sowerbutts, G. Alsop. Middle row: J. Edwards, J. Hays, G. Perrett, R. Bruce, R. Rodger, C. Cowie, J. Carter, R. MacPherson (trainer). Front row: J. Williams, A. Mulraney, J. Taylor, J. McLuckie (captain), A. Scott Duncan (manager), O. Parry, F. Jones, J. Little, L. Asthill.

v. Crystal Palace

Season	League	Date	Result	Ipswich	Crystal P	Date	Result	Ipswich	Crystal P	Ipswich	Crystal P
		Home						**Away**		*Final Positions*	
1938-39	Division 3S	18 January	Won	2	1	1 April	Lost	0	3	7th	2nd
1946-47	Division 3S	8 February	Drew	1	1	5 October	Drew	1	1	6th	18th
1947-48	Division 3S	22 November	Won	3	0	10 April	Lost	1	2	4th	13th
1948-49	Division 3S	5 February	Won	3	2	18 September	Drew	1	1	7th	22nd
1949-50	Division 3S	24 December	Drew	4	4	27 August	Lost	0	2	17th	7th
1950-51	Division 3S	7 April	Drew	1	1	18 November	Won	3	1	8th	24th
1951-52	Division 3S	8 March	Drew	1	1	20 October	Lost	1	3	17th	19th
1952-53	Division 3S	1 October	Won	2	0	22 April	Drew	1	1	16th	13th
1953-54	Division 3S	16 April	Won	2	0	19 April	Drew	1	1	1stP	22nd
1955-56	Division 3S	1 October	Drew	3	3	11 February	Lost	0	1	3rd	23rd
1956-57	Division 3S	6 April	Won	4	2	24 November	Won	3	1	1stP	20th
1964-65	Division 2	24 April	Won	3	2	7 October	Drew	1	1	5th	7th
1965-66	Division 2	11 February	Drew	2	2	27 December	Lost	1	3	15th	11th
1966-67	Division 2	28 March	Won	2	0	27 March	Won	2	0	5th	7th
1967-68	Division 2	30 March	Drew	2	2	1 May	Won	3	1	1stP	11th
1969-70	Division 1	15 November	Won	2	0	28 March	Drew	1	1	18th	20th
1970-71	Division 1	5 December	Lost	1	2	6 February	Lost	0	1	19th	18th
1971-72	Division 1	4 March	Lost	0	2	13 November	Drew	1	1	13th	20th
1972-73	Division 1	9 December	Won	2	1	14 April	Drew	1	1	4th	21stR
1979-80	Division 1	19 February	Won	3	0	29 September	Lost	1	4	3rd	13th
1980-81	Division 1	7 February	Won	3	2	13 September	Won	2	1	2nd	22ndR
1986-87	Division 2	27 December	Won	3	0	15 November	Drew	3	3	5th	6th
1987-88	Division 2	26 December	Lost	2	3	26 September	Won	2	1	8th	6th
1988-89	Division 2	4 February	Lost	1	2	4 October	Lost	0	2	8th	3rdP
1992-93	Premiership	24 October	Drew	2	2	1 May	Lost	1	3	16th	20thR
1994-95	Premiership	4 February	Lost	0	2	5 November	Lost	0	3	22ndR	19thR
1995-96	Division 1	19 August	Won	1	0	13 January	Drew	1	1	7th	3rd
1996-97	Division 1	26 December	Won	3	1	10 September	Drew	0	0	4th	6thP
1998-99	Division 1	3 October	Won	3	0	9 March	Lost	2	3	3rd	14th
1999-00	Division 1	25 April	Won	1	0	7 December	Drew	2	2	3rdP	15th
2002-03	Division 1	3 November	Lost	1	2	11 March	Drew	1	1	7th	14th
2003-04	Division 1	28 December	Lost	1	3	21 October	Won	4	3	5th	6thP

FA Cup

										Division	
1957-58	Round 3					4 January	Won	1	0	Div 2	Div 3S

League Cup

										Division	
1996-97	Round 3	22 October	Won	4	1					Div 1	Div 1

- Ipswich were unbeaten in their first 16 home games against the Eagles.
- There has never been a goalless draw between the sides at Portman Road.

Summary	P	W	D	L	F	A
Ipswich's home league record	32	17	8	7	64	43
Ipswich's away league record	32	7	13	12	41	53
Ipswich's cup record	2	2	0	0	5	1
TOTAL	**66**	**26**	**21**	**19**	**110**	**97**

Ipswich's top scorers vs Palace
Sam McCrory, Alex Mathie 5
Tommy Parker, John Wark, Kevin Wilson 4

Ipswich hat-tricks vs Palace
18 November 1950 Sam McCrory
15 November 1986 Kevin Wilson

Played for both clubs

Charlie Fletcher	Palace 1928-29	Ipswich 1938-39 to 1939-40
Ossie Parry	Palace 1931-32 to 1935-36	Ipswich 1938-39 to 1948-49
George Rumbold	Palace 1935-36	Ipswich 1946-47 to 1949-50
Ian Gillespie	Palace 1936-37 to 1938-39	Ipswich 1946-47
Roy Bailey	Palace 1949-50 to 1955-56	Ipswich 1955-56 to 1964-65
Peter Berry	Palace 1953-54 to 1957-58	Ipswich 1958-59 to 1959-60
Jim Belcher	Palace 1954-55 to 1957-58	Ipswich 1958-59 to 1959-60
Bobby Kellard	Palace 1963-64 to 1965-66 & 1971-72 to 1972-73	Ipswich 1965-66
Charlie Woods	Palace 1964-65 to 1965-66	Ipswich 1966-67 to 1969-70
John Jackson	Palace 1964-65 to 1973-74	Ipswich 1981-82
Bobby Bell	Ipswich 1968-69 to 1971-72	Palace 1971-72 to 1973-74
Mick Hill	Ipswich 1969-70 to 1972-73	Palace 1973-74 to 1975-76
Glenn Pennyfather	Palace 1987-88 to 1988-89	Ipswich 1989-90 to 1992-93
David Whyte	Palace 1991-92 to 1995-96	Ipswich 1997-98
Jason Cundy	Palace 1995-96	Ipswich 1996-97 to 1998-99
Hermann Hreidarsson	Palace 1997-98 to 1998-99	Ipswich 2001-02 to 2003-04

Northern Ireland international Kevin Wilson (seen here taking on the Stoke defence) signed from Derby in 1984 for £100,000 and scored a total of 49 goals for Ipswich over three seasons before his big money transfer to Chelsea. In 1986 his hat-trick secured a point against the Eagles of Crystal Palace. The season ended in personal glory for the tricky striker as he topped the scoring charts with 25 goals, more than double that of his nearest rival (John Deehan on 12), but for Ipswich it meant play-off despair as they lost to Charlton in the semi-final second leg 2–1 following a 0-0 stalemate in the home leg.

v. Dagenham & Redbridge

FA Cup						Date	Result	Away Ipswich Dagenham	Division Ipswich	Dagenham
2001-02 Round 3						5 January	Won	4 1	Prem	Non L

Summary	P	W	D	L	F	A
Ipswich's cup record	1	1	0	0	4	1
TOTAL	**1**	**1**	**0**	**0**	**4**	**1**

Ipswich's top scorers vs Dagenham
Sixto Peralta 2

Ipswich have played the Daggers only once, in an FA Cup tie in January 2002.
Argentinian midfielder Sixto Peralta (seen fending off Arsenal's Patrick Vieira) scored
two of the four goals in the easy win. Jim Magilton and Marcus Stewart were also on
target that day.

v. Darlington

League Cup		Date	Result	Home Ipswich Darlington		Date	Result	Away Ipswich Darlington		Division Ipswich	Darlington
1965-66	Round 4	3 November	Won	2	0					Div 2	Div 4
1985-86	Round 2	23 September	Won	3	1	8 October	Won	4	1	Div 1	Div 3

Summary	P	W	D	L	F	A
Ipswich's cup record	3	3	0	0	9	2
TOTAL	3	3	0	0	9	2

FACT FILE

- **Darlington are the only team Ipswich have played three times against whilst maintaining a 100 percent record.**

Ipswich's top scorers vs Darlington
Kevin Wilson 5
Gerry Baker 2

Ipswich hat-tricks vs Darlington
8 October 1985 Kevin Wilson (cup)

Played for both clubs

David Geddis	Ipswich 1976-77 to 1978-79	Darlington 1990-91
Frederick Barber	Darlington 1982-83 to 1985-86	Ipswich 1995-96
Ian Juryeff	Ipswich 1988-89	Darlington 1992-93
Jason De Vos	Darlington 1996-97 to 1998-99	Ipswich 2004-05
Bobby Petta	Ipswich 1996-97 to 1998-99	Darlington 2004-05
Alun Armstrong	Ipswich 2000-01 to 2003-04	Darlington 2004-05

Alun Armstrong made an immediate impact when George Burley signed the former Stockport County man from Middlesborough for £500,000 in December 2000, scoring eight goals in his first 17 full appearances. However, he struggled in his second season (seven goals in 24 starts) and subsequently never held down a regular place, being used mainly as a substitute. After a spell at Bradford on loan, Armstrong signed for Darlington in September 2004 on a free transfer.

v. Derby County

		Home				Away				Final Positions	
Season	League	Date	Result	Ipswich	Derby	Date	Result	Ipswich	Derby	Ipswich	Derby
1954-55	Division 2	26 March	Won	2	1	6 November	Lost	0	2	21stR	22ndR
1957-58	Division 2	8 February	Drew	2	2	28 September	Drew	2	2	8th	16th
1958-59	Division 2	10 September	Drew	1	1	17 September	Lost	2	3	16th	7th
1959-60	Division 2	9 April	Drew	1	1	21 November	Lost	0	3	11th	18th
1960-61	Division 2	27 August	Won	4	1	24 April	Won	4	1	1stP	12th
1964-65	Division 2	24 October	Won	2	1	17 April	Won	3	2	5th	9th
1965-66	Division 2	23 October	Drew	2	2	15 January	Drew	2	2	15th	8th
1966-67	Division 2	6 September	Won	4	3	28 September	Drew	2	2	5th	17th
1967-68	Division 2	14 October	Won	4	0	1 March	Won	3	2	1stP	18th
1969-70	Division 1	12 August	Lost	0	1	20 August	Lost	1	3	18th	4th
1970-71	Division 1	16 January	Lost	0	1	26 August	Lost	0	2	19th	9th
1971-72	Division 1	31 August	Drew	0	0	22 March	Lost	0	1	13th	1st
1972-73	Division 1	21 October	Won	3	1	30 April	Lost	0	3	4th	7th
1973-74	Division 1	10 November	Won	3	0	23 March	Lost	0	2	4th	3rd
1974-75	Division 1	25 February	Won	3	0	23 November	Lost	0	2	3rd	1st
1975-76	Division 1	24 April	Lost	2	6	4 October	Lost	0	1	6th	4th
1976-77	Division 1	18 December	Drew	0	0	14 May	Drew	0	0	3rd	15th
1977-78	Division 1	31 December	Lost	1	2	24 August	Drew	0	0	18th	12th
1978-79	Division 1	16 April	Won	2	1	28 February	Won	1	0	6th	19th
1979-80	Division 1	29 March	Drew	1	1	17 November	Won	1	0	3rd	21stR
1986-87	Division 2	4 April	Lost	0	2	8 November	Lost	1	2	5th	1stP
1991-92	Division 2	28 March	Won	2	1	16 November	Lost	0	1	1stP	3rd
1995-96	Division 1	1 April	Won	1	0	14 October	Drew	1	1	7th	2ndP
2000-01	Premiership	1 December	Lost	0	1	19 May	Drew	1	1	5th	17th
2001-02	Premiership	21 August	Won	3	1	19 January	Won	3	1	18thR	19thR
2002-03	Division 1	28 September	Lost	0	1	4 May	Won	4	1	7th	18th
2003-04	Division 1	6 December	Won	2	1	8 November	Drew	2	2	5th	20th
2004-05	Champ'ship	1 April	Won	3	2	14 August	Lost	2	3	3rd	4th

FA Cup										Division	
2003-04	Round 3	3 January	Won	3	0					Div 1	Div 1

League Cup											
1984-85	Round 2	25 September	Won	4	2	10 October	Drew	1	1	Div 1	Div 3
1991-92	Round 2	8 October	Lost	0	2	25 September	Drew	0	0	Div 2	Div 2

FACT FILE

- In the 1-1 draw in March 1980, Ipswich goalkeeper Paul Cooper saved two penalties, bringing his final tally for the season to eight saves from 10 penalties.
- Between 1970 and 1977, Ipswich failed to score in eight visits to Derby.

Summary	P	W	D	L	F	A
Ipswich's home league record	28	14	7	7	48	34
Ipswich's away league record	28	7	8	13	35	45
Ipswich's cup record	5	2	2	1	8	5
TOTAL	**61**	**23**	**17**	**21**	**91**	**84**

Ipswich's top scorers vs Derby
Ray Crawford, Gerry Baker, Frank Brogan 5
Eddie Spearritt, Darren Bent, Tommy Miller 4

Played for both clubs
Dave Bell	Derby 1934-35 to 1938-39	Ipswich 1938-39 to 1949-50
Trevor Whymark	Ipswich 1969-70 to 1978-79	Derby 1979-80
Kevin Wilson	Derby 1979-80 to 1984-85	Ipswich 1984-85 to 1986-87
Graham Harbey	Derby 1983-84 to 1986-87	Ipswich 1987-88 to 1989-90
Geraint Williams	Derby 1984-85 to 1991-92	Ipswich 1992-93 to 1997-98
Paul Goddard	Derby 1988-89 to 1989-90	Ipswich 1990-91 to 1993-94
Jonathan Hunt	Derby 1997-98 to 1998-99	Ipswich 1998-99
Chris Makin	Ipswich 2000-01 to 2003-04	Derby 2004-05

Chris Makin is one of only two players to have joined Derby after playing for Ipswich, the other being Trevor Whymark. A £1.4 million signing from Sunderland, Makin made his Town debut against Aston Villa at Villa Park before going on to make 91 (+1) league and cup appearances before his free transfer to Leicester City in August 2004. Makin never settled at the Walker's Stadium and he re-joined George Burley at Derby County on a short-term contract in 2005, where he almost helped them back into the Premiership. He played every game for the Rams after he joined except the final league game of the season and the play-off semi-finals, all of which were against Preston North End.

v. Doncaster Rovers

Season	League	Date	Result	Home Ipswich Doncaster R	Date	Result	Away Ipswich Doncaster R	Final Positions Ipswich Doncaster R
1954-55	Division 2	30 October	Won	5 1	19 March	Drew	1 1	21stR 18th
1957-58	Division 2	14 December	Won	2 0	26 April	Drew	1 1	8th 22ndR

League Cup								Division
2004-05	Round 2				21 September	Lost	0 2	Champ Lg 1

Summary	P	W	D	L	F	A
Ipswich's home league record	2	2	0	0	7	1
Ipswich's away league record	2	0	2	0	2	2
Ipswich's cup record	1	0	0	1	0	2
TOTAL	**5**	**2**	**2**	**1**	**9**	**5**

FACT FILE

- A shock League Cup exit in 2004 ended Ipswich's unbeaten record against Doncaster.

Ipswich's top scorers vs Doncaster
Tom Garneys 5

Ipswich hat-tricks vs Doncaster
30 October 1954 Tom Garneys (4)

Played for both clubs

Tony Kinsella	Ipswich 1982-83 to 1983-84	Doncaster 1986-87 to 1987-88
Ian Atkins	Ipswich 1985-86 to 1987-88	Doncaster 1993-94
John Moncur	Doncaster 1986-87	Ipswich 1991-92
Neil Woods	Ipswich 1987-88 to 1989-90	Doncaster 1982-83 to 1986-87
Chris Swailes	Doncaster 1993-94 to 1994-95	Ipswich 1994-95 to 1997-98
Jermaine Wright	Doncaster 1996-97	Ipswich 1999-00 to 2003-04

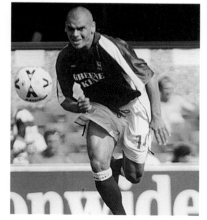

Londoner Jermaine Wright started his career as a trainee at Millwall before a £60,000 transfer to Wolves in 1994. During his time at Molineux, he failed to break into the first team regularly and so had a loan spell at Doncaster Rovers. Dario Gradi spotted his potential and snapped him up on a free transfer for Crewe in 1998. In only 15 months, Gradi had turned Wright into a £500,000 player when Ipswich signed the energetic midfielder. Wright gave good service at Portman Road, making 180 appearances and scoring 11 goals in his five years at the club before joining Leeds United on a free transfer in June 2004.

v. Eastern Counties United

			Home			Division	
				Ipswich	Eastern	Ipswich	Eastern
FA Cup		Date	Result				
1936-37	Prelim	19 September	Won	7	0	Non L	Non L

Summary	P	W	D	L	F	A
Ipswich's cup record	1	1	0	0	7	0
TOTAL	1	1	0	0	7	0

FACT FILE

● This match marked the start of a goal-crazy cup run for Ipswich, and their easy victory set up a clash against Stowmarket.

Ipswich's top scorers vs Eastern
Jack Blackwell 3
George Dobson 2

Ipswich hat-tricks vs Eastern
19 September 1936 Jack Blackwell (cup)

Jack Blackwell and George Dobson won the main plaudits following this easy 7-0 win in the FA Cup, but neither were at the club when the 1937-38 season kicked off. The other two scorers in the match, Jock Carter and Bobby Bruce (pictured) both made it into A. Scott Duncan's team after his appointment as manager following Mick O'Brien's resignation.

v. Everton

Season	League	Date	Result	Ipswich	Everton	Date	Result	Ipswich	Everton	Ipswich	Everton
		Home				**Away**				*Final Positions*	
1961-62	Division 1	3 February	Won	4	2	16 September	Lost	2	5	1st	4th
1962-63	Division 1	19 March	Lost	0	3	27 October	Lost	1	3	17th	1st
1963-64	Division 1	14 September	Drew	0	0	18 January	Drew	1	1	22ndR	3rd
1968-69	Division 1	9 November	Drew	2	2	18 January	Drew	2	2	12th	3rd
1969-70	Division 1	20 September	Lost	0	3	10 January	Lost	0	3	18th	1st
1970-71	Division 1	6 April	Drew	0	0	12 September	Lost	0	2	19th	14th
1971-72	Division 1	14 August	Drew	0	0	16 October	Drew	1	1	13th	15th
1972-73	Division 1	24 March	Lost	0	1	28 October	Drew	2	2	4th	17th
1973-74	Division 1	1 January	Won	3	0	1 September	Lost	0	3	4th	7th
1974-75	Division 1	7 September	Won	1	0	22 March	Drew	1	1	3rd	4th
1975-76	Division 1	27 March	Won	1	0	6 December	Drew	3	3	6th	11th
1976-77	Division 1	15 January	Won	2	0	24 August	Drew	1	1	3rd	9th
1977-78	Division 1	19 November	Drew	3	3	15 April	Lost	0	1	18th	3rd
1978-79	Division 1	14 October	Lost	0	1	24 February	Won	1	0	6th	4th
1979-80	Division 1	22 September	Drew	1	1	9 February	Won	4	0	3rd	19th
1980-81	Division 1	30 August	Won	4	0	17 January	Drew	0	0	2nd	15th
1981-82	Division 1	6 March	Won	3	0	17 October	Lost	1	2	2nd	8th
1982-83	Division 1	11 December	Lost	0	2	14 May	Drew	1	1	9th	7th
1983-84	Division 1	6 September	Won	3	0	17 March	Lost	0	1	12th	7th
1984-85	Division 1	29 December	Lost	0	2	4 September	Drew	1	1	17th	1st
1985-86	Division 1	16 November	Lost	3	4	19 April	Lost	0	1	20thR	2nd
1992-93	Premiership	28 November	Won	1	0	24 March	Lost	0	3	16th	13th
1993-94	Premiership	30 October	Lost	0	2	12 February	Drew	0	0	19th	17th
1994-95	Premiership	9 May	Lost	0	1	31 December	Lost	1	4	22ndR	15th
2000-01	Premiership	24 February	Won	2	0	30 September	Won	3	0	5th	16th
2001-02	Premiership	13 October	Drew	0	0	1 February	Won	2	1	18thR	15th

FA Cup

										Division	
1952-53	Round 3					10 January	Lost	2	3	Div 3S	Div 2
1968-69	Round 3					4 January	Lost	1	2	Div 1	Div 1
1979-80	Q'ter-Final					8 March	Lost	1	2	Div 1	Div 1
1984-85	Q'ter-Final	13 March	Lost	0	1	9 March	Drew	2	2	Div 1	Div 1
1998-99	Round 4					23 January	Lost	0	1	Div 1	Prem

League Cup

1981-82	Round 4					15 December	Won	3	2	Div 1	Div 1

FACT FILE

- It took Ipswich 16 attempts to claim a first win at Goodison Park.
- Ipswich have won 15 matches against Everton. Everton have scored in just three of these.

Summary	P	W	D	L	F	A
Ipswich's home league record	26	10	7	9	33	27
Ipswich's away league record	26	4	11	11	28	42
Ipswich's cup record	7	1	1	5	9	13
TOTAL	**59**	**15**	**19**	**25**	**70**	**82**

Ipswich's top scorers vs Everton
Paul Mariner, John Wark 6
Trevor Whymark, Eric Gates, Alan Brazil 5
Ray Crawford 4
Doug Moran, Clive Woods 3

Played for both clubs

Jimmy McGourty	Everton 1932-33 to 1933-34	Ipswich 1938-39
David Johnson	Everton 1970-71 to 1972-73 & 1982-83 to 1983-84	Ipswich 1972-73 to 1975-76
Rod Belfitt	Ipswich 1971-72 to 1972-73	Everton 1972-73
Bryan Hamilton	Ipswich 1971-72 to 1975-76	Everton 1975-76 to 1976-77
Glenn Keeley	Ipswich 1972-73 to 1973-74	Everton 1982-83
Neil Rimmer	Everton 1984-85	Ipswich 1985-86 to 1987-88
Ian Atkins	Everton 1984-85 to 1985-86	Ipswich 1985-86 to 1987-88
Ian Marshall	Everton 1985-86 to 1987-88	Ipswich 1993-94 to 1996-97
Eddie Youds	Everton 1990-91	Ipswich 1991-92 to 1994-95
David Unsworth	Everton 1991-92 to 1996-97 & 1998-99 to 2003-04	Ipswich 2004-05
Claus Thomsen	Ipswich 1994-95 to 1996-97	Everton 1996-97 to 1997-98
Richard Wright	Ipswich 1994-95 to 2000-01	Everton 2002-03 to 2004-05
Paul Gerrard	Everton 1996-97 to 2002-03	Ipswich 2002-03
Marcus Bent	Ipswich 2001-02 to 2003-04	Everton 2004-05

Scouse striker Ian Marshall (seen here fending off Everton's Dave Watson) started his career on Merseyside, joining Everton as an 18-year-old apprentice in 1984, but it was during his time at Oldham Athletic under current Ipswich and former Everton manager Joe Royle that Marshall's career really took off. Marshall had great strength and presence, exactly what Ipswich were looking for when they paid the Latics £750,000 for him in 1993. Marshall's three seasons at Portman Road yielded 38 goals in 92 (+5) appearances in total, but it was his 19 goals in 39 appearances in 1995-96 that prompted Leicester City to pay £800,000 for him in August 1996.

v. Exeter City

		Home				Away				Final Positions	
Season	League	Date	Result	Ipswich	Exeter City	Date	Result	Ipswich	xeter City	Ipswich	xeter City
1938-39	Division 3S	31 December	Drew	2	2	3 September	Lost	0	3	7th	14th
1946-47	Division 3S	22 March	Won	2	1	16 November	Drew	0	0	6th	15th
1947-48	Division 3S	17 September	Won	2	0	10 September	Lost	0	1	4th	11th
1948-49	Division 3S	16 April	Drew	2	2	20 November	Won	3	1	7th	12th
1949-50	Division 3S	4 February	Won	1	0	24 September	Drew	1	1	17th	16th
1950-51	Division 3S	20 January	Won	1	0	16 September	Lost	0	2	8th	14th
1951-52	Division 3S	16 February	Lost	2	4	6 October	Lost	1	2	17th	23rd
1952-53	Division 3S	7 March	Lost	0	1	18 October	Drew	1	1	16th	17th
1953-54	Division 3S	14 November	Drew	1	1	3 April	Won	2	1	1stP	9th
1955-56	Division 3S	3 December	Drew	2	2	14 April	Drew	2	2	3rd	16th
1956-57	Division 3S	1 December	Won	3	0	1 April	Won	2	1	1stP	21st

FA Cup

										Division	
1951-52	Round 2	15 December	Won	4	0					Div 3S	Div 3S

League Cup

										Division	
1998-99	Round 1	18 August	Won	5	1	11 August	Drew	1	1	Div 1	Div 3

Summary	P	W	D	L	F	A
Ipswich's home league record	11	5	4	2	18	13
Ipswich's away league record	11	3	4	4	12	15
Ipswich's cup record	3	2	1	0	10	2
TOTAL	**25**	**10**	**9**	**6**	**40**	**30**

Ipswich's top scorers vs Exeter City
Bill Jennings, Tom Garneys 5
Tommy Parker 3

Played for both clubs

Angus Mackay	Ipswich 1946-47	Exeter 1947-48 to 1954-55
Dermot Curtis	Ipswich 1958-59 to 1962-63	Exeter 1963-64 to 1965-66
		& 1967-68 to 1968-69
Ken Thompson	Ipswich 1964-65 to 1965-66	Exeter 1966-67
Steve Stacey	Ipswich 1968-69	Exeter 1971-72 to 1972-73
Chris O'Donnell	Ipswich 1986-87 to 1988-89	Exeter 1991-92
Simon Milton	Exeter 1987-88	Ipswich 1987-88 to 1997-98
Brian Gayle	Ipswich 1989-90 to 1991-92	Exeter 1996-97
Lee Hodges	Exeter 1996-97	Ipswich 1998-99

FACT FILE

● **An easy League Cup win in 1998 brought Ipswich's unbeaten run in the series to eight matches. Matt Holland scored in both legs**

v. Frost Athletic

			Home							Division	
FA Cup		*Date*	*Result*	Ipswich	Frost					Ipswich	Frost
1934-35	2nd Qual	13 October	Won	**2**	**0**					Non L	Non L

Summary	*P*	*W*	*D*	*L*	*F*	*A*
Ipswich's cup record	1	1	0	0	2	0
TOTAL	1	1	0	0	2	0

FACT FILE

● Goals from Green and Stopher took Ipswich through.

v. Fulham

Season	League	Home Date	Result	Ipswich	Fulham	Away Date	Result	Ipswich	Fulham	Final Positions Ipswich	Fulham
1954-55	Division 2	16 October	Lost	2	4	5 March	Lost	1	4	21stR	14th
1957-58	Division 2	11 September	Drew	1	1	18 September	Drew	0	0	8th	5th
1958-59	Division 2	17 January	Lost	1	2	6 September	Lost	2	3	16th	1stP
1961-62	Division 1	23 September	Lost	2	4	10 February	Won	2	1	1st	20th
1962-63	Division 1	1 March	Lost	0	1	13 October	Drew	1	1	17th	16th
1963-64	Division 1	28 December	Won	4	2	26 December	Lost	1	10	22ndR	15th
1999-00	Division 1	25 March	Won	1	0	26 December	Drew	0	0	3rdP	9th
2001-02	Premiership	30 January	Won	1	0	21 October	Drew	1	1	18thR	13th

FA Cup

										Division	
1956-57	Round 3	5 January	Lost	2	3					Div 3S	Div 2

League Cup

										Division	
1973-74	Round 3	14 November	Won	2	1	31 October	Drew	2	2	Div 1	Div 2
1996-97	Round 2	24 September	Won	4	2	17 September	Drew	1	1	Div 1	Div 3

Summary

	P	W	D	L	F	A
Ipswich's home league record	8	3	1	4	12	14
Ipswich's away league record	8	1	4	3	8	20
Ipswich's cup record	5	2	2	1	11	9
TOTAL	**21**	**6**	**7**	**8**	**31**	**43**

Bobby Petta, seen here challenging for the ball against Sunderland in 1999, made just five full appearances for Fulham, one for each month of his loan spell at Craven Cottage. He also made eight appearances from the bench in that time, but failed to find the back of the net in any game.

FACT FILE

- Fulham are the only team to reach double figures (1-10) against Ipswich. It happened on Boxing Day 1963, a day that has gone down in football folklore. The other top flight scorelines that day were as follows: 3-3, 2-8, 1-5, 3-0, 6-1, 2-0, 6-1, 3-3 and 4-4.
- In this match, Graham Leggat of Fulham scored a hat-trick in three minutes, the fastest top-flight hat-trick since the war.
- Two days later Town had to face Fulham again, but this time they won 4-2.
- In October 1954, Town suffered their club record 10th league defeat in a row against Fulham.
- Ipswich have played 11 home games against Fulham. They won none of their first six, but have won all of their last five.

Ipswich's top scorers vs Fulham
Ray Crawford 3
Tom Garneys, Basil Acres, Bill Baxter, Gerry Baker, Alex Mathie 2

Played for both clubs

Rod Belfitt	Ipswich 1971-72 to 1972-73	Fulham 1974-75
Brian Talbot	Ipswich 1973-74 to 1978-79	Fulham 1990-91
Kevin Steggles	Ipswich 1980-81 to 1985-86	Fulham 1986-87
Mark Grew	Ipswich 1984-85	Fulham 1985-86
Michael Cole	Ipswich 1984-85 to 1987-88	Fulham 1987-88 to 1990-91
Gus Uhlenbeek	Ipswich 1995-96 to 1997-98	Fulham 1998-99 to 1999-00
Bobby Petta	Ipswich 1996-97 to 1998-99	Fulham 2003-04

v. Gateshead

FA Cup		Date	Result	Home		Date	Result	Away		Division	
				Ipswich	Gateshead			Ipswich	Gateshead	Ipswich	Gateshead
1951-52	Round 3	12 January	Drew	2	2	16 January	Drew*	3	3	Div 3S	Div 3N
		21 January	Bramall Lane (2nd replay)				Lost*	1	3		

Summary	P	W	D	L	F	A
Ipswich's cup record	3	0	2	1	6	7
TOTAL	3	0	2	1	6	7

FACT FILE

- Ipswich have not played anyone else as often without claiming at least one win.
- In this long running cup tie, Mick Burns became the oldest player to represent Ipswich in a first-team fixture at 43 years and 219 days old.

Ipswich's top scorers vs Gateshead
Peter Dobson, Tom Garneys 2

v. Gillingham

| | | | **Home** | | | | **Away** | | | **Final Positions** | |
Season	League	Date	Result	Ipswich	Gillingham	Date	Result	Ipswich	Gillingham	Ipswich	Gillingham
1950-51	Division 3S	17 February	Won	5	1	30 September	Won	1	0	8th	22nd
1951-52	Division 3S	14 April	Drew	1	1	11 April	Drew	1	1	17th	22nd
1952-53	Division 3S	8 November	Drew	1	1	28 March	Drew	1	1	16th	21st
1953-54	Division 3S	9 September	Won	6	1	16 September	Drew	1	1	1stP	10th
1955-56	Division 3S	25 February	Drew	1	1	15 October	Drew	0	0	3rd	10th
1956-57	Division 3S	8 September	Drew	1	1	12 January	Drew	1	1	1stP	22nd
2002-03	Division 1	26 October	Lost	0	1	29 March	Won	3	1	7th	11th
2003-04	Division 1	1 November	Lost	3	4	17 April	Won	2	1	5th	21st
2004-05	Champ'ship	7 August	Won	2	1	19 March	Drew	0	0	3rd	22ndR

FA Cup

								Division	
1984-85	Round 4	26 January	Won	3	2			Div 1	Div 3

League Cup

								Division	
1996-97	Round 4	26 November	Won	1	0			Div 1	Div 2

Summary	P	W	D	L	F	A
Ipswich's home league record	9	3	4	2	20	12
Ipswich's away league record	9	3	6	0	10	6
Ipswich's cup record	2	2	0	0	4	2
TOTAL	**20**	**8**	**10**	**2**	**34**	**20**

FACT FILE

- Ipswich have never lost at the Gills' home ground of Priestfield.
- Ipswich were unbeaten in their first 14 games in the series.

Ipswich's top scorers vs Gillingham
Tommy Parker 4
Pablo Counago 3

Played for both clubs

Eddie Spearritt	Ipswich 1965-66 to 1968-69	Gillingham 1976-77
George Burley	Ipswich 1973-74 to 1985-86	Gillingham 1988-89
Irvin Gernon	Ipswich 1981-82 to 1986-87	Gillingham 1986-87 to 1987-88
Scott Houghton	Ipswich 1990-91	Gillingham 1996-97
Keith Branagan	Gillingham 1991-92	Ipswich 2000-01 to 2001-02
Andy Marshall	Gillingham 1996-97	Ipswich 2001-02 to 2002-03

v. Gorleston

FA Cup		Date	Result	Away Ipswich	Gorleston	Division Ipswich	Gorleston
1933-34	ExPrelim	1 September	Lost	2	3	Non L	Non L
1934-35	3rd Qual	27 October	Lost	0	2	Non L	Non L

Summary	P	W	D	L	F	A
Ipswich's cup record	2	0	0	2	2	5
TOTAL	2	0	0	2	2	5

FACT FILE

● Gorleston, who reached the FA Cup competition proper in 1951-52 and 1957-58, were not the first team to knock Ipswich out of the cup two years in succession; Old Westminsters had done so in the 19th century.

v. Grimsby Town

			Home				Away		Final Positions	
Season	League	Date	Result	Ipswich	Grimsby	Date	Result	Ipswich	Grimsby	Ipswich	Grimsby
1957-58	Division 2	19 October	Won	3	2	1 March	Won	2	0	8th	13th
1958-59	Division 2	11 April	Won	2	1	22 November	Won	3	2	16th	21stR
1986-87	Division 2	23 August	Drew	1	1	24 January	Drew	1	1	5th	21stR
1991-92	Division 2	21 April	Drew	0	0	28 September	Won	2	1	1stP	19th
1995-96	Division 1	4 November	Drew	2	2	8 April	Lost	1	3	7th	17th
1996-97	Division 1	27 August	Drew	1	1	31 March	Lost	1	2	4th	22ndR
1998-99	Division 1	9 January	Lost	0	1	9 August	Drew	0	0	3rd	11th
1999-00	Division 1	30 October	Won	2	0	1 October	Lost	1	2	3rdP	20th
2002-03	Division 1	22 February	Drew	2	2	8 October	Lost	0	3	7th	24thR

FA Cup

										Division	
1982-83	Round 4	29 January	Won	2	0					Div 1	Div 2
1992-93	Round 5	13 February	Won	4	0					Prem	Div 1

League Cup

										Division	
1985-86	Round 3					29 October	Won	2	0	Div 1	Div 2

Summary	P	W	D	L	F	A
Ipswich's home league record	9	3	5	1	13	10
Ipswich's away league record	9	3	2	4	11	14
Ipswich's cup record	3	3	0	0	8	0
TOTAL	21	9	7	5	32	24

Ipswich's top scorers vs Grimsby
Ray Crawford, Paul Mason 4
Bontcho Guentchev 3

Ipswich hat-tricks vs Grimsby
13 February 1993 Bontcho Guentchev (cup)

Played for both clubs

Colin Harper	Ipswich 1965-66 to 1974-75	Grimsby 1976-77
Ron Wigg	Ipswich 1967-68 to 1969-70	Grimsby 1974-75 to 1976-77
Trevor Whymark	Ipswich 1969-70 to 1978-79	Grimsby 1980-81 to 1983-84
Tommy Parkin	Grimsby 1975-76	Ipswich 1977-78 to 1986-87
Neil Woods	Ipswich 1987-88 to 1989-90	Grimsby 1990-91 to 1997-98
Gary Croft	Grimsby 1990-91 to 1995-96	Ipswich 1999-00 to 2000-01
Georges Santos	Grimsby 2002-03	Ipswich 2003-04

FACT FILE

- Ipswich were undefeated in their first 12 meetings with Grimsby.
- In every season in which the sides have been in the same division, Ipswich have finished in the higher league position.

v. Halifax Town

FA Cup	Date	Result	Home				Division	
			Ipswich	Halifax			Ipswich	Halifax
1975-76 Round 3	3 January	Won	3	1			Div 1	Div 3

Summary	P	W	D	L	F	A
Ipswich's cup record	1	1	0	0	3	1
TOTAL	1	1	0	0	3	1

FACT FILE

● Ipswich's only match against Halifax provided Mick Lambert's only hat-trick for the club.

Ipswich's top scorers vs Halifax
Mick Lambert 3

Ipswich hat-tricks vs Halifax
3 January 1976 Mick Lambert (cup)

Played for both clubs

Bob Smythe	Ipswich 1946-47 to 1947-48	Halifax 1950-51
Frank Brogan	Ipswich 1964-65 to 1969-70	Halifax 1971-72 to 1972-73
Terry Shanahan	Ipswich 1970-71	Halifax 1971-72 to 1974-75
Ian Juryeff	Ipswich 1988-89	Halifax 1989-90
		& 1990-91 to 1992-93
Scott Houghton	Ipswich 1990-91	Halifax 2001-02
Darren Edmonds	Ipswich 1991-92	Halifax 1992-93

The 1976-77 squad prepare for the start of the new season. Back row, left to right: John Wark, Paul Cooper, John Peddelty, Laurie Sivell, Pat Sharkey. Middle row: Dave Johnson, Eric Gates, Terry Austin, Colin Viljoen, Keith Bertschin, Alan Hunter, Kevin Beattie, Trevor Whymark. Front row: Cyril Lea (coach), Brian Talbot, Clive Woods, Mick Mills, Roger Osborne, George Burley, Mick Lambert and Bobby Robson (manager). Winger Mick Lambert scored all three goals in the only fixture between these two sides.

v. Hartlepool United

FA Cup		Date	Home Result	Ipswich	Hartlepool	Date	Away Result	Ipswich	Hartlepool	Division Ipswich	Hartlepool
1977-78	Round 4	28 January	Won	4	1					Div 1	Div 4
1991-92	Round 3	4 January	Drew	1	1	15 January	Won	2	0	Div 2	Div 3

Summary	P	W	D	L	F	A
Ipswich's cup record	3	2	1	0	7	2
TOTAL	3	2	1	0	7	2

Ipswich's top scorers vs Hartlepool
Colin Viljoen, Jason Dozzell 2

Played for both clubs
John Brownlow	Ipswich 1946-47	Hartlepool 1948-49
David Linighan	Hartlepool 1981-82 to 1985-86	Ipswich 1988-89 to 1995-96
Mark Venus	Hartlepool 1984-85	Ipswich 1997-98 to 2002-03
Kelvin Davis	Hartlepool 1997-98	Ipswich 2003-04 to 2004-05
Tommy Miller	Hartlepool 1997-98 to 2000-01	Ipswich 2001-02 to 2004-05

Sunderland fan Tommy Miller made his name in the North-East at Hartlepool United where his goalscoring exploits attracted interest from many clubs. His 44 goals from 155 starts prompted George Burley to splash out £750,000 on the 22-year-old in 2001. Miller had no time to adjust to life at the top, with Burley throwing him straight in at the deep end in the away fixture against Torpedo Moscow in the UEFA Cup first round. Miller didn't really establish himself in the first team until the following season and subsequently become a mainstay of the team. In 2004–05 he made 45 league appearances, scoring 13 goals in the process. In the close season of 2005, Miller signed for his boyhood heroes Sunderland. Remarkably, he never missed a penalty for Ipswich, the most consistent record since John Wark.

v. Harwich & Parkeston

FA Cup	Date	Result	Home Ipswich Harwich					Division Ipswich Harwich
1930-31 ExPrelim	6 September	Won	**5**	**0**				Non L Non L

Summary	P	W	D	L	F	A
Ipswich's cup record	1	1	0	0	5	0
TOTAL	**1**	**1**	**0**	**0**	**5**	**0**

Ipswich's top scorers vs Harwich
Fred Birtchnell, Dammo Green 2

FACT FILE

- This match was Town's first FA Cup tie for 37 years. Harwich had met Ipswich many times previously in regional competitions.

v. Hastings United

			Home						Division	
FA Cup	*Date*	*Result*	Ipswich	Hastings					Ipswich	Hastings
1956-57 Round 1	17 November	Won	**4**	**0**					Div 3S	Non L

Summary	P	W	D	L	F	A
Ipswich's cup record	1	1	0	0	4	0
TOTAL	1	1	0	0	4	0

Ipswich's top scorers vs Hastings
Ted Phillips 2

FACT FILE

● Hastings enjoyed a reasonable amount of FA Cup success in the 1950's, but they were no match for an Ipswich side on their way to promotion.

Ted Phillips is arguably Ipswich's best-ever striker, scoring 173 goals in 276 appearances, a phenomenal strike rate, including a club record 46 goals in the 1956-57 season. Phillips and teammates John Elsworthy, Larry Carberry, Roy Bailey and Jimmy Leadbetter were the first and still the only players who have won First, Second and Third Division championship medals with the same club.

v. Hereford United

League Cup	Date	Result	Ipswich	Hereford		Division	Ipswich	Hereford
1974-75 Round 3	8 October	Won	4	1			Div 1	Div 3

Summary	P	W	D	L	F	A
Ipswich's cup record	1	1	0	0	4	1
TOTAL	1	1	0	0	4	1

FACT FILE

● **Goals from Johnson, Talbot, Hunter and Whymark were more than enough for the Blues.**

Played for both clubs

Bobby Kellard	Ipswich 1965-66	Hereford 1974-75
Derek Jefferson	Ipswich 1967-68 to 1972-73	Hereford 1976-77 to 1977-78
John Jackson	Ipswich 1981-82	Hereford 1982-83
Ian Juryeff	Ipswich 1988-89	Hereford 1989-90 to 1990-91
David Gregory	Ipswich 1988-89 to 1994-95	Hereford 1994-95

David Gregory was always the nearly man at Ipswich. In his seven seasons at the club, after graduating from the youth team, Gregory made just 23 starts for Ipswich, scoring six goals. His final game for Town was against Chelsea in the Premier League when he came on as substitute in the 2-0 defeat at Stamford Bridge in 1994. Gregory had a spell at Hereford on loan, before signing for Peterborough United in July 1995.

v. Hoffman Athletic

FA Cup					Date	Result	Away Ipswich Hoffman		Division Ipswich Hoffman	
1937-38 4th Qual					13 November	Won	3	0	Non L	Non L

Summary	P	W	D	L	F	A
Ipswich's cup record	1	1	0	0	3	0
TOTAL	1	1	0	0	3	0

FACT FILE

● With entry into the Football League awaiting at the end of the season, this was to be Ipswich's last-ever FA Cup qualifying match.

Ipswich's top scorers vs Hoffman
Ambrose Mulraney 2

Ambrose Mulraney (2) and Gilbert Alsop scored the goals in this FA Cup fixture. Ipswich were knocked out of the competition when they lost their first round match 2-1 to Yeovil and Petters United.

v. Huddersfield Town

Season	League	Date	Result	Home Ipswich	Huddersfield	Date	Result	Away Ipswich	Huddersfield	Final Positions Ipswich	Huddersfield
1957-58	Division 2	5 April	Won	4	0	12 October	Lost	0	3	8th	9th
1958-59	Division 2	18 October	Drew	0	0	7 March	Lost	0	3	16th	14th
1959-60	Division 2	22 August	Lost	1	4	19 December	Lost	1	3	11th	6th
1960-61	Division 2	26 November	Won	4	2	1 April	Won	3	1	1stP	20th
1964-65	Division 2	26 December	Won	3	2	28 December	Drew	0	0	5th	8th
1965-66	Division 2	31 August	Drew	2	2	24 August	Lost	0	1	15th	4th
1966-67	Division 2	23 August	Won	3	0	30 August	Lost	0	1	5th	6th
1967-68	Division 2	20 January	Won	2	0	16 September	Won	4	1	1stP	14th
1970-71	Division 1	17 April	Won	2	0	10 October	Lost	0	1	19th	15th
1971-72	Division 1	20 November	Won	1	0	8 April	Won	3	1	13th	22ndR
1986-87	Division 2	1 November	Won	3	0	11 April	Won	2	1	5th	17th
1987-88	Division 2	3 November	Won	3	0	8 April	Won	2	1	8th	23rdR
1995-96	Division 1	1 May	Won	2	1	9 September	Lost	1	2	7th	8th
1996-97	Division 1	7 September	Lost	1	3	28 December	Lost	0	2	4th	20th
1997-98	Division 1	14 February	Won	5	1	13 September	Drew	2	2	5th	16th
1998-99	Division 1	13 March	Won	3	0	7 November	Drew	2	2	3rd	10th
1999-00	Division 1	12 February	Won	2	1	1 November	Lost	1	3	3rdP	8th

FA Cup

							Division	
1958-59	Round 3	10 January	Won	1	0	Div 2	Div 2

Summary

	P	W	D	L	F	A
Ipswich's home league record	17	13	2	2	41	16
Ipswich's away league record	17	5	3	9	21	28
Ipswich's cup record	1	1	0	0	1	0
TOTAL	**35**	**19**	**5**	**11**	**63**	**44**

Alex Mathie (pictured) stands just below Ted Phillips, Ray Crawford and David Johnson in the scoring charts versus Huddersfield. One of these goals came in the 5-1 demolition of the Terriers on Valentine's Day 1998 at Portman Road, Ipswich's record score against the Yorkshire club. The other Town scorers that day were Matt Holland, David Johnson (2) and Richard Naylor. Mathie carried on his goalscoring run just seven days later, scoring a hat-trick in the 5-0 trouncing of arch-rivals Norwich.

FACT FILE

- Between 1966 and 1996, Ipswich won seven home games in a row against Huddersfield, keeping clean sheets in the first six of these.
- Both sides have failed to win in a home game just once each.

Ipswich's top scorers vs Huddersfield
Ted Phillips, Ray Crawford, David Johnson (II) 4
Alex Mathie 3

Played for both clubs

Jackie Williams	Huddersfield 1932-33 to 1935-36	Ipswich 1938-39
Tom Lang	Huddersfield 1934-35 to 1935-36	Ipswich 1946-47
Harry Baird	Huddersfield 1938-39	Ipswich 1946-47 to 1951-52
Rod Belfitt	Ipswich 1971-72 to 1972-73	Huddersfield 1974-75 to 1975-76
Mark Stuart	Ipswich 1989-90	Huddersfield 1992-93
Eddie Youds	Ipswich 1991-92 to 1994-95	Huddersfield 2002-03
Marcus Stewart	Huddersfield 1996-97 to 1999-00	Ipswich 1999-00 to 2002-03
Alun Armstrong	Huddersfield 1999-00	Ipswich 2000-01 to 2003-04

v. Hull City

Season	League	Date	Result	Home Ipswich	Hull	Date	Result	Away Ipswich	Hull	Final Positions Ipswich	Hull
1954-55	Division 2	18 April	Won	2	0	4 September	Lost	2	4	21stR	19th
1959-60	Division 2	31 October	Won	2	0	30 April	Lost	0	2	11th	21stR
1966-67	Division 2	22 October	Won	5	4	18 March	Drew	1	1	5th	12th
1967-68	Division 2	16 April	Won	2	0	15 April	Drew	1	1	1stP	17th
1986-87	Division 2	28 March	Drew	0	0	4 October	Lost	1	2	5th	14th
1987-88	Division 2	12 March	Won	2	0	10 October	Lost	0	1	8th	15th
1988-89	Division 2	8 April	Drew	1	1	31 December	Drew	1	1	8th	21st
1989-90	Division 2	21 March	Lost	0	1	1 May	Lost	3	4	9th	14th
1990-91	Division 2	23 February	Won	2	0	10 November	Drew	3	3	14th	24thR

Summary	P	W	D	L	F	A
Ipswich's home league record	9	6	2	1	16	6
Ipswich's away league record	9	0	4	5	12	19
TOTAL	**18**	**6**	**6**	**6**	**28**	**25**

Ipswich's top scorers vs Hull
Ray Crawford 5
Frank Brogan 4
David Lowe, Ian Redford 3

Ipswich hat-tricks vs Hull
22 October 1966 Ray Crawford

Played for both clubs
Billy Baxter	Ipswich 1960-61 to 1970-71	Hull 1970-71 to 1971-72
Dale Roberts	Ipswich 1974-75 to 1978-79	Hull 1979-80 to 1984-85
Neil Thompson	Hull 1981-82 to 1982-83	Ipswich 1989-90 to 1995-96
Richard Appleby	Ipswich 1995-96	Hull 2002-03

FACT FILE

- Ipswich never won at Boothferry Park.
- Four of Hull's six goals at Portman Road came in the same match - and they still lost.

Geordie centre-half Dale Roberts (pictured) came through the Ipswich youth team, making his debut as an 18-year-old against Birmingham City on 28 December 1974. He was at Portman Road for six years, but couldn't establish himself in the first team, making only 22 (+1) appearances in that time. In February 1980 he joined Hull City, where he made 149 (+4) appearances before a pelvic injury eventually forced his early retirement from playing. Roberts later achieved success at Ipswich in his role as part of George Burley's backroom team, guiding the reserves to the FA Premiership Reserve League South title in 2002.

v. Huntington County

FA Cup	Date	Result	Home Ipswich	Huntington	Division Ipswich	Huntington
1890-91 3rd Qual	15 November	Won	5	2	Non L	Non L

Summary	P	W	D	L	F	A
Ipswich's cup record	1	1	0	0	5	2
TOTAL	1	1	0	0	5	2

Ipswich's top scorers vs Huntington
Percy Turner 2

George S. Sherrington scored one of the goals in the 5-2 win over Huntington County. Sherrington joined the club from Ipswich School with his brother W.S. Sherrington, scoring four goals on his debut in 1878. The following season he captained the club while still at school and later played for Cambridge University, Crusaders and Corinthians. Sherrington was one of the most prominent figures in the development of football in Suffolk.

v. Kidderminster Harriers

		Home							Division	
League Cup	_Date_	_Result_	Ipswich	Harriers					Ipswich	Harriers
2003-04 Round 1	13 August	Won*	**1**	**0**					Div 1	Div 3

Summary	_P_	_W_	_D_	_L_	_F_	_A_
Ipswich's cup record	1	1	0	0	1	0
TOTAL	**1**	**1**	**0**	**0**	**1**	**0**

FACT FILE

● **An extra-time goal from Dean Bowditch allowed Ipswich to sneak past Harriers.**

Played for both clubs

Richard Appleby   Ipswich 1995-96   Kidderminster 2001-02 to 2004-05

Third division Kidderminster Harriers should have been a straightforward tie to negotiate at home, hence the attendance of a mere 11,118 versus the 24,830 that had attended the first game of the season against Reading just four days earlier. However, Ipswich struggled to break through. England Under-17 international Dean Bowditch (pictured) came to the rescue just 30 seconds into extra-time, when his left-foot shot beat the Harriers keeper Stuart Brock, setting up a second-round match away at Notts County. This time Ipswich weren't as lucky, losing 2-1 at Meadow Lane.

v. Kirkley

FA Cup		Date	Result	Home Ipswich	Kirkley	Date	Result	Away Ipswich	Kirkley	Division Ipswich	Kirkley
1932-33	ExPrelim	3 September	Drew	0	0	8 September	Won	3	2	Non L	Non L

Summary	P	W	D	L	F	A
Ipswich's cup record	2	1	1	0	3	2
TOTAL	2	1	1	0	3	2

FACT FILE

- Jones, Rodwell and Groom scored the goals in the second of Ipswich's three participations in the extra preliminary round of the FA Cup.

v. Leeds United

Season	League	Date	Result	Ipswich	Leeds	Date	Result	Ipswich	Leeds	Ipswich	Leeds
		Home					**Away**			**Final Positions**	
1954-55	Division 2	25 September	Lost	1	2	12 February	Lost	1	4	21stR	4th
1960-61	Division 2	18 February	Won	4	0	1 October	Won	5	2	1stP	14th
1968-69	Division 1	20 August	Lost	2	3	12 February	Lost	0	2	12th	1st
1969-70	Division 1	21 April	Won	3	2	8 November	Lost	0	4	18th	2nd
1970-71	Division 1	23 February	Lost	2	4	12 December	Drew	0	0	19th	2nd
1971-72	Division 1	28 August	Lost	0	2	8 January	Drew	2	2	13th	2nd
1972-73	Division 1	4 November	Drew	2	2	23 August	Drew	3	3	4th	3rd
1973-74	Division 1	8 December	Lost	0	3	20 April	Lost	2	3	4th	1st
1974-75	Division 1	12 October	Drew	0	0	19 April	Lost	1	2	3rd	9th
1975-76	Division 1	13 December	Won	2	1	23 August	Lost	0	1	6th	5th
1976-77	Division 1	20 November	Drew	1	1	16 April	Lost	1	2	3rd	10th
1977-78	Division 1	4 February	Lost	0	1	10 September	Lost	1	2	18th	9th
1978-79	Division 1	1 December	Lost	2	3	7 April	Drew	1	1	6th	5th
1979-80	Division 1	14 March	Won	1	0	6 October	Lost	1	2	3rd	11th
1980-81	Division 1	4 October	Drew	1	1	31 March	Lost	0	3	2nd	9th
1981-82	Division 1	26 September	Won	2	1	20 February	Won	2	0	2nd	20thR
1986-87	Division 2	1 January	Won	2	0	18 April	Lost	2	3	5th	4th
1987-88	Division 2	5 September	Won	1	0	6 February	Lost	0	1	8th	7th
1988-89	Division 2	5 November	Lost	0	1	11 March	Won	4	2	8th	10th
1989-90	Division 2	17 February	Drew	2	2	9 September	Drew	1	1	9th	1stP
1992-93	Premiership	3 October	Won	4	2	27 February	Lost	0	1	16th	17th
1993-94	Premiership	17 October	Drew	0	0	15 January	Drew	0	0	19th	5th
1994-95	Premiership	1 November	Won	2	0	5 April	Lost	0	4	22ndR	5th
2000-01	Premiership	3 February	Lost	1	2	16 September	Won	2	1	5th	4th
2001-02	Premiership	30 September	Lost	1	2	6 March	Lost	0	2	18thR	5th
2004-05	Champ'ship	13 November	Won	1	0	23 April	Drew	1	1	3rd	14th

FA Cup

Season	Round	Date	Result	Ipswich	Leeds	Date	Result	Ipswich	Leeds	Division	
1974-75	Q'ter-Final	8 March	Drew	0	0	11 March	Drew*	1	1	Div 1	Div 1
		25 March				Filbert Street (2nd replay)	Drew*	0	1		
		27 March				Filbert Street (3rd replay)	Won	3	3		
1989-90	Round 3					6 January	Won	1	0	Div 2	Div 2

League Cup

Season	Round	Date	Result	Ipswich	Leeds	Date	Result	Ipswich	Leeds	Division	
1973-74	Round 2	8 October	Won	2	0					Div 1	Div 1
1975-76	Round 2					9 September	Lost	2	3	Div 1	Div 1
1981-82	Round 2	27 October	Won	3	0	7 October	Won	1	0	Div 1	Div 1

Summary

	P	W	D	L	F	A
Ipswich's home league record	26	10	6	10	37	35
Ipswich's away league record	26	4	7	15	30	49
Ipswich's cup record	9	5	3	1	13	6
TOTAL	**61**	**19**	**16**	**26**	**80**	**90**

FACT FILE

- The 1975 cup tie is the only one in which Ipswich have gone to three replays. A magnificent winning goal from Clive Woods eventually saw the men from Suffolk into the FA Cup semi-finals for the very first time.
- This tie produced another record when the 0-0 draw in the first match was seen by Portman Road's largest ever attendance – 38,010.
- Ipswich failed to win in 15 visits to Leeds from 1969 to 1981.

Ipswich's top scorers vs Leeds
John Wark 7
Ray Crawford 5
Bryan Hamilton, Eric Gates, Paul Mariner 4
Ted Phillips, David Johnson (I), Brian Talbot 3

Ipswich hat-tricks vs Leeds
1 October 1960 Ray Crawford

Played for both clubs

Rod Belfitt	Leeds 1964-65 to 1971-72	Ipswich 1971-72 to 1972-73
Chris O'Donnell	Ipswich 1986-87 to 1988-89	Leeds 1989-90
Lee Chapman	Leeds 1989-90 to 1992-93 & 1995-96	Ipswich 1994-95 to 1995-96
David Kerslake	Leeds 1992-93	Ipswich 1997-98
Jermaine Wright	Ipswich 1999-00 to 2003-04	Leeds 2004-05

Steve Palmer fends off Leeds United's Gary Speed as Rod Wallace looks on.

v. Leicester City

Season	League	Date	Result	Ipswich	Leicester	Date	Result	Ipswich	Leicester	Ipswich	Leicester
		Home					**Away**			**Final Positions**	
1961-62	Division 1	26 December	Won	1	0	28 March	Won	2	0	1st	14th
1962-63	Division 1	6 October	Lost	0	1	23 February	Lost	0	3	17th	4th
1963-64	Division 1	30 March	Drew	1	1	31 March	Lost	1	2	22ndR	11th
1968-69	Division 1	3 May	Won	2	1	17 August	Won	3	1	12th	21stR
1971-72	Division 1	11 September	Lost	1	2	25 March	Lost	0	1	13th	12th
1972-73	Division 1	30 September	Lost	0	2	24 April	Drew	1	1	4th	16th
1973-74	Division 1	25 August	Drew	1	1	19 January	Lost	0	5	4th	9th
1974-75	Division 1	29 March	Won	2	1	20 December	Won	1	0	3rd	18th
1975-76	Division 1	18 October	Drew	1	1	22 November	Drew	0	0	6th	7th
1976-77	Division 1	11 September	Drew	0	0	19 February	Lost	0	1	3rd	11th
1977-78	Division 1	17 December	Won	1	0	12 November	Lost	1	2	18th	22ndR
1980-81	Division 1	15 November	Won	3	1	16 August	Won	1	0	2nd	21stR
1983-84	Division 1	22 October	Drew	0	0	25 February	Lost	0	2	12th	15th
1984-85	Division 1	23 April	Won	2	0	8 September	Lost	1	2	17th	15th
1985-86	Division 1	8 April	Lost	0	2	28 September	Lost	0	1	20thR	19th
1987-88	Division 2	20 February	Lost	0	2	30 September	Drew	1	1	8th	13th
1988-89	Division 2	1 January	Won	2	0	10 September	Won	1	0	8th	15th
1989-90	Division 2	3 March	Drew	2	2	18 November	Won	1	0	9th	13th
1990-91	Division 2	4 May	Won	3	2	27 October	Won	2	1	14th	22nd
1991-92	Division 2	14 March	Drew	0	0	1 November	Drew	2	2	1stP	4th
1994-95	Premiership	1 January	Won	4	1	29 April	Lost	0	2	22ndR	21stR
1995-96	Division 1	3 March	Won	4	2	13 March	Won	2	0	7th	5thP
2000-01	Premiership	14 January	Won	2	0	6 September	Lost	1	2	5th	13th
2001-02	Premiership	26 December	Won	2	0	8 September	Drew	1	1	18thR	20thR
2002-03	Division 1	18 August	Won	6	1	26 December	Won	2	1	7th	2ndP
2004-05	Champ'ship	12 February	Won	2	1	19 October	Drew	2	2	3rd	15th

FA Cup

										Division	
1962-63	Round 4					30 January	Lost	1	3	Div 1	Div 1

League Cup

1996-97	Q'ter-Final	21 January	Lost	0	1					Div 1	Prem

Summary

	P	W	D	L	F	A
Ipswich's home league record	26	14	7	5	42	24
Ipswich's away league record	26	9	6	11	26	33
Ipswich's cup record	2	0	0	2	1	4
TOTAL	**54**	**23**	**13**	**18**	**69**	**61**

Ipswich's top scorers vs Leicester City

John Wark 4

Ray Crawford, Trevor Whymark, Micky Stockwell, Chris Kiwomya, Ian Marshall 3

- **Ipswich are unbeaten in their last 10 league games against Leicester, having won the last six of them.**
- **There has been just one goalless draw in the last 28 meetings between the sides.**

Played for both clubs

Roy Stephenson	Leicester 1958-59 to 1959-60	Ipswich 1960-61 to 1964-65
Bobby Kellard	Ipswich 1965-66	Leicester 1970-71 to 1971-72
Billy Houghton	Ipswich 1966-67 to 1968-69	Leicester 1969-70
Paul Cooper	Ipswich 1973-74 to 1986-87	Leicester 1987-88 to 1988-89
Russell Osman	Ipswich 1977-78 to 1984-85	Leicester 1985-86 to 1987-88
Mich D'Avray	Ipswich 1979-80 to 1989-90	Leicester 1986-87
Mark Grew	Leicester 1983-84	Ipswich 1984-85
Mark Venus	Leicester 1985-86 to 1987-88	Ipswich 1997-98 to 2002-03
David Lowe	Ipswich 1987-88 to 1991-92	Leicester 1992-93 to 1995-96
Ian Marshall	Ipswich 1993-94 to 1996-97	Leicester 199-697 to 1999-00
James Scowcroft	Ipswich 1995-96 to 2000-01 & 2004-05	Leicester 2001-02 to 2004-05
Matt Elliott	Leicester 1996-97 to 2004-05	Ipswich 2003-04
Chris Makin	Ipswich 2000-01 to 2003-04	Leicester 2004-05
Marcus Bent	Ipswich 2001-02 to 2003-04	Leicester 2003-04

Trevor Whymark (pictured falling to the ground) fires off a shot at Portman Road against Leicester City, as Steve Kember, Keith Weller and Dennis Rofe challenge for the ball.

v. Leiston Works

FA Cup		Home				Away			Division	
		Date	Result	Ipswich	Leiston	Date	Result	Ipswich	Leiston	Ipswich	Leiston
1930-31	Prelim	20 September	Won	5	2					Non L	Non L
1931-32	Prelim					19 September	Lost	2	3	Non L	Non L

Summary	P	W	D	L	F	A
Ipswich's cup record	2	1	0	1	7	5
TOTAL	2	1	0	1	7	5

Ipswich's top scorers vs Leiston
Dammo Green 2

v. Leyton Orient

			Home				Away			Final Positions	
Season	League	Date	Result	Ipswich	Leyton O	Date	Result	Ipswich	Leyton O	Ipswich	Leyton O
1938-39	Division 3S	22 April	Won	3	0	17 December	Drew	1	1	7th	20th
1939-40	Division 3S					26 August	Drew	2	2		
1946-47	Division 3S	28 December	Drew	0	0	31 August	Drew	2	2	6th	19th
1947-48	Division 3S	29 March	Won	1	0	26 March	Drew	1	1	4th	17th
1948-49	Division 3S	13 November	Drew	2	2	9 April	Drew	1	1	7th	19th
1949-50	Division 3S	17 September	Drew	4	4	21 January	Lost	0	4	17th	18th
1950-51	Division 3S	23 August	Drew	2	2	31 August	Lost	0	2	8th	19th
1951-52	Division 3S	22 March	Won	1	0	3 November	Lost	0	2	17th	18th
1952-53	Division 3S	25 March	Lost	0	1	26 December	Lost	1	3	16th	14th
1953-54	Division 3S	5 September	Won	3	1	16 January	Won	2	1	1stP	11th
1955-56	Division 3S	21 April	Won	2	0	3 May	Won	2	1	3rd	1stP
1957-58	Division 2	30 November	Won	5	3	12 April	Lost	0	2	8th	12th
1958-59	Division 2	27 August	Won	2	1	4 September	Lost	0	2	16th	17th
1959-60	Division 2	1 January	Won	6	3	29 August	Lost	1	4	11th	10th
1960-61	Division 2	17 December	Won	6	2	20 August	Won	3	1	1stP	19th
1962-63	Division 1	13 April	Drew	1	1	10 November	Won	2	1	17th	22ndR
1964-65	Division 2	10 April	Drew	1	1	28 November	Drew	0	0	5th	19th
1965-66	Division 2	11 April	Won	3	2	8 April	Won	4	1	15th	22ndR

FA Cup										Division	
1950-51	Round 1					25 November	Won	2	1	Div 3S	Div 3S
1978-79	Round 4	27 January	Drew	0	0	30 January	Won	2	0	Div 1	Div 2

League Cup										Division	
1988-89	Round 3	1 November	Won	2	0					Div 2	Div 4

Summary	P	W	D	L	F	A
Ipswich's home league record	17	10	6	1	42	23
Ipswich's away league record	18	5	6	7	22	31
Ipswich's cup record	4	3	1	0	6	1
TOTAL	39	18	13	8	70	55

FACT FILE

- Micky Stockwell and Jason Dozzell scored the goals the last time the sides met.
- Orient have not won in their last 11 visits to Suffolk. They have also not won in their last 11 games home or away against the Blues.
- Ipswich were unbeaten in their first 10 games in the series, although eight of these were drawn.

Ipswich's top scorers vs Leyton Orient

Ray Crawford 7
Doug Milward 6
Ted Phillips 5
Jackie Little, Jimmy Leadbetter, Derek Rees 3

Ipswich hat-tricks vs Leyton Orient

2 January 1960 Doug Milward
17 December 1960 Ray Crawford

Played for both clubs

Charlie Fletcher	Orient 1930-31 to 1932-33	Ipswich 1938-39 to 1939-40
George Rumbold	Orient 1937-38 to 1938-39	Ipswich 1946-47 to 1949-50
Ted Pole	Ipswich 1946-47 to 1950-51	Orient 1951-52 to 1952-53
Ted Phillips	Ipswich 1953-54 to 1963-64	Orient 1963-64 to 1964-65
Cyril Lea	Orient 1957-58 to 1964-65	Ipswich 1964-65 to 1968-69
Andy Nelson	Ipswich 1959-60 to 1964-65	Orient 1964-65 to 1965-66
Dave Harper	Ipswich 1964-65 to 1966-67	Orient 1967-68 to 1970-71
John Jackson	Orient 1973-74 to 1978-79	Ipswich 1981-82
Trevor Putney	Ipswich 1982-83 to 1985-86	Orient 1993-94
Ian Juryeff	Orient 1984-85 to 1988-89	Ipswich 1988-89
Ron Fearon	Ipswich 1987-88 to 1988-89	Orient 1995-96
Scott Houghton	Ipswich 1990-91	Orient 2000-01 to 2001-02
Chris Bart-Williams	Orient 1990-91 to 1991-92	Ipswich 2003-04
Darren Currie	Orient 1995-96	Ipswich 2004-05
Jamie Clapham	Orient 1996-97	Ipswich 1997-98 to 2002-03
Lee Hodges	Orient 1996-97	Ipswich 1998-99

Midfielder Darren Currie had played for seven different clubs before ending up at Portman Road in a £250,000 move from Brighton and Hove Albion. He signed as a trainee at West Ham United in 1993 but failed to make the first team. His loan spell at Orient in 1995 followed two similar spells at Shrewsbury, but Currie's career seemed to be going backwards when he signed for Barnet on a free transfer in 1998. Good spells at Barnet, Wycombe and Brighton gave Joe Royle all he needed to try the player at the higher level of football.

v. Lincoln City

Season	League	Date	Result	Home Ipswich	Lincoln C	Date	Result	Away Ipswich	Lincoln C	Final Positions Ipswich	Lincoln C
1954-55	Division 2	11 September	Lost	1	2	27 April	Drew	1	1	21stR	16th
1957-58	Division 2	18 January	Drew	1	1	14 September	Lost	1	2	8th	20th
1958-59	Division 2	13 September	Won	4	1	31 January	Lost	1	3	16th	19th
1959-60	Division 2	5 September	Won	3	0	16 January	Won	1	0	11th	13th
1960-61	Division 2	12 November	Won	3	1	15 April	Won	4	1	1stP	22ndR

Summary	P	W	D	L	F	A
Ipswich's home league record	5	3	1	1	12	5
Ipswich's away league record	5	2	1	2	8	7
TOTAL	**10**	**5**	**2**	**3**	**20**	**12**

FACT FILE

● **Ipswich have never failed to score against Lincoln.**

Ipswich's top scorers vs Lincoln City
Jimmy Leadbetter, Ray Crawford 3

Played for both clubs

Laurie Sivell	Ipswich 1969-70 to 1983-84	Lincoln 1978-79
David Hill	Ipswich 1988-89 to 1990-91	Lincoln 1993-94 to 1994-95

Only two players have played for both Ipswich Town and Lincoln City, Laurie Sivell and David Hill (pictured). Nottingham-born Hill spent much of his early career at Scunthorpe United, punctuated by a three-season stay at Portman Road, where the midfielder made 62 (+5) appearances. Following his second spell at Scunthorpe, Hill moved inland to Lincoln City, where he scored six goals in his 52 starts for the Imps.

v. Liverpool

Season	League	Date (Home)	Result	Ipswich	Liverpool	Date (Away)	Result	Ipswich	Liverpool	Ipswich	Liverpool
1954-55	Division 2	27 December	Won	2	0	25 December	Lost	2	6	21stR	11th
1957-58	Division 2	16 November	Won	3	1	29 March	Lost	1	3	8th	4th
1958-59	Division 2	29 November	Won	2	0	18 April	Lost	1	3	16th	4th
1959-60	Division 2	23 April	Lost	0	1	5 December	Lost	1	3	11th	3rd
1960-61	Division 2	10 September	Won	1	0	21 January	Drew	1	1	1stP	3rd
1962-63	Division 1	5 March	Drew	2	2	15 September	Drew	1	1	17th	8th
1963-64	Division 1	26 October	Lost	1	2	7 March	Lost	0	6	22ndR	1st
1968-69	Division 1	14 September	Lost	0	2	19 April	Lost	0	4	12th	2nd
1969-70	Division 1	18 October	Drew	2	2	24 March	Lost	0	2	18th	5th
1970-71	Division 1	24 October	Won	1	0	29 March	Lost	1	2	19th	5th
1971-72	Division 1	4 December	Drew	0	0	22 April	Lost	0	2	13th	3rd
1972-73	Division 1	16 December	Drew	1	1	24 February	Lost	1	2	4th	1st
1973-74	Division 1	13 April	Drew	1	1	17 November	Lost	2	4	4th	2nd
1974-75	Division 1	1 November	Won	1	0	8 February	Lost	2	5	3rd	2nd
1975-76	Division 1	13 September	Won	2	0	10 January	Drew	3	3	6th	1st
1976-77	Division 1	4 December	Won	1	0	30 April	Lost	1	2	3rd	1st
1977-78	Division 1	17 September	Drew	1	1	18 April	Drew	2	2	18th	2nd
1978-79	Division 1	22 August	Lost	0	3	24 March	Lost	0	2	6th	1st
1979-80	Division 1	13 October	Lost	1	2	23 February	Drew	1	1	3rd	1st
1980-81	Division 1	13 December	Drew	1	1	11 October	Drew	1	1	2nd	5th
1981-82	Division 1	12 September	Won	2	0	6 February	Lost	0	4	2nd	1st
1982-83	Division 1	1 October	Won	1	0	12 February	Lost	0	1	9th	1st
1983-84	Division 1	26 November	Drew	1	1	28 April	Drew	2	2	12th	1st
1984-85	Division 1	27 April	Drew	0	0	24 November	Lost	0	2	17th	2nd
1985-86	Division 1	1 February	Won	2	1	26 August	Lost	0	5	20thR	1st
1992-93	Premiership	25 August	Drew	2	2	20 February	Drew	0	0	16th	6th
1993-94	Premiership	1 January	Lost	1	2	9 April	Lost	0	1	19th	8th
1994-95	Premiership	29 October	Lost	1	3	14 January	Won	1	0	22ndR	4th
2000-01	Premiership	10 April	Drew	1	1	10 December	Won	1	0	5th	3rd
2001-02	Premiership	9 February	Lost	0	6	11 May	Lost	0	5	18thR	2nd

FA Cup

Season	Round	Date (Home)	Result	Ipswich	Liverpool	Date (Away)	Result	Ipswich	Liverpool	Division Ipswich	Division Liverpool
1973-74	Round 5					16 February	Lost	0	2	Div 1	Div 1
1974-75	Round 4	25 January	Won	1	0					Div 1	Div 1
1978-79	Q'ter-Final	10 March	Lost	0	1					Div 1	Div 1
1991-92	Round 5	16 February	Drew	0	0	26 February	Lost*	2	3	Div 2	Div 1

League Cup

Season	Round	Date (Home)	Result	Ipswich	Liverpool	Date (Away)	Result	Ipswich	Liverpool	Division Ipswich	Division Liverpool
1981-82	Semi-Final	1 February	Lost	0	2	9 February	Drew	2	2	Div 1	Div 1
1982-83	Round 2	4 October	Lost	1	2	26 October	Lost	0	2	Div 1	Div 1
1985-86	Q'ter-Final					21 January	Lost	0	3	Div 1	Div 1
1993-94	Round 3					27 October	Lost	2	3	Prem	Prem
2002-03	Round 4					4 December	Drew*	1	1	Div 1	Prem

(lost 4-5 pens)

FACT FILE

- Not surprisingly, no club has a better record against Ipswich than Liverpool, at least not among teams that have faced Ipswich more than three times.
- No other club has played as many as 12 cup matches against Ipswich.
- Ipswich's heaviest-ever home league defeat came at the hands of Liverpool in 2002.
- In December 2002, Ipswich lost their second penalty shoot-out inside three weeks, having been knocked out of the UEFA Cup by Slovan Liberec. Their current record in penalty shoot-outs stands at played five, lost five.
- In the 2001-02 season, Liverpool beat Ipswich twice by an aggregate of 11-0.
- When Adam Tanner scored Ipswich's winner at Anfield in January 1995, it provided possibly the biggest shock in Premiership history. It was Ipswich's first-ever win at Anfield, at the 34th time of asking, and came in possibly the worst season in Ipswich's history.
- Liverpool failed to win at Portman Road in 10 visits between 1969 and 1977.

Summary	P	W	D	L	F	A
Ipswich's home league record	30	11	11	8	34	35
Ipswich's away league record	30	2	8	20	25	75
Ipswich's cup record	12	1	3	8	9	21
TOTAL	72	14	22	36	68	131

(+ one penalty shoot-out defeat)

Ipswich's top scorers vs Liverpool
Trevor Whymark 6
Ted Phillips, Eric Gates 5
John Wark 4
Ray Crawford, Mick Lambert, David Johnson (I) 3

Played for both clubs

Charlie Ashcroft	Liverpool 1946-47 to 1954-55	Ipswich 1955-56
David Johnson	Ipswich 1972-73 to 1975-76	Liverpool 1976-77 to 1981-82
John Wark	Ipswich 1974-75 to 1983-84, 1987-88 to 1989-90 & 1991-92 to 1996-97	Liverpool 1983-84 to 1987-88
John Scales	Liverpool 1994-95 to 1996-97	Ipswich 2000-01

Dave Johnson (pictured here keeping a close eye on the ball despite the attention of Liverpool 'keeper Ray Clemence) was a hero at both Ipswich and Liverpool. Born on Merseyside, Johnson actually signed as an apprentice for Everton in April 1969, but it was at Portman Road that he made his name, playing 174 (+4) matches in only four seasons, a staggering number. In that time, he netted 46 times, three of which were against Liverpool. In 1976 he returned to the North-West as Liverpool's big summer signing, for their then record fee of £200,000. He won a title medal in his first season at the club, and again in 1978-79, eventually ending with four championship medals and a European Cup-winners' medal before rejoining Everton in 1982. He shares with Peter Beardsley the distinction of scoring winning Merseyside derby goals for both clubs.

v. Lowestoft Town

FA Cup		Date	Result	Home Ipswich	Lowestoft	Date	Result	Away Ipswich	Lowestoft	Division Ipswich	Lowestoft
1936-37	2nd Qual	21 October	Won	7	1	17 October	Drew	1	1	Non L	Non L

Summary	P	W	D	L	F	A
Ipswich's cup record	2	1	1	0	8	2
TOTAL	2	1	1	0	8	2

Ipswich's top scorers vs Lowestoft
George Perrett 3
Jackie Williams 2

Ipswich hat-tricks vs Lowestoft
21 October 1936 George Perrett (cup)

Lowestoft Town probably thought that they stood a chance in the replay at neighbours Ipswich following their 1-1 draw on 17 October 1937. Four days later they left Portman Road on the wrong end of a 7-1 thrashing with George Perrett (pictured) notching a hat-trick.

v. Luton Town

Season	League	Date	Result	Home Ipswich	Luton	Date	Result	Away Ipswich	Luton	Final Positions Ipswich	Luton
1954-55	Division 2	28 August	Won	3	1	1 January	Lost	2	3	21stR	2ndP
1960-61	Division 2	25 March	Lost	0	1	5 November	Lost	2	3	1stP	13th
1974-75	Division 1	26 December	Lost	0	1	14 September	Won	4	1	3rd	20thR
1982-83	Division 1	26 February	Won	3	0	16 October	Drew	1	1	9th	18th
1983-84	Division 1	31 March	Won	3	0	13 March	Lost	1	2	12th	16th
1984-85	Division 1	28 August	Drew	1	1	30 March	Lost	1	3	17th	13th
1985-86	Division 1	28 December	Drew	1	1	1 October	Lost	0	1	20thR	9th
1995-96	Division 1	22 October	Lost	0	1	30 March	Won	2	1	7th	24thR

FA Cup

										Division	
1958-59	Round 5	14 February	Lost	2	5					Div 2	Div 1
1961-62	Round 3	6 January	Drew	1	1	10 January	Drew*	1	1	Div 1	Div 2
		15 January	Highbury (2nd replay)				Won	5	1		
1981-82	Round 4					23 January	Won	3	0	Div 1	Div 2

League Cup

1987-88	Round 4	17 November	Lost	0	1					Div 2	Div 1
1998-99	Round 2	15 September	Won	2	1	22 September	Lost*	2	4	Div 1	Div 2

Summary

	P	W	D	L	F	A
Ipswich's home league record	8	3	2	3	11	6
Ipswich's away league record	8	2	1	5	13	15
Ipswich's cup record	8	3	2	3	16	14
TOTAL	**24**	**8**	**5**	**11**	**40**	**35**

Ipswich's top scorers vs Luton
Eric Gates 5
Ted Phillips 4
Alan Brazil, Trevor Putney 3

Played for both clubs

Allenby Driver	Luton 1946-47 to 1947-48	Ipswich 1949-50 to 1950-52
Joe O'Brien	Luton 1947-48 to 1948-49	Ipswich 1949-50 to 1950-51
Willie Havenga	Luton 1950-51 to 1951-52	Ipswich 1951-52 to 1952-53
Ted Phillips	Ipswich 1953-54 to 1963-64	Luton 1964-65
John O'Rourke	Luton 1963-64 to 1965-66	Ipswich 1967-68 to 1969-70
David Geddis	Luton 1976-77 & 1982-83	Ipswich 1976-77 to 1978-79
Mark Stein	Luton 1983-84 to 1987-88 & 2000-01	Ipswich 1997-98
Raphael Meade	Luton 1988-89	Ipswich 1989-90
Gavin Johnson	Ipswich 1988-89 to 1994-95	Luton 1995-96
Scott Houghton	Ipswich 1990-91	Luton 1993-94 to 1994-95
Andrew Petterson	Ipswich 1992-93 & 1995-96	Luton 1992-93 to 1993-94
Bontcho Guentchev	Ipswich 1992-93 to 1994-95	Luton 1995-96 to 1996-97
Kelvin Davies	Luton 1993-94 to 1998-99	Ipswich 2003-04 to 2004-05
Neil Midgley	Ipswich 1999-00	Luton 1999-00

v. Manchester City

		Home				Away				Final Positions	
Season	League	Date	Result	Ipswich	Man C	Date	Result	Ipswich	Man C	Ipswich	Man C
1961-62	Division 1	26 August	Lost	2	4	23 December	Lost	0	3	1st	12th
1962-63	Division 1	11 September	Drew	0	0	5 September	Lost	1	2	17th	21stR
1964-65	Division 2	27 March	Won	4	1	14 November	Lost	0	4	5th	11th
1965-66	Division 2	23 April	Drew	1	1	27 November	Lost	1	2	15th	1stP
1968-69	Division 1	11 March	Won	2	1	31 August	Drew	1	1	12th	13th
1969-70	Division 1	1 November	Drew	1	1	28 February	Lost	0	1	18th	10th
1970-71	Division 1	26 February	Won	2	0	31 October	Lost	0	2	19th	11th
1971-72	Division 1	18 April	Won	2	1	11 December	Lost	0	4	13th	4th
1972-73	Division 1	7 April	Drew	1	1	1 December	Drew	1	1	4th	11th
1973-74	Division 1	24 November	Won	2	1	6 April	Won	3	1	4th	14th
1974-75	Division 1	26 October	Drew	1	1	23 April	Drew	1	1	3rd	8th
1975-76	Division 1	7 April	Won	2	1	25 October	Drew	1	1	6th	8th
1976-77	Division 1	23 October	Won	1	0	1 April	Lost	1	2	3rd	2nd
1977-78	Division 1	5 November	Won	1	0	1 April	Lost	1	2	18th	4th
1978-79	Division 1	31 March	Won	2	1	25 November	Won	2	1	6th	15th
1979-80	Division 1	8 December	Won	4	0	3 May	Lost	1	2	3rd	17th
1980-81	Division 1	25 April	Won	1	0	6 December	Drew	1	1	2nd	12th
1981-82	Division 1	28 November	Won	2	0	24 April	Drew	1	1	2nd	10th
1982-83	Division 1	13 November	Won	1	0	26 March	Won	1	0	9th	20thR
1985-86	Division 1	12 April	Drew	0	0	9 November	Drew	1	1	20thR	15th
1987-88	Division 2	17 October	Won	3	0	5 March	Lost	0	2	8th	9th
1988-89	Division 2	8 October	Won	1	0	11 February	Lost	0	4	8th	2ndP
1992-93	Premiership	12 December	Won	3	1	3 April	Lost	1	3	16th	9th
1993-94	Premiership	29 March	Drew	2	2	5 February	Lost	1	2	19th	16th
1994-95	Premiership	3 December	Lost	1	2	22 February	Lost	0	2	22ndR	17th
1996-97	Division 1	22 April	Won	1	0	16 August	Lost	0	1	4th	14th
1997-98	Division 1	4 October	Won	1	0	18 February	Won	2	1	5th	22ndR
1999-00	Division 1	26 September	Won	2	1	27 October	Lost	0	1	3rdP	2ndP
2000-01	Premiership	7 May	Won	2	1	25 November	Won	3	2	5th	18thR

FA Cup

										Division	
1966-67	Round 5	11 March	Drew	1	1	14 March	Lost	0	3	Div 2	Div 1
1980-81	Semi-Final	11 April	Villa Park				Lost*	0	1	Div 1	Div 1
2001-02	Round 4	27 January	Lost	1	4					Prem	Div 1

League Cup

1961-62	Round 1	11 September	Won	4	2					Div 1	Div 1
1977-78	Round 4	29 November	Lost	1	2					Div 1	Div 1
2000-01	Q'ter-Final					19 December	Won*	2	1	Prem	Prem

Summary	P	W	D	L	F	A
Ipswich's home league record	29	20	7	2	48	21
Ipswich's away league record	29	5	7	17	25	51
Ipswich's cup record	7	2	1	4	9	14
TOTAL	**65**	**27**	**15**	**23**	**82**	**86**

FACT FILE

- Having been knocked out of the first League Cup in 1960-61 by Barnsley in the first round, Town's first win in the competition came against Man City the following season.
- Man City were the last lower league team to knock Ipswich out of the FA Cup, doing so in 2002.
- Defeat to Man City on the final day of the 1979-80 season ended a club record sequence of 23 league games unbeaten. Unfortunately, they had won only three of their first 15 games that season, so had to settle for third place.
- In 1981, City were fighting for silverware on three fronts, but succeeded only once. In the FA Cup, they lost in the semi-finals to Paul Power's free-kick. Ipswich became the first team to lose an FA Cup semi-final in extra-time without a replay.
- Ipswich have a phenomenal home record against City. They have won 15 of the last 18 league meetings there, and have lost one of the last 28.

Ipswich's top scorers vs Manchester City
Trevor Whymark 7
Ray Crawford 6
Bryan Hamilton, Eric Gates 4
John Wark 3

Ipswich hat-tricks vs Manchester City
8 December 1979 Eric Gates

Played for both clubs

Billy Dale	Man City 1931-32 to 1937-38	Ipswich 1938-39 to 1939-40
Jimmy McLuckie	Man City 1933-34 to 1934-35	Ipswich 1938-39 to 1939-40
Gerard Baker	Man City 1960-61 to 1961-62	Ipswich 1963-64 to 1967-68
Colin Viljoen	Ipswich 1966-67 to 1977-78	Man City 1978-79 to 1979-80
Geoff Hammond	Ipswich 1970-71 to 1973-74	Man City 1974-75 to 1975-76
David Johnson	Ipswich 1972-73 to 1975-76	Man City 1983-84
Paul Cooper	Ipswich 1973-74 to 1986-87	Man City 1988-89 to 1989-90
Mark Brennan	Ipswich 1983-84 to 1987-88	Man City 1990-91 to 1991-92
Nigel Gleghorn	Ipswich 1985-86 to 1987-88	Man City 1988-89 to 1989-90
Dalian Atkinson	Ipswich 1985-86 to 1988-89	Man City 1996-97
Brian Gayle	Man City 1988-89 to 1989-90	Ipswich 1989-90 to 1991-92
Tony Vaughan	Ipswich 1994-95 to 1996-97	Man City 1997-98 to 1999-00
Gerry Creaney	Man City 1995-96 to 1997-98	Ipswich 1996-97
Kevin Horlock	Man City 1996-97 to 2002-03	Ipswich 2004-05

v. Manchester United

		Home				Away			Final Positions	
Season	League	Date	Result	Ipswich	Man U	Date	Result	Ipswich	Man U	Ipswich	Man U
1961-62	Division 1	18 November	Won	4	1	7 April	Lost	0	5	1st	15th
1962-63	Division 1	3 November	Lost	3	5	23 March	Won	1	0	17th	19th
1963-64	Division 1	3 September	Lost	2	7	28 August	Lost	0	2	22ndR	2nd
1968-69	Division 1	1 February	Won	1	0	16 November	Drew	0	0	12th	11th
1969-70	Division 1	10 February	Lost	0	1	11 October	Lost	1	2	18th	8th
1970-71	Division 1	19 September	Won	4	0	24 April	Lost	2	3	19th	8th
1971-72	Division 1	18 December	Drew	0	0	4 September	Lost	0	1	13th	8th
1972-73	Division 1	17 February	Won	4	1	12 August	Won	2	1	4th	18th
1973-74	Division 1	8 September	Won	2	1	29 December	Lost	0	2	4th	21stR
1975-76	Division 1	10 April	Won	3	0	20 September	Lost	0	1	6th	3rd
1976-77	Division 1	3 January	Won	2	1	30 October	Won	1	0	3rd	6th
1977-78	Division 1	14 January	Lost	1	2	27 August	Drew	0	0	18th	10th
1978-79	Division 1	26 August	Won	3	0	18 November	Lost	0	2	6th	9th
1979-80	Division 1	1 March	Won	6	0	20 October	Lost	0	1	3rd	2nd
1980-81	Division 1	18 October	Drew	1	1	21 March	Lost	1	2	2nd	8th
1981-82	Division 1	20 April	Won	2	1	5 September	Won	2	1	2nd	3rd
1982-83	Division 1	5 February	Drew	1	1	11 September	Lost	1	3	9th	3rd
1983-84	Division 1	10 December	Lost	0	2	7 May	Won	2	1	12th	4th
1984-85	Division 1	1 September	Drew	1	1	22 December	Lost	0	3	17th	4th
1985-86	Division 1	20 August	Lost	0	1	7 December	Lost	0	1	20thR	4th
1992-93	Premiership	30 January	Won	2	1	22 August	Drew	1	1	16th	1st
1993-94	Premiership	1 May	Lost	1	2	24 November	Drew	0	0	19th	1st
1994-95	Premiership	24 September	Won	3	2	4 March	Lost	0	9	22ndR	2nd
2000-01	Premiership	22 August	Drew	1	1	23 December	Lost	0	2	5th	1st
2001-02	Premiership	27 April	Lost	0	1	22 September	Lost	0	4	18thR	3rd

FA Cup

										Division	
1957-58	Round 4					25 January	Lost	0	2	Div 2	Div 1
1969-70	Round 3	3 January	Lost	0	1					Div 1	Div 1
1973-74	Round 4					26 January	Won	1	0	Div 1	Div 1
1987-88	Round 3	10 January	Lost	1	2					Div 2	Div 1

League Cup

										Division	
1971-72	Round 2	7 September	Lost	1	3					Div 1	Div 1
1997-98	Round 3	14 October	Won	2	0					Div 1	Prem

Summary

	P	W	D	L	F	A
Ipswich's home league record	25	12	5	8	47	33
Ipswich's away league record	25	5	4	16	14	47
Ipswich's cup record	6	2	0	4	5	8
TOTAL	56	19	9	28	66	88

FACT FILE

- United have been responsible both for Ipswich's heaviest home defeat and joint heaviest away defeat in league history. The former was a 7-2 defeat in 1963, and the latter a truly diabolical 9-0 reverse in 1995 – still the Premiership's biggest-ever scoreline. On both occasions, United finished second and Ipswich finished bottom.
- It hasn't always been so bad against United. In March 1980, the Blues won 6-0 in a match those who were there still talk about. Ipswich were third at the time and United second, but there was no sign of that as Ipswich tore into their opponents. As well as scoring six, they missed at least one sitter, not to mention two penalties (one of which was retaken and missed again)!
- The last time the Blues won at Old Trafford, Mich D'Avray and Alan Sunderland were the scorers.

Ipswich's top scorers vs Manchester United
Paul Mariner 8
John Wark 4
Colin Viljoen, Trevor Whymark, Bryan Hamilton,
    Alan Brazil, Chris Kiwomya 3

Ipswich hat-tricks vs Manchester United
1 March 1980 Paul Mariner

Played for both clubs

Billy Dale	Man United 1928-29 to 1931-32	Ipswich 1938-39 to 1939-40
Tom Lang	Man United 1935-36 to 1936-37	Ipswich 1946-47
Harry Baird	Man United 1936-37 to 1937-38	Ipswich 1946-47 to 1951-52
Alan Brazil	Ipswich 1977-78 to 1982-83	Man United 1984-85 to 1985-86
Arnold Muhren	Ipswich 1978-79 to 1981-82	Man United 1982-83 to 1984-85
Michael Clegg	Man United 1996-97 to 1999-00	Ipswich 1999-00

Both Arnold Muhren and Alan Brazil (seen here v Bristol City) later played for the Red Devils after success at Ipswich. This is not the only link between Brazil and United. He actually made his Ipswich debut against them on 14 January 1978 (United won the game 2-1, Paul Mariner scoring the Ipswich goal) and he also scored a brace in Ipswich's biggest win against United, 6-0 in 1980, only overshadowed by Mariner's hat-trick in the same game.

v. Mansfield Town

			Home				Away		Final Positions	
Season	League	Date	Result	Ipswich Mansfield	Date	Result	Ipswich Mansfield		Ipswich	Mansfield
1938-39	Division 3S	26 December	Won	5 1	27 December	Won	1	0	7th	16th
1946-47	Division 3S	7 April	Won	2 1	4 April	Lost	3	4	6th	22nd

FA Cup									Division	
1962-63	Round 3				9 January	Won	3	2	Div 1	Div 4

Summary	P	W	D	L	F	A
Ipswich's home league record	2	2	0	0	7	2
Ipswich's away league record	2	1	0	1	4	4
Ipswich's cup record	1	1	0	0	3	2
TOTAL	**5**	**4**	**0**	**1**	**14**	**8**

Ipswich's top scorers vs Mansfield
Fred Chadwick, Jimmy Leadbetter 3
Ted Pole 2

Ipswich hat-tricks vs Mansfield
9 January 1963 Jimmy Leadbetter

Played for both clubs

John Roy	Mansfield 1936-37	Ipswich 1946-47
Peter Morris	Mansfield 1960-61 to 1967-68 & 1976-77 to 1977-78	Ipswich 1967-68 to 1973-74
John Miller	Ipswich 1968-69 to 1973-74	Mansfield 1976-77 to 1979-80
Pat Sharkey	Ipswich 1975-76 to 1976-77	Mansfield 1977-78
Ian Juryeff	Mansfield 1983-84	Ipswich 1988-89
Neil Woods	Ipswich 1987-88 to 1989-90	Mansfield 1997-98
David Linighan	Ipswich 1988-89 to 1995-96	Mansfield 1998-99 to 1999-00
Tony Vaughan	Ipswich 1994-95 to 1996-97	Mansfield 2002-03 to 2003-04

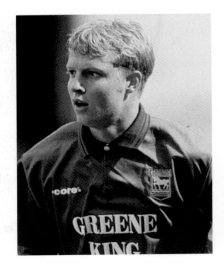

Manchester-born midfielder Tony Vaughan (right) came through the ranks at Ipswich, making his debut in a 2-0 defeat at Stamford Bridge in December 1994 against Chelsea. In his first season, Vaughan made 10 appearances in the relegated side, and seemed to be firmly in George Burley's plans, when he appeared in nearly half of the games in the two subsequent seasons. However in August 2000 he returned to his home town, signing for Manchester City. A move to Forest followed a frustrating spell at City, the only transfer in his career to attract a fee (£350,000), but again the move didn't work out. Since Forest, Vaughan has appeared for Scunthorpe, Mansfield Town (twice), Motherwell and Barnsley.

v. Merthyr Tydfil

		Home				Away	Division			
FA Cup	*Date*	*Result*	Ipswich	Merthyr	*Date*	*Result*	Ipswich	Merthyr	Ipswich	Merthyr
1951-52 Round 1	5 December	Won	1	0	29 November	Drew*	2	2	Div 3S	Non L

Summary	P	W	D	L	F	A
Ipswich's cup record	2	1	1	0	3	2
TOTAL	2	1	1	0	3	2

FACT FILE

● Jimmy Roberts scored Town's winner in the replay against the Welshmen.

Tom Garneys (pictured) scored one of the goals in the first round of the 1951-52 FA Cup, as did Sam McCrory. This surprise draw against non-league Merthyr Tydfil was rectified in the Division Three South side's favour in the replay.

v. Middlesbrough

			Home				Away		Final Positions	
Season	League	Date	Result	Ipswich	M'boro	Date	Result	Ipswich M'boro	Ipswich	M'boro
1954-55	Division 2	1 September	Won	6	1	25 August	Won	1 0	21stR	12th
1957-58	Division 2	22 February	Drew	1	1	23 November	Lost	2 5	8th	7th
1958-59	Division 2	25 April	Won	2	1	6 December	Won	3 2	16th	13th
1959-60	Division 2	14 November	Won	1	0	1 April	Lost	1 4	11th	5th
1960-61	Division 2	31 March	Won	3	1	3 April	Lost	1 3	1stP	5th
1964-65	Division 2	6 February	Won	5	2	26 September	Won	4 2	5th	17th
1965-66	Division 2	7 September	Won	2	1	14 September	Lost	2 3	15th	21stR
1967-68	Division 2	16 December	Lost	1	2	19 August	Won	2 0	1stP	6th
1974-75	Division 1	11 January	Won	2	0	7 December	Lost	0 3	3rd	7th
1975-76	Division 1	27 September	Lost	0	3	3 April	Lost	0 2	6th	13th
1976-77	Division 1	23 April	Lost	0	1	27 November	Won	2 0	3rd	12th
1977-78	Division 1	21 March	Drew	1	1	24 September	Drew	1 1	18th	14th
1978-79	Division 1	21 November	Won	2	1	1 September	Drew	0 0	6th	12th
1979-80	Division 1	27 October	Won	1	0	11 March	Drew	1 1	3rd	9th
1980-81	Division 1	17 February	Won	1	0	1 May	Lost	1 2	2nd	14th
1981-82	Division 1	1 May	Won	3	1	5 December	Won	1 0	2nd	22ndR
1987-88	Division 2	23 April	Won	4	0	20 October	Lost	1 3	8th	3rdP
1989-90	Division 2	30 December	Won	3	0	25 April	Won	2 1	9th	21st
1990-91	Division 2	26 December	Lost	0	1	30 March	Drew	1 1	14th	7th
1991-92	Division 2	24 August	Won	2	1	11 January	Lost	0 1	1stP	2ndP
1992-93	Premiership	1 March	Lost	0	1	1 September	Drew	2 2	16th	21stR
1997-98	Division 1	1 December	Drew	1	1	17 January	Drew	1 1	5th	2ndP
2000-01	Premiership	28 October	Won	2	1	16 April	Won	2 1	5th	14th
2001-02	Premiership	24 April	Won	1	0	25 November	Drew	0 0	18thR	12th

League Cup									Division	
1980-81	Round 2	1 September	Won	3	0	26 August	Lost	1 3	Div 1	Div 1
2002-03	Round 3	6 November	Won	3	1				Div 1	Prem

Summary	P	W	D	L	F	A
Ipswich's home league record	24	16	3	5	44	21
Ipswich's away league record	24	8	7	9	31	38
Ipswich's cup record	3	2	0	1	7	4
TOTAL	**51**	**26**	**10**	**15**	**82**	**63**

FACT FILE

- Ipswich's hopes of winning their second league title in 1981 ended when they lost 2-1 at Ayresome Park. This handed the title to Aston Villa, despite the Midlanders losing 2-0 to Arsenal. A few weeks earlier, Ipswich had been top of the league, but extended runs in the UEFA Cup (which they won) and the FA Cup (in which they reached the semi-finals) took their toll.
- There has never been a goalless draw between the sides in Ipswich.

Ipswich's top scorers vs Middlesbrough
Ray Crawford 7
Paul Mariner 6
Tom Garneys 5
Ted Phillips, John Wark 4

Ipswich hat-tricks vs Middlesbrough
23 April 1988 Dalian Atkinson

Played for both clubs

Mick McNeil	Middlesbrough 1958-59 to 1963-64	Ipswich 1964-65 to 1971-72
John O'Rourke	Middlesbrough 1966-67 to 1967-68	Ipswich 1967-68 to 1969-70
Kevin Beattie	Ipswich 1972-73 to 1980-81	Middlesbrough 1982-83
John Wark	Ipswich 1974-75 to 1984-85, 1987-88 to 1989-90 & 1991-92 to 1996-97	Middlesbrough 1990-91
Trevor Putney	Ipswich 1982-83 to 1985-86	Middlesbrough 1989-90 to 1990-91
Tony Mowbray	Middlesbrough 1982-83 to 1991-92	Ipswich 1995-96 to 1999-00
Mark Brennan	Ipswich 1983-84 to 1987-88	Middlesbrough 1988-89 to 1989-90
Phil Whelan	Ipswich 1991-92 to 1994-95	Middlesbrough 1995-96 to 1996-97
Alun Armstrong	Middlesbrough 1997-98 to 1999-00	Ipswich 2000-01 to 2003-04

Tony Mowbray guaranteed his place in Ipswich folklore by scoring one of his eight Ipswich goals in the play-off final v Barnsley in 2000. Mowbray was signed in 1995 at the ripe old age of 32 but still gave five years service to the club, his final match coming on that great day at Wembley. An England 'B' international, Mowbray made his name alongside Gary Pallister at Middlesborough before moving to Celtic for £1 million in 1991. Following George Burley's sacking, Mowbray acted as caretaker manager at Portman Road until Joe Royle's appointment. Mowbray returned to Scotland, and now manages Hibernian.

v. Millwall

Season	League	Date	Result	Ipswich	Millwall	Date	Result	Ipswich	Millwall	Ipswich	Millwall
			Home				**Away**			**Final Positions**	
1948-49	Division 3S	30 October	Won	1	0	26 March	Drew	0	0	7th	8th
1949-50	Division 3S	8 April	Lost	0	3	19 November	Lost	1	3	17th	22nd
1950-51	Division 3S	25 December	Won	2	1	26 December	Lost	0	4	8th	5th
1951-52	Division 3S	29 August	Won	3	0	22 August	Lost	0	4	17th	4th
1952-53	Division 3S	21 March	Lost	1	6	1 November	Lost	2	3	16th	2nd
1953-54	Division 3S	1 January	Drew	1	1	29 August	Won	2	1	1stP	12th
1955-56	Division 3S	22 October	Won	6	2	3 March	Won	5	0	3rd	22nd
1956-57	Division 3S	25 August	Lost	0	2	22 December	Drew	2	2	1stP	17th
1966-67	Division 2	8 April	Won	4	1	12 November	Lost	0	1	5th	8th
1967-68	Division 2	26 December	Won	2	1	30 December	Drew	1	1	1stP	7th
1986-87	Division 2	21 April	Drew	0	0	26 December	Lost	0	1	5th	16th
1987-88	Division 2	1 January	Drew	1	1	12 September	Lost	1	2	8th	1stP
1990-91	Division 2	1 February	Lost	0	3	15 September	Drew	1	1	14th	5th
1991-92	Division 2	19 October	Drew	0	0	1 February	Won	3	2	1stP	15th
1995-96	Division 1	5 May	Drew	0	0	11 November	Lost	1	2	7th	22ndR
2002-03	Division 1	1 January	Won	4	1	24 August	Drew	1	1	7th	9th
2003-04	Division 1	13 March	Lost	1	3	13 December	Drew	0	0	5th	10th
2004-05	Champ'ship	12 September	Won	2	0	26 December	Lost	1	3	3rd	10th

FA Cup										**Division**	
1977-78	Q'ter-Final					11 March	Won	6	1	Div 1	Div 2

League Cup											
2000-01	Round 2	26 September	Won*	5	0	19 September	Lost	0	2	Prem	Div 2

Summary	P	W	D	L	F	A
Ipswich's home league record	18	8	5	5	28	25
Ipswich's away league record	18	3	6	9	21	31
Ipswich's cup record	3	2	0	1	11	3
TOTAL	**39**	**13**	**11**	**15**	**60**	**59**

FACT FILE

- Ipswich have won once in their last 11 league trips to Millwall.
- Both sides have managed to score six in away games – Millwall in 1953, Ipswich on their way to FA Cup glory in 1978.

Ipswich's top scorers vs Millwall
Wilf Grant 6
Tommy Parker 4
Tom Garneys, Frank Brogan, Paul Mariner,
  Darren Bent 3

Ipswich hat-tricks vs Millwall
22 October 1955	Wilf Grant
3 March 1956	Wilf Grant
11 March 1978	Paul Mariner (cup)

Played for both clubs

Fred Jones	Millwall 1934-35 to 1935-36	Ipswich 1938-39
Angus Mackay	Ipswich 1946-47	Millwall 1955-56
Len Tyler	Millwall 1946-47 to 1949-50	Ipswich 1950-51 to 1951-52
Dave Harper	Millwall 1957-58 to 1964-65	Ipswich 1964-65 to 1966-67
Joe Broadfoot	Millwall 1958-59 to 1963-64	Ipswich 1963-64 to 1965-66
	& 1966-67	& 1966-67 to 1967-68
Bobby Hunt	Millwall 1966-67 to 1967-68	Ipswich 1967-68 to 1970-71
Terry Shanahan	Ipswich 1970-71	Millwall 1976-77
Bryan Hamilton	Ipswich 1971-72 to 1975-76	Millwall 1977-78 to 978-79
Pat Sharkey	Ipswich 1975-76 to 1976-77	Millwall 1976-77
Kevin O'Callaghan	Millwall 1978-79 to 1979-80	Ipswich 1979-80 to 1984-85
	& 1987-88 to 1990-91	
Tony Kinsella	Millwall 1978-79 to 1980-81	Ipswich 1982-83 to 1983-84
	& 1984-85 to 1985-86	
John Jackson	Millwall 1979-80 to 1980-81	Ipswich 1981-82
Paul Goddard	Millwall 1989-90 to 1990-91	Ipswich 1990-91 to 1993-94
Keith Branagan	Millwall 1989-90 to 1991-92	Ipswich 2000-01 to 2001-02
Richard Naylor	Ipswich 1996-97 to 2004-05	Millwall 2001-02
Andy Marshall	Ipswich 2001-02 to 2002-03	Millwall 2003-04 to 2004-05

Republic of Ireland international Kevin O'Callaghan (seen here striking the ball, closely watched by John McGovern, Viv Anderson and Martin O'Neill of Nottingham Forest) started his career at Millwall before being signed by Ipswich in January 1980. Left-winger O'Callaghan made only 72 league starts for Ipswich in a six-season spell, scoring a mere four goals. O'Callaghan also became famous as the prison camp goalkeeper, Tony Lewis, in the film Escape to Victory, who volunteered to have his arm broken so that Sylvester 'Hatch' Stallone could be freed from isolation. The film also featured John Wark, Laurie Sivell and Russell Osman.

v. Morecambe

FA Cup		Date	Result	Ipswich	Morecambe	Date	Result	Ipswich	Morecambe	Ipswich	Morecambe
				Home				**Away**		*Division*	
2000-01	Round 3					6 January	Won	3	0	Prem	Non L
2002-03	Round 3	4 January	Won	4	0					Div 1	Non L

Summary	P	W	D	L	F	A
Ipswich's home league record:	31	16	9	6	65	39
Ipswich's cup record	2	2	0	0	7	0
TOTAL	2	2	0	0	7	0

FACT FILE

- Ipswich were given third round ties against Conference opposition three years in succession (2001-03).
- Incredibly, Morecambe, who have reached the third round only twice since 1962, drew Ipswich on both occasions.

Ipswich's top scorers vs Morecambe
Darren Bent 2

Darren Bent (pictured) joined Ipswich Town at the age of 14 and has not looked back since. A meteoric rise through the youth ranks of both club and country (he has been capped for England at Under-15, Under-16, Under-17 and Under-19 level) saw him stake a place in the first team aged just 17 in a UEFA Cup game against Helsingborg IF in November 2001. His goalscoring record of 55 goals in 115 starts always meant that he would be coveted by other clubs, and Town's failure to achieve promotion in 2005 sparked his departure to Charlton Athletic in a £3 million move. In January 2003, Bent scored a brace against Morecambe in an easy win for Ipswich, with Jamie Clapham and Darren Ambrose also on the scoresheet.

v. Newcastle United

Season	League	Date	Result	Home Ipswich	Newcastle	Date	Result	Away Ipswich	Newcastle	Final Positions Ipswich	Newcastle
1964-65	Division 2	3 October	Won	3	1	13 February	Drew	2	2	5th	1stP
1968-69	Division 1	12 October	Lost	1	4	14 December	Lost	1	2	12th	9th
1969-70	Division 1	6 September	Won	2	0	20 December	Lost	0	4	18th	7th
1970-71	Division 1	13 March	Won	1	0	14 November	Drew	0	0	19th	12th
1971-72	Division 1	25 September	Drew	0	0	5 April	Won	1	0	13th	11th
1972-73	Division 1	6 January	Won	1	0	26 August	Won	2	1	4th	9th
1973-74	Division 1	4 September	Lost	1	3	12 September	Lost	1	3	4th	15th
1974-75	Division 1	15 March	Won	5	4	28 September	Lost	0	1	3rd	15th
1975-76	Division 1	16 August	Lost	0	3	20 December	Drew	1	1	6th	15th
1976-77	Division 1	7 May	Won	2	0	9 March	Drew	1	1	3rd	5th
1977-78	Division 1	1 October	Won	2	1	25 February	Won	1	0	18th	21stR
1984-85	Division 1	23 March	Drew	1	1	6 October	Lost	0	3	17th	14th
1985-86	Division 1	12 October	Drew	2	2	15 March	Lost	1	3	20thR	11th
1989-90	Division 2	7 October	Won	2	1	17 March	Lost	1	2	9th	3rd
1990-91	Division 2	20 October	Won	2	1	20 April	Drew	2	2	14th	11th
1991-92	Division 2	11 April	Won	3	2	17 September	Drew	1	1	1stP	20th
1993-94	Premiership	31 August	Drew	1	1	23 March	Lost	0	2	19th	3rd
1994-95	Premiership	28 February	Lost	0	2	26 November	Drew	1	1	22ndR	6th
2000-01	Premiership	14 April	Won	1	0	4 November	Lost	1	2	5th	11th
2001-02	Premiership	9 December	Lost	0	1	16 March	Drew	2	2	18thR	4th

FA Cup

Season	Round	Date	Result	Ipswich	Newcastle	Date	Result	Ipswich	Newcastle	Division Div 1	Div 1
1970-71	Round 3	13 January	Won	2	1	11 January	Drew	1	1	Div 1	Div 1

League Cup

Season	Round	Date	Result	Ipswich	Newcastle	Date	Result	Ipswich	Newcastle	Division	
1984-85	Round 3	30 October	Drew	1	1	7 November	Won	2	1	Div 1	Div 1
2001-02	Round 4	27 November	Lost	1	4					Prem	Prem

FACT FILE

- Ipswich have not won on Tyneside since a Clive Woods goal gave them victory in 1978.
- There have only ever been two goalless draws between the sides, both in the early 1970s.
- The most famous link between the teams is not any of the players listed below, but Sir Bobby Robson. He managed Ipswich from 1969 to 1982 and Newcastle from 1999 to 2004, and of course nearly led England to the World Cup in between. Two managers have taken England to World Cup semi-finals, and they both managed Ipswich.

Summary	P	W	D	L	F	A
Ipswich's home league record	20	11	4	5	30	27
Ipswich's away league record	20	3	8	9	19	33
Ipswich's cup record	5	2	2	1	7	8
TOTAL	**45**	**16**	**14**	**15**	**56**	**68**

Ipswich's top scorers vs Newcastle
Chris Kiwomya 5
Eric Gates, John Wark 4
John O'Rourke, Trevor Whymark, Bryan Hamilton 3

Ipswich hat-tricks vs Newcastle
15 March 1975   Bryan Hamilton

Played for both clubs
Mick Burns	Newcastle 1927-28 to 1935-36	Ipswich 1938-39 to 1951-52
Tom Lang	Newcastle 1927-28 to 1934-35	Ipswich 1946-47
Dave Bell	Newcastle 1931-32 to 1933-34	Ipswich 1938-39 to 1949-50
Charlie Woods	Newcastle 1960-61 to 1961-62	Ipswich 1966-67 to 1969-70
Glenn Keeley	Ipswich 1972-73 to 1973-74	Newcastle 1974-75 to 1975-76
Paul Goddard	Newcastle 1986-87 to 1987-88	Ipswich 1990-91 to 1993-94
Alex Mathie	Newcastle 1993-94 to 1994-95	Ipswich 1994-95 to 1998-99
Kieron Dyer	Ipswich 1996-97 to 1998-99	Newcastle 1999-00 to 2004-05
Titus Bramble	Ipswich 1998-99 to 2001-02	Newcastle 2002-03 to 2004-05
Darren Ambrose	Ipswich 2001-02 to 2002-03	Newcastle 2002-03 to 2004-05

Sir Bobby Robson, seen here returning to Portman Road with Porto, is one of Ipswich Town's favourite sons. A player at Fulham and West Bromwich Albion, Robson was good enough to be capped by England 20 times. But it is as a manager that he will be best remembered. Starting his managerial career at his old club Fulham, Robson shot to fame as manager at Portman Road in 1969. Over the next 13 years, Ipswich enjoyed a period of success not seen since Alf Ramsey's team of the 1960s, winning the FA Cup, UEFA Cup and finishing runners-up in Division One twice. At the time, Ipswich were every football fan's second team. In 1982, Robson succeeded Ron Greenwood as England manager, and despite pressure from the tabloids, steered England to firstly the quarter-finals and then the semi-finals of the World Cup. After resigning from the England job, success followed him abroad to club football in Holland, Portugal and Spain (with the mighty Barcelona), before an emotional return to club football managing his boyhood team Newcastle United.

v. Newport County

Season	League	Date	Result	Home Ipswich	Newport	Date	Result	Away Ipswich	Newport	Final Positions Ipswich	Newport
1938-39	Division 3S	15 October	Lost	1	4	18 February	Lost	2	3	7th	1stP
1947-48	Division 3S	27 December	Won	3	0	25 December	Lost	1	3	4th	12th
1948-49	Division 3S	28 August	Won	5	1	1 January	Lost	0	3	7th	15th
1949-50	Division 3S	11 March	Won	1	0	22 October	Lost	0	1	17th	21st
1950-51	Division 3S	21 April	Won	2	1	1 December	Won	2	1	8th	11th
1951-52	Division 3S	22 December	Won	3	1	25 August	Lost	1	2	17th	6th
1952-53	Division 3S	21 February	Won	3	0	4 October	Won	3	1	16th	15th
1953-54	Division 3S	13 March	Lost	1	2	26 April	Won	2	1	1stP	15th
1955-56	Division 3S	24 December	Won	3	2	27 August	Lost	1	2	3rd	19th
1956-57	Division 3S	23 February	Won	5	0	13 October	Lost	0	1	1stP	12th

League Cup										Division	
1972-73	Round 2					5 September	Won	3	0	Div 1	Div 4

Summary

	P	W	D	L	F	A
Ipswich's home league record	10	8	0	2	27	11
Ipswich's away league record	10	3	0	7	12	18
Ipswich's cup record	1	1	0	0	3	0
TOTAL	21	12	0	9	42	29

FACT FILE

- Lambert, Collard and Miller scored the goals that won the 1972-73 League Cup tie for Ipswich.
- Neither side has failed to score at home in a league game
- Newport dropped out of the league in 1988.

Ipswich's top scorers vs Newport
Tom Garneys 5
Sam McCrory 3

Played for both clubs

Matt O'Mahoney	Newport 1935-36	Ipswich 1939-40 to 1948-49
Fred Chadwick	Newport 1936-37 to 1938-39	Ipswich 1938-39 to 1946-47
Ken Wookey	Newport 1946-47	Ipswich 1950-51

v. 93rd Highlanders

			Home					*Division*
FA Cup	*Date*	*Result*	Ipswich Highlanders					Ipswich Highlanders
1890-91 4th Qual	6 December	Lost	1 4					Non L Non L

Summary	P	W	D	L	F	A
Ipswich's cup record	1	0	0	1	1	4
TOTAL	1	0	0	1	1	4

FACT FILE

- The 93rd Highlanders put an end to Ipswich's first FA Cup campaign, in the last round before the competition proper began.

v. Northampton Town

Season	League	Date		Result	Ipswich	N'hampton	Date		Result	Ipswich	N'hampton	Ipswich	N'hampton
			Home					**Away**				**Final Positions**	
1938-39	Division 3S	21 January	Won		2	0	17 September	Lost		0	2	7th	17th
1946-47	Division 3S	26 October	Lost		1	2	31 May	Drew		2	2	6th	13th
1947-48	Division 3S	21 April	Won		5	2	24 April	Lost		2	4	4th	14th
1948-49	Division 3S	5 March	Won		4	2	9 October	Drew		1	1	7th	20th
1949-50	Division 3S	25 February	Drew		2	2	8 October	Won		2	1	17th	2nd
1950-51	Division 3S	19 August	Drew		1	1	16 December	Lost		1	2	8th	21st
1951-52	Division 3S	5 January	Won		3	2	8 September	Lost		0	1	17th	8th
1952-53	Division 3S	6 April	Drew		1	1	7 April	Lost		0	2	16th	3rd
1953-54	Division 3S	1 May	Won		2	1	25 March	Lost		0	1	1stP	5th
1955-56	Division 3S	17 September	Won		1	0	21 January	Won		5	0	3rd	11th
1956-57	Division 3S	23 March	Lost		0	1	10 November	Lost		1	2	1stP	14th
1964-65	Division 2	15 September	Drew		0	0	29 September	Lost		2	3	5th	2ndP
1966-67	Division 2	5 November	Won		6	1	1 April	Drew		1	1	5th	21stR

League Cup

													Division
1977-78	Round 2	30 August	Won		5	0						Div 1	Div 4
1987-88	Round 2	22 September	Drew		1	1	7 October	Won*		4	2	Div 2	Div 3

Summary

	P	W	D	L	F	A
Ipswich's home league record	13	7	4	2	28	15
Ipswich's away league record	13	2	3	8	17	22
Ipswich's cup record	3	2	1	0	10	3
TOTAL	**29**	**11**	**8**	**10**	**55**	**40**

Tommy Parker (pictured) is Ipswich's top-scorer against Northampton with five goals. Parker was a one club man, holding the record for most Ipswich appearances (475) until the record was broken by Mick Mills in the 1970s. A talented rugby player, Parker was an England schoolboy international, playing against Wales at Cardiff Arms Park in 1938 before serving his country in World War Two. Parker holds two 'firsts' for Ipswich, becoming Alf Ramsey's first captain, and retiring from the administration side of the club in 1985 as its first commercial manager. Parker died in 1996.

- **The home match in May 1954 was played in a celebratory atmosphere, as three days earlier a dropped point by Brighton had confirmed Ipswich's promotion to Division Two for the first time.**

Ipswich's top scorers vs Northampton	*Ipswich hat-tricks vs Northampton*
Tommy Parker 5	21 January 1956 Tom Garneys
Stan Parker, Bill Jennings 4	5 November 1966 Frank Brogan
Tom Garneys, Frank Brogan 3	

Played for both clubs

Bill Jennings	Northampton 1938-39 to 1946-47	Ipswich 1947-48 to 1950-51
Billy Baxter	Ipswich 1960-61 to 1970-71	Northampton 1972-73
Joe Broadfoot	Ipswich 1963-64 to 1965-66 & 1966-67 to 1967-68	Northampton 1965-66
Bobby Hunt	Northampton 1963-64 to 1965-66 & 1972-73	Ipswich 1967-68 to 1970-71
Irvin Gernon	Ipswich 1981-82 to 1986-87	Northampton 1986-87 & 1989-90 to 1991-92
Jason Dozzell	Ipswich 1983-84 to 1992-93 & 1997-98	Northampton 1997-98
Kevin Wilson	Ipswich 1984-85 to 1986-87	Northampton 1997-98 to 2000-01
Nigel Gleghorn	Ipswich 1985-86 to 1987-88	Northampton 1997-98
Chris O'Donnell	Ipswich 1986-87 to 1988-89	Northampton 1987-88
Nabil Abidallah	Ipswich 2000-01	Northampton 2003-04

v. Norwich City

Season	League	Date	Result	Home Ipswich	Home Norwich	Date	Result	Away Ipswich	Away Norwich	Final Positions Ipswich	Final Positions Norwich
1939-40	Division 3S	1 September	Drew	1	1						
1946-47	Division 3S	7 September	Won	5	0	4 January	Won	1	0	6th	21st
1947-48	Division 3S	31 January	Lost	1	2	13 September	Won	5	1	4th	21st
1948-49	Division 3S	16 October	Lost	1	2	12 March	Lost	0	2	7th	10th
1949-50	Division 3S	15 October	Won	3	0	4 March	Drew	1	1	17th	11th
1950-51	Division 3S	11 April	Lost	0	1	28 April	Won	3	1	8th	2nd
1951-52	Division 3S	25 December	Lost	0	2	26 December	Lost	0	2	17th	3rd
1952-53	Division 3S	27 August	Won	2	1	3 September	Lost	0	1	16th	4th
1953-54	Division 3S	28 November	Drew	1	1	20 March	Won	2	1	1stP	7th
1955-56	Division 3S	30 March	Won	4	1	1 April	Lost	2	3	3rd	7th
1956-57	Division 3S	22 April	Won	3	1	19 April	Won	2	1	1stP	24th
1960-61	Division 2	27 December	Won	4	1	26 December	Won	3	0	1stP	4th
1964-65	Division 2	1 January	Won	3	0	5 September	Lost	1	2	5th	6th
1965-66	Division 2	19 March	Won	2	0	25 September	Lost	0	1	15th	13th
1966-67	Division 2	18 April	Lost	0	2	3 September	Won	2	1	5th	11th
1967-68	Division 2	23 September	Drew	0	0	3 February	Won	4	3	1stP	9th
1972-73	Division 1	15 August	Lost	1	2	11 November	Drew	0	0	4th	20th
1973-74	Division 1	1 March	Drew	1	1	26 December	Won	2	1	4th	22ndR
1975-76	Division 1	23 September	Won	2	0	31 March	Lost	0	1	6th	10th
1976-77	Division 1	15 February	Won	5	0	9 April	Won	1	0	3rd	16th
1977-78	Division 1	27 March	Won	4	0	26 December	Lost	0	1	18th	13th
1978-79	Division 1	26 December	Drew	1	1	14 April	Won	1	0	6th	16th
1979-80	Division 1	5 April	Won	4	2	26 December	Drew	3	3	3rd	12th
1980-81	Division 1	26 December	Won	2	0	20 April	Lost	0	1	2nd	20thR
1982-83	Division 1	27 December	Lost	2	3	4 April	Drew	0	0	9th	14th
1983-84	Division 1	23 April	Won	2	0	27 December	Drew	0	0	12th	14th
1984-85	Division 1	1 January	Won	2	0	8 April	Won	2	0	17th	20thR
1992-93	Premiership	19 April	Won	3	1	21 December	Won	2	0	16th	3rd
1993-94	Premiership	18 December	Won	2	1	25 August	Lost	0	1	19th	12th
1994-95	Premiership	19 September	Lost	1	2	20 March	Lost	0	3	22ndR	20thR
1995-96	Division 1	14 April	Won	2	1	19 November	Lost	1	2	7th	16th
1996-97	Division 1	18 April	Won	2	0	11 October	Lost	1	3	4th	13th
1997-98	Division 1	21 February	Won	5	0	26 September	Lost	1	2	5th	15th
1998-99	Division 1	20 October	Lost	0	1	11 April	Drew	0	0	3rd	9th
1999-00	Division 1	19 March	Lost	0	2	21 November	Drew	0	0	3rdP	12th
2002-03	Division 1	15 September	Drew	1	1	1 March	Won	2	0	7th	8th
2003-04	Division 1	21 December	Lost	0	2	7 March	Lost	1	3	5th	1stP

FA Cup										Division	
1961-62	Round 4	30 January	Lost	1	2	27 January	Drew	1	1	Div 1	Div 2
1982-83	Round 5					19 February	Lost	0	1	Div 1	Div 1

			Home				Away		Division	
League Cup	Date	Result	Ipswich	Norwich	Date	Result	Ipswich	Norwich	Ipswich	Norwich
1968-69 Round 2	3 September	Lost	2	4					Div 1	Div 2
1974-75 Q'ter-Final	10 December	Lost	1	2	4 December	Drew	1	1	Div 1	Div 2
1980-81 Round 3	23 September	Drew	1	1	8 October	Won	3	1	Div 1	Div 1
1983-84 Round 4	30 November	Lost	0	1					Div 1	Div 1
1984-85 Semi-Final	23 February	Won	1	0	6 March	Lost	0	2	Div 1	Div 1

Summary	P	W	D	L	F	A
Ipswich's home league record	37	20	6	11	72	35
Ipswich's away league record	36	14	7	15	43	41
Ipswich's cup record	11	2	3	6	11	16
TOTAL	84	36	16	32	126	92

FACT FILE

- Ipswich have played more competitive matches against Norwich than against any other club.
- Ipswich's cup record against Norwich makes for disappointing reading, but they did beat the Canaries 4-2 on aggregate to win the final of the 1973 Texaco Cup, a competition for English and Scottish sides.
- Ipswich have beaten Norwich 5-0 on three separate occasions, most recently in 1998 when Alex Mathie scored a first-half hat-trick.
- Ipswich's first-ever league meeting with their friends from Norfolk came just one day before the outbreak of World War Two. Fred Chadwick scored Town's goal in a 1-1 draw.
- Three times the sides have met in cup competition when Ipswich were in Division One and Norwich were in Division Two, and three times the lower league side prevailed. Indeed, Ipswich were on their way to the league title when Norwich beat them in the 1962 FA Cup.
- Ipswich have won once in their last eight meetings with Norwich.
- Norwich have completed the league double over Ipswich four times, most recently in 2004.
- Ipswich have completed the league double over Norwich six times, most recently in 1993.
- In terms of league wins, Ipswich currently lead 34-26. Norwich last led the series in 1954.

Ipswich's top scorers vs Norwich
John Wark 9
Ray Crawford 8
Tom Garneys, Ted Phillips, Trevor Whymark, Paul Mariner 5
Tommy Parker, Albert Day, Stan Parker, Gerry Baker 4

Ipswich hat-tricks vs Norwich
7 September 1946 Albert Day
15 October 1949 Jackie Brown
3 Feb 1968 Colin Viljoen
15 Feb 1977 Trevor Whymark
5 April 1980 John Wark
21 Feb 1998 Alex Mathie

Played for both clubs

John Roy	Norwich 1934-35 to 1935-36	Ipswich 1946-47
Allenby Driver	Norwich 1947-48 to 1949-50	Ipswich 1949-50 to 1951-52
Peter Morris	Ipswich 1967-68 to 1973-74	Norwich 1974-75 to 1975-76
Bobby Bell	Ipswich 1968-69 to 1971-72	Norwich 1971-72
John Miller	Ipswich 1968-69 to 1973-74	Norwich 1974-75 to 1975-76
Clive Woods	Ipswich 1969-70 to 1979-80	Norwich 1979-80 to 1981-82
Keith Bertschin	Ipswich 1975-76 to 1976-77	Norwich 1981-82 to 1984-85
Clive Baker	Norwich 1977-78 to 1980-81	Ipswich 1992-93 to 1994-95
John Deehan	Norwich 1981-82 to 1985-86	Ipswich 1986-87 to 1987-88
Trevor Putney	Ipswich 1982-83 to 1985-86	Norwich 1986-87 to 1988-89
Louie Donowa	Norwich 1982-83 to 1985-86	Ipswich 1989-90
Andy Marshall	Norwich 1994-95 to 2000-01	Ipswich 2001-02 to 2002-03

Graham Harbey and Jason Dozzell look on as a free-kick heads towards the Norwich goal in the (now defunct) Full Members Cup second round on 20 December 1988 (not within the scope of this book), 18,024 fans turned up to see the old enemy beaten 1-0 by a Simon Milton goal in extra-time. Ipswich eventually lost 3-1 at home to Nottingham Forest in the quarter-final.

v. Norwich St Barnabas

FA Cup		Date	Result	Home Ipswich	Norwich				Division Ipswich	Norwich
1934-35	Prelim	15 September	Won	3	2				Non L	Non L

Summary	P	W	D	L	F	A
Ipswich's cup record	1	1	0	0	3	2
TOTAL	1	1	0	0	3	2

FACT FILE

- An own goal, along with goals from Tubby and Groom booked a meeting in the first qualifying round with another Norwich outfit, the YMCA.

v. Norwich Thorpe

FA Cup					Date	Result	Away Ipswich	Norwich	Division Ipswich	Norwich
1890-91 2nd Qual					25 October	Won	4	0	Non L	Non L

Summary	P	W	D	L	F	A
Ipswich's cup record	1	1	0	0	4	0
TOTAL	**1**	**1**	**0**	**0**	**4**	**0**

v. Norwich YMCA

FA Cup		Date	Result	Home Ipswich	Norwich	Date	Result	Ipswich	Norwich	Division Ipswich	Norwich
1934-35	1st Qual	29 September	Drew	1	1	3 October	Won	4	2	Non L	Non L
	(both matches at home)										

Summary	P	W	D	L	F	A
Ipswich's cup record	2	1	1	0	5	3
TOTAL	2	1	1	0	5	3

Ipswich's top scorers vs Norwich YMCA
Jock Sowerby 2

v. Nottingham Forest

Season	League	Date	Result	Ipswich	N'Forest	Date	Result	Ipswich	N'Forest	Ipswich	N'Forest
				Home			**Away**			**Final Positions**	
1949-50	Division 3S	1 October	Lost	1	2	18 February	Lost	0	2	17th	4th
1950-51	Division 3S	24 February	Lost	1	3	7 October	Drew	0	0	8th	1stP
1954-55	Division 2	9 March	Won	2	1	1 October	Lost	0	2	21stR	15th
1961-62	Division 1	4 November	Won	1	0	24 March	Drew	1	1	1st	19th
1962-63	Division 1	1 September	Drew	1	1	10 May	Lost	1	2	17th	9th
1963-64	Division 1	28 March	Won	4	3	1 November	Lost	1	3	22ndR	13th
1968-69	Division 1	21 December	Lost	2	3	19 October	Won	2	1	12th	18th
1969-70	Division 1	9 August	Drew	0	0	10 April	Lost	0	1	18th	15th
1970-71	Division 1	22 August	Drew	0	0	19 December	Won	1	0	19th	16th
1971-72	Division 1	9 October	Drew	1	1	11 March	Won	2	0	13th	21stR
1977-78	Division 1	25 April	Lost	0	2	4 October	Lost	0	4	18th	1st
1978-79	Division 1	3 March	Drew	1	1	21 October	Lost	0	1	6th	2nd
1979-80	Division 1	18 August	Lost	0	1	3 November	Lost	0	2	3rd	5th
1980-81	Division 1	10 January	Won	2	0	22 November	Won	2	1	2nd	7th
1981-82	Division 1	15 May	Lost	1	3	17 March	Drew	1	1	2nd	12th
1982-83	Division 1	19 March	Won	2	0	6 November	Lost	1	2	9th	5th
1983-84	Division 1	14 April	Drew	2	2	19 November	Lost	1	2	12th	3rd
1984-85	Division 1	6 April	Won	1	0	26 December	Lost	0	2	17th	9th
1985-86	Division 1	8 March	Won	1	0	5 October	Lost	1	3	20thR	8th
1992-93	Premiership	8 May	Won	2	1	31 October	Won	1	0	16th	22ndR
1994-95	Premiership	20 August	Lost	0	1	10 December	Lost	1	4	22ndR	3rd
1997-98	Division 1	29 November	Lost	0	1	5 April	Lost	1	2	5th	1stP
1999-00	Division 1	7 August	Won	3	1	5 December	Won	1	0	3rdP	14th
2002-03	Division 1	5 April	Lost	3	4	30 November	Lost	1	2	7th	6th
2003-04	Division 1	24 April	Lost	1	2	3 December	Drew	1	1	5th	14th
2004-05	Champ'ship	12 March	Won	6	0	11 August	Drew	1	1	3rd	23rdR

FA Cup

										Division	
1980-81	Q'ter-Final	10 March	Won	1	0	7 March	Drew	3	3	Div 1	Div 1
1988-89	Round 3					7 January	Lost	0	3	Div 2	Div 1
1996-97	Round 3					4 January	Lost	0	3	Div 1	Prem

FACT FILE

- In 1982, Ipswich finished second in the league for the second year running. This time, the title was decided on 15 May, when Ipswich lost to Forest, although it didn't matter as Liverpool's victory over Spurs on the same day would have clinched the title anyway.
- The sides have not played out a goalless draw since 1970.
- Ipswich had never beaten Forest by more than two until March 2005, when they put that right in stunning fashion.

Summary	P	W	D	L	F	A
Ipswich's home league record	26	10	6	10	38	33
Ipswich's away league record	26	6	5	15	21	40
Ipswich's cup record	4	1	1	2	4	9
TOTAL	**56**	**17**	**12**	**27**	**63**	**82**

Ipswich's top scorers vs Forest
Paul Mariner, Tommy Miller 4
Alan Brazil, Darren Bent 3

Played for both clubs
Frank Shufflebottom	Ipswich 1938-39	Forest 1946-47
Ron Blackman	Forest 1954-55	Ipswich 1955-56 to 1957-58
Frans Thijssen	Ipswich 1978-79 to 1983-84	Forest 1983-84
Lee Chapman	Forest 1988-89 to 1989-90	Ipswich 1994-95 to 1995-96
Tony Vaughan	Ipswich 1994-95 to 1996-97	Forest 1999-00 to 2002-03
Robert Howe	Forest 1993-94 to 1996-97	Ipswich 1996-97
Danny Sonner	Ipswich 1996-97 to 1998-99	Forest 2003-04
David Johnson	Ipswich 1997-98 to 2000-01	Forest 2000-01 to 2004-05
Marlon Harewood	Forest 1997-98 to 2003-04	Ipswich 1998-99
Paul Gerrard	Ipswich 2002-03	Forest 2003-04 to 2004-05
Chris Bart-Williams	Forest 1995-96 to 2001-02	Ipswich 2003-04

Ipswich and Forest's golden eras coincided in 1978 with Ipswich winning the FA Cup and Forest the Division One championship. Over the next four years Ipswich finished higher than Brian Clough's side three times, even though Forest won two back to back European Cups in that period. Pictured is the battle of the left-wingers as Forest's John Robertson is chased by Town's Kevin O'Callaghan in a clash from that era.

Season	League	Date	Result	Home Ipswich	Notts C	Date	Result	Away Ipswich	Notts C	Final Positions Ipswich	Notts C
1938-39	Division 3S	25 February	Lost	0	2	22 October	Lost	1	2	7th	11th
1946-47	Division 3S	17 May	Lost	1	2	19 October	Won	2	1	6th	12th
1947-48	Division 3S	23 August	Won	2	0	15 April	Won	1	0	4th	6th
1948-49	Division 3S	15 September	Won	3	2	9 September	Lost	2	9	7th	11th
1949-50	Division 3S	27 December	Lost	0	4	26 December	Lost	0	2	17th	1stP
1954-55	Division 2	11 December	Lost	0	1	30 April	Lost	1	2	21stR	7th
1957-58	Division 2	7 September	Won	2	1	11 January	Won	3	0	8th	21stR
1981-82	Division 1	30 January	Lost	1	3	19 September	Won	4	1	2nd	15th
1982-83	Division 1	9 April	Drew	0	0	25 September	Won	6	0	9th	15th
1983-84	Division 1	31 December	Won	1	0	3 September	Won	2	0	12th	21stR
1990-91	Division 2	17 November	Drew	0	0	7 May	Lost	1	3	14th	4thP

League Cup

									Division	
2003-04	Round 2					23 August	Lost	1	2	Div 1 Div 2

Summary

	P	W	D	L	F	A
Ipswich's home league record	11	4	2	5	10	15
Ipswich's away league record	11	6	0	5	23	20
Ipswich's cup record	1	0	0	1	1	2
TOTAL	**23**	**10**	**2**	**11**	**34**	**37**

FACT FILE

- In 1955, one year after promotion to Division Two for the first time, Ipswich soon looked doomed to go straight back down. However, an improvement in results gave them hope, but a final-day defeat at Meadow Lane confirmed the relegation.
- Games at Meadow Lane between the sides have averaged nearly four goals per game; a 9-2 defeat and a 6-0 win contributing to this in no small part.

Ipswich's top scorers vs Notts Co.
Tommy Parker 5
Paul Mariner 4
Alan Brazil 3

Played for both clubs

John Roy	Notts Co 1937-38 to 1938-39	Ipswich 1946-47
Kevin Wilson	Ipswich 1984-85 to 1986-87	Notts Co 1991-92 to 1993-94
Andrew Legg	Notts Co 1993-94 to 1995-96	Ipswich 1997-98
Gerry Creaney	Ipswich 1996-97	Notts Co 1998-99

v. Old Westminsters

FA Cup			Date	Result	Away Ipswich Westminster	Division Ipswich Westminster
1891-92	1st Qual		3 October	Lost	0 5	Non L Non L
1892-93	2nd Qual		29 October	Lost	1 4	Non L Non L

Summary	P	W	D	L	F	A
Ipswich's cup record	2	0	0	2	1	9
TOTAL	2	0	0	2	1	9

FACT FILE

- After the second of their defeats to Old Westminsters, Ipswich did not enter the FA Cup again until 1930. They were still an amateur club throughout this time and concentrated instead on regional and amateur competitions; in particular the Suffolk Senior Cup, which they won 13 times.
- Old Westminsters were FA Cup quarter-finalists three times between 1884 and 1887.

v. Old Wykehamists

		Home			**Division**

FA Cup		Date	Result	Ipswich Wykehamists		Ipswich Wykehamists
1892-93	1st Qual	15 October	Won	4 0		Non L Non L

Summary	P	W	D	L	F	A
Ipswich's cup record	1	1	0	0	4	0
TOTAL	1	1	0	0	4	0

FACT FILE

- Old Wykehamists, who had some decent cup runs in the 1880s, never entered the FA Cup again after this defeat.

Ipswich's top scorers vs Old Wykehamists
Stanley Turner 2

v. Oldham Athletic

Season	League	Date	Result	Ipswich	Oldham A	Date	Result	Ipswich	Oldham A	Ipswich	Oldham A
			Home				Away			Final Positions	
1986-87	Division 2	1 September	Lost	0	1	14 February	Lost	1	2	5th	3rd
1987-88	Division 2	21 November	Won	2	0	30 April	Lost	1	3	8th	10th
1988-89	Division 2	16 December	Won	2	1	4 April	Lost	0	4	8th	16th
1989-90	Division 2	25 November	Drew	1	1	24 February	Lost	1	4	9th	8th
1990-91	Division 2	27 April	Lost	1	2	23 October	Lost	0	2	14th	1stP
1992-93	Premiership	9 January	Lost	1	2	19 September	Lost	2	4	16th	19th
1993-94	Premiership	4 December	Drew	0	0	14 August	Won	3	0	19th	21stR
1995-96	Division 1	19 March	Won	2	1	12 September	Drew	1	1	7th	18th
1996-97	Division 1	5 April	Won	4	0	31 August	Drew	3	3	4th	23rdR

FA Cup

Season		Date	Result			Date	Result			Division	
1953-54	Round 3	9 January	Drew	3	3	12 January	Won	1	0	Div 3S	Div 2
1963-64	Round 3	4 January	Won	6	3					Div 1	Div 3

Summary

	P	W	D	L	F	A
Ipswich's home league record	9	4	2	3	13	8
Ipswich's away league record	9	1	2	6	12	23
Ipswich's cup record	3	2	1	0	10	6
TOTAL	**21**	**7**	**5**	**9**	**35**	**37**

Ipswich's top scorers vs Oldham
Gerry Baker, John Wark, Chris Kiwomya,
Paul Mason 3

Ipswich hat-tricks vs Oldham
4 January 1964 Gerry Baker (cup)

Played for both clubs

David Best	Oldham 1966-67 to 1968-69	Ipswich 1968-69 to 1973-74
Allan Hunter	Oldham 1966-67 to 1968-69	Ipswich 1971-72 to 1980-81
Glenn Keeley	Ipswich 1972-73 to 1973-74	Oldham 1987-88
Mark Grew	Oldham 1983-84	Ipswich 1984-85
Mark Brennan	Ipswich 1983-84 to 1987-88	Oldham 1992-93 to 1995-96
Jon Hallworth	Ipswich 1985-86 to 1987-88	Oldham 1988-89 to 1996-97
Ian Marshall	Oldham 1987-88 to 1992-93	Ipswich 1993-94 to 1996-97
Neil Thompson	Ipswich 1989-90 to 1995-96	Oldham 1997-98
Paul Gerrard	Oldham 1992-93 to 1995-96	Ipswich 2002-03
Chris Makin	Oldham 1993-94 to 1995-96	Ipswich 2000-01 to 2003-04
Gerry Creaney	Oldham 1995-96	Ipswich 1996-97
Michael Clegg	Ipswich 1999-00	Oldham 2001-02 to 2003-04

v. Oxford United

League Cup

Summary	P	W	D	L	F	A
Ipswich's home league record	8	6	1	1	17	10
Ipswich's away league record	8	0	4	4	12	17
Ipswich's cup record	2	2	0	0	4	2
TOTAL	**18**	**8**	**5**	**5**	**33**	**29**

Scottish international centre-half, Matt Elliott started his career in the lower reaches of the football ladder with Epsom and Ewell before spells at Charlton, Torquay and Scunthorpe resulted in a £150,000 move to Oxford, the springboard to Elliott's career. After 171 games for Oxford, Leicester splashed the cash, spending £1.6 million securing his signature. It was a great investment as captain Elliott typified Martin O'Neill's succesful Leicester side, culminating in two League Cup final appearances, one of which gave Leicester their first trophy in years. Ipswich gave Elliott a home on loan at the end of the 2003-04 season, when economics dictated that Leicester were forced to cut costs, but after only 10 appearances Elliott returned to the Midlands, where he eventually retired in January 2005.

FACT FILE

- The 3-2 win over relegation rivals over Oxford in April 1986 seemed to have ensured Ipswich's safety. However, four days later a bitterly contested penalty condemned Town to defeat by West Ham, and, on the same day, Oxford beat championship contenders Everton with a last-minute goal. When Ipswich lost their final game of the season to Sheffield Wednesday, it left them needing Arsenal to do them a favour against Oxford. Arsenal lost 3-0, and Town were down.
- However, they were back six years later as a draw at the Manor Ground clinched promotion. Their return coincided with the advent of Premier League football.
- Neither side has managed more than one away win in the series.

Ipswich's top scorers vs Oxford
Jason Dozzell, David Johnson (II) 4
Matt Holland 2

Ipswich hat-tricks vs Oxford
24 February 1998 David Johnson (II)

Played for both clubs

Mark Stein	Oxford 1989-90 to 1991-92	Ipswich 1997-98
Jim Magilton	Oxford 1990-91 to 1993-94	Ipswich 1998-99 to 2004-05
Phil Whelan	Ipswich 1991-92 to 1994-95	Oxford 1997-98 to 1999-00
Matt Elliott	Oxford 1993-94 to 1996-97	Ipswich 2003-04
Paul Gerrard	Oxford 1998-99	Ipswich 2002-03

v. Peterborough United

Summary	P	W	D	L	F	A
Ipswich's cup record	3	1	0	2	5	6
TOTAL	3	1	0	2	5	6

FACT FILE

- Twice in five seasons, Ipswich were eliminated from the FA Cup by non-league Peterborough. However, within two and a half years of the second ignominy, Ipswich were champions of England.

Played for both clubs

Roger Wosahlo	Ipswich 1967-68 & 1969-70	Peterborough 1968-69
Peter Morris	Ipswich 1967-68 to 1973-74	Peterborough 1979-80
Mick Lambert	Ipswich 1968-69 to 1978-79	Peterborough 1979-80 to 1980-81
Trevor Whymark	Ipswich 1969-70 to 1978-79	Peterborough 1985-86
Pat Sharkey	Ipswich 1975-76 to 1976-77	Peterborough 1978-79 to 1979-80
Tommy Parkin	Peterborough 1976-77	Ipswich 1977-78 to 1986-87
David Gregory	Ipswich 1988-89 to 1994-95	Peterborough 1995-96
Frederick Barber	Peterborough 1989-90 & 1991-92 to 1994-95	Ipswich 1995-96
Louie Donowa	Ipswich 1989-90	Peterborough 1996-97
Scott Houghton	Ipswich 1990-91	Peterborough 1996-97 to 1998-99
Neil Gregory	Ipswich 1994-95 to 1997-98	Peterborough 1997-98
Danny Sonner	Ipswich 1996-97 to 1998-99	Peterborough 2004-05
Andrew Legg	Ipswich 1997-98	Peterborough 1998-99 & 2003-04 to 2004-05
Richard Logan	Ipswich 1998-99 to 1999-00	Peterborough 2003-04 to 2004-05
James Pullen	Ipswich 2002-03	Peterborough 2003-04

Colin Viljoen (pictured) scored one of the goals in Ipswich's only win over Peterborough, in the 1972 FA Cup third round. Mick Hill scored the other as a potential upset was avoided. The run came to a halt in the next round with a 1-0 defeat at home by Birmingham City.

v. Plymouth Argyle

Season	League	Date	Result	Home Ipswich	Plymouth	Date	Result	Away Ipswich	Plymouth	Final Positions Ipswich	Plymouth
1950-51	Division 3S	26 August	Won	2	0	23 December	Lost	1	2	8th	4th
1951-52	Division 3S	29 September	Drew	2	2	9 February	Lost	0	2	17th	1stP
1954-55	Division 2	27 November	Won	2	1	16 April	Lost	0	2	21stR	20th
1956-57	Division 3S	20 April	Won	2	1	27 October	Won	2	1	1stP	18th
1959-60	Division 2	28 November	Drew	3	3	19 March	Lost	1	3	11th	19th
1960-61	Division 2	10 December	Won	3	1	18 March	Won	2	1	1stP	11th
1964-65	Division 2	16 January	Drew	2	2	12 September	Drew	1	1	5th	15th
1965-66	Division 2	4 September	Won	4	1	19 February	Lost	0	3	15th	18th
1966-67	Division 2	4 March	Drew	1	1	29 October	Drew	1	1	5th	16th
1967-68	Division 2	25 November	Drew	1	1	20 April	Won	1	0	1stP	22ndR
1986-87	Division 2	19 December	Won	3	0	21 October	Lost	0	2	5th	7th
1987-88	Division 2	13 February	Lost	1	2	18 August	Drew	0	0	8th	16th
1988-89	Division 2	3 December	Drew	2	2	1 May	Won	1	0	8th	18th
1989-90	Division 2	21 October	Won	3	0	31 March	Lost	0	1	9th	16th
1990-91	Division 2	22 March	Won	3	1	6 October	Drew	0	0	14th	18th
1991-92	Division 2	29 February	Won	2	0	7 December	Lost	0	1	1stP	22ndR
2004-05	Champ'ship	25 September	Won	3	2	3 January	Won	2	1	3rd	17th

FA Cup

										Division	
1992-93	Round 3	12 January	Won	3	1					Prem	Div 2

Summary	P	W	D	L	F	A
Ipswich's home league record	17	10	6	1	39	20
Ipswich's away league record	17	5	4	8	12	21
Ipswich's cup record	1	1	0	0	3	1
TOTAL	**35**	**16**	**10**	**9**	**54**	**42**

FACT FILE

● Plymouth have won just once in 18 visits to Ipswich. Ipswich have scored in all 18 home games.

Ipswich's top scorers vs Plymouth
Ted Phillips, Ray Crawford 4
Frank Brogan, Chris Kiwomya 3

Played for both clubs

Fred Mitcheson	Plymouth 1935-36 to 1938-39	Ipswich 1939-40
Charlie Fletcher	Plymouth 1937-38 to 1938-39	Ipswich 1939-40
Sam McCrory	Ipswich 1949-50 to 1951-52	Plymouth 1952-53 to 1954-55
Andy Nelson	Ipswich 1959-60 to 1964-65	Plymouth 1965-66 to 1967-68
John Peddelty	Ipswich 1972-73 to 1976-77	Plymouth 1976-77 to 1977-78
Paul Mariner	Plymouth 1973-74 to 1976-77	Ipswich 1976-77 to 1983-84
Terry Austin	Ipswich 1974-75 to 1975-76	Plymouth 1976-77 to 1977-78
Lee Chapman	Plymouth 1978-79	Ipswich 1994-95 to 1995-96
Steve McCall	Ipswich 1979-80 to 1986-87	Plymouth 1991-92 to 1995-96
		& 1998-99 to 1999-00
Mark Stuart	Plymouth 1988-89 to 1989-90	Ipswich 1989-90
Raphael Meade	Ipswich 1989-90	Plymouth 1990-91
Andrew Petterson	Ipswich 1992-93 & 1995-96	Plymouth 1995-96
Earl Jean	Ipswich 1996-97	Plymouth 1997-98 to 1998-99
Lee Hodges	Plymouth 1997-98	Ipswich 1998-99
Darren Currie	Plymouth 1997-98	Ipswich 2004-05

Bolton-born Paul Mariner, pictured scoring past Liverpool's Ray Clemence, joined Ipswich from Plymouth Argyle in 1976 after three successful years on the south-west coast. Mariner is one of Ipswich's all-time greats, scoring 135 goals in 340 appearances over eight seasons. His transfer to Arsenal in 1984 marked the end of a great Ipswich career. Mariner's ability was recognised by England 35 times.

v. Port Vale

				Home					Away		Final Positions	
Season	League	Date	Result	Ipswich	Port Vale	Date	Result	Ipswich	Port Vale		Ipswich	Port Vale
1938-39	Division 3S	12 November	Won	2	0	18 March	Drew	0	0		7th	18th
1946-47	Division 3S	23 November	Won	2	1	29 March	Lost	0	1		6th	10th
1947-48	Division 3S	20 March	Won	2	1	1 November	Lost	1	4		4th	8th
1948-49	Division 3S	19 March	Won	4	1	23 October	Won	2	1		7th	13th
1949-50	Division 3S	6 May	Won	2	1	5 September	Drew	2	2		17th	13th
1950-51	Division 3S	13 September	Drew	2	2	4 September	Lost	0	1		8th	12th
1951-52	Division 3S	15 September	Won	2	0	19 January	Drew	0	0		17th	13th
1954-55	Division 2	12 March	Won	1	0	23 October	Drew	3	3		21stR	17th
1989-90	Division 2	14 April	Won	3	2	1 January	Lost	0	5		9th	11th
1990-91	Division 2	13 October	Won	3	0	18 March	Won	2	1		14th	15th
1991-92	Division 2	20 August	Won	2	1	1 January	Won	2	1		1stP	24thR
1995-96	Division 1	1 January	Won	5	1	23 March	Lost	1	2		7th	12th
1996-97	Division 1	23 November	Won	2	1	15 February	Drew	2	2		4th	8th
1997-98	Division 1	18 April	Won	5	1	20 December	Won	3	1		5th	19th
1998-99	Division 1	30 January	Won	1	0	31 August	Won	3	0		3rd	21st
1999-00	Division 1	8 April	Won	3	0	3 January	Won	2	1		3rdP	23rdR

League Cup

											Division	
1988-89	Round 2	10 October	Won	3	0	26 September	Lost	0	1		Div 2	Div 3

Summary

	P	W	D	L	F	A
Ipswich's home league record	16	15	1	0	41	12
Ipswich's away league record	16	6	5	5	23	25
Ipswich's cup record	2	1	0	1	3	1
TOTAL	**34**	**22**	**6**	**6**	**67**	**38**

Ipswich's top scorers vs Port Vale
Alex Mathie, David Johnson (II) 5
Jackie Brown 4
Sam McCrory, Simon Milton, Chris Kiwomya,
  Neil Thompson, James Scowcroft, Matt Holland 3

Ipswich hat-tricks vs Port Vale
19 March 1949 Jackie Brown

FACT FILE

● Ipswich are unbeaten in their last eight games of the series; they have won seven of these.
● A 2-2 draw in 1950 spoiled an otherwise perfect home record for the Blues.

Played for both clubs

Fred Mitcheson	Port Vale 1933-34 to 1935-36	Ipswich 1939-40
Ken Hancock	Port Vale 1958-59 to 1964-65	Ipswich 1964-65 to 1968-69
Dave Mitchell	Port Vale 1964-65 to 1965-66	Ipswich 1966-67
Colin Harper	Ipswich 1965-66 to 1974-75	Port Vale 1977-78
John Miller	Ipswich 1968-69 to 1973-74	Port Vale 1980-81
Kevin Steggles	Ipswich 1980-81 to 1985-86	Port Vale 1987-88
Mark Grew	Ipswich 1984-85	Port Vale 1986-87 to 1991-92
Michael Cole	Ipswich 1984-85 to 1987-88	Port Vale 1987-88
David Lowe	Ipswich 1987-88 to 1991-92	Port Vale 1991-92 & 1993-94
Alex Mathie	Port Vale 1992-93	Ipswich 1994-95 to 1998-99
Danny Sonner	Ipswich 1996-97 to 1998-99	Port Vale 2004-05
Marcus Bent	Port Vale 1998-99 to 1999-00	Ipswich 2001-02 to 2003-04
Tony Dinning	Ipswich 2004-05	Port Vale 2004-05

Alex Mathie (pictured) made the briefest of stops at Port Vale, just three substitute appearances, on his way south to Newcastle United from Scottish football. When Ipswich paid £500,000 for Mathie in February 1995, they took a chance as he had made just eight full appearances for the Geordies, but it was a good decision. When Mathie transferred to Dundee United in October 1998, he had scored 47 goals in only 108 starts, a great ratio for a striker. Mathie is also the club's top scorer against Port Vale, with five goals, three of which came in the 1997-98 season alone.

v. Portsmouth

Season	League	Date	Result	Ipswich	Portsmouth	Date	Result	Ipswich	Portsmouth	Ipswich	Portsmouth
				Home				**Away**		*Final Positions*	
1959-60	Division 2	13 February	Drew	1	1	26 September	Won	2	0	11th	20th
1960-61	Division 2	8 April	Drew	2	2	19 November	Lost	0	1	1stP	21stR
1964-65	Division 2	7 November	Won	7	0	20 March	Won	2	0	5th	20th
1965-66	Division 2	26 February	Won	1	0	11 September	Lost	0	1	15th	12th
1966-67	Division 2	25 March	Won	4	2	15 October	Lost	2	4	5th	14th
1967-68	Division 2	9 December	Lost	1	2	4 May	Won	2	1	1stP	5th
1986-87	Division 2	7 February	Lost	0	1	30 August	Drew	1	1	5th	2ndP
1988-89	Division 2	25 October	Lost	0	1	28 February	Won	1	0	8th	20th
1989-90	Division 2	10 April	Lost	0	1	28 October	Won	3	2	9th	12th
1990-91	Division 2	1 April	Drew	2	2	21 December	Drew	1	1	14th	17th
1991-92	Division 2	8 February	Won	5	2	26 October	Drew	1	1	1stP	9th
1995-96	Division 1	25 November	Won	3	2	27 April	Won	1	0	7th	21st
1996-97	Division 1	19 October	Drew	1	1	25 April	Won	1	0	4th	7th
1997-98	Division 1	13 December	Won	2	0	13 April	Won	1	0	5th	20th
1998-99	Division 1	26 December	Won	3	0	22 August	Drew	0	0	3rd	19th
1999-00	Division 1	4 March	Lost	0	1	11 September	Drew	1	1	3rdP	18th
2002-03	Division 1	18 April	Won	3	0	21 December	Drew	1	1	7th	1stP

League Cup										*Division*	
1992-93	Round 3					27 October	Won	1	0	Prem	Div 1

Summary	P	W	D	L	F	A
Ipswich's home league record	17	8	4	5	35	18
Ipswich's away league record	17	8	6	3	20	14
Ipswich's cup record	1	1	0	0	1	0
TOTAL	**35**	**17**	**10**	**8**	**56**	**32**

Midfielder Danny Hegan, pictured, was twice on the scoresheet on 7 November 1964, as Ipswich thrashed Portsmouth 7-0, by far their biggest victory against their south coast opposition. His brace was overshadowed – by Frank Brogan, hat-trick hero that day. Also scoring in the game were Joe Broadfoot and Gerard Baker. Hegan finished the season on seven goals.

FACT FILE

- Ipswich have not lost in their last 13 visits to Fratton Park.
- Ipswich have lost to Portsmouth once in their last 17 meetings.

Ipswich's top scorers vs Portsmouth

Simon Milton 5
Gerry Baker, Jason Dozzell 4
Danny Hegan, Frank Brogan, Colin Viljoen,
  Neil Thompson 3

Ipswich hat-tricks vs Portsmouth

7 November 1964 Frank Brogan
25 March 1967 Colin Viljoen
7 September 1963 Harry Burrows

Played for both clubs

Reg Pickett	Portsmouth 1949-50 to 1956-57	Ipswich 1957-58 to 1962-63
Derek Rees	Portsmouth 1954-55 to 1956-57	Ipswich 1957-58 to 1960-61
Ray Crawford	Portsmouth 1957-58 to 1958-59	Ipswich 1958-59 to 1963-64
		& 1965-66 to 1968-69
Bobby Kellard	Ipswich 1965-66	Portsmouth 1965-66 to 1967-68
		& 1972-73 to 1974-75
David Best	Ipswich 1968-69 to 1973-74	Portsmouth 1973-74 to 1974-75
Ian Collard	Ipswich 1969-70 to 1974-75	Portsmouth 1975-76
Paul Mariner	Ipswich 1976-77 to 1983-84	Portsmouth 1986-87 to 1987-88
Kevin O'Callaghan	Ipswich 1979-80 to 1984-85	Portsmouth 1984-85 to 1986-87
John Moncur	Portsmouth 1988-89	Ipswich 1991-92
Andrew Petterson	Ipswich 1992-93 & 1995-96	Portsmouth 1998-99 to 2000-01
Lee Chapman	Portsmouth 1993-94	Ipswich 1994-95 to 1995-96
Gerry Creaney	Portsmouth 1993-94 to 1995-96	Ipswich 1996-97
Jason Cundy	Ipswich 1996-97 to 1998-99	Portsmouth 1999-00
Paolo Vernazza	Ipswich 1998-99	Portsmouth 1999-00
Mark Burchill	Ipswich 2000-01	Portsmouth 2001-02 to 2002-03
David Unsworth	Ipswich 2004-05	Portsmouth 2004-05

v. Preston North End

		Home					Away		Final Positions	
Season	League	Date	Result	Ipswich	Preston	Date	Result	Ipswich	Preston	Ipswich	Preston

Season	League	Date	Result	Ipswich	Preston	Date	Result	Ipswich	Preston	Ipswich	Preston
1964-65	Division 2	29 August	Lost	1	5	19 December	Lost	1	4	5th	12th
1965-66	Division 2	21 August	Won	1	0	29 January	Won	1	0	15th	17th
1966-67	Division 2	22 April	Drew	0	0	26 November	Lost	0	2	5th	13th
1967-68	Division 2	16 March	Won	4	0	21 October	Drew	1	1	1stP	20th
2002-03	Division 1	18 January	Won	3	0	1 September	Drew	0	0	7th	12th
2003-04	Division 1	28 February	Won	2	0	25 October	Drew	1	1	5th	15th
2004-05	Champ'ship	30 October	Won	3	0	18 February	Drew	1	1	3rd	5th

FA Cup

										Division	
1953-54	Round 5					20 February	Lost	1	6	Div 3S	Div 1
1979-80	Round 3					5 January	Won	3	0	Div 1	Div 2

Summary

	P	W	D	L	F	A
Ipswich's home league record	7	5	1	1	14	5
Ipswich's away league record	7	1	4	2	5	9
Ipswich's cup record	2	1	0	1	4	6
TOTAL	**16**	**7**	**5**	**4**	**23**	**20**

FACT FILE

● Having scored five on their first visit to Ipswich, Preston have not scored there since.

Ipswich's top scorers vs Preston
Darren Bent, Tommy Miller 3
Ray Crawford, Joe Broadfoot, Paul Mariner 2

Played for both clubs

Mick Burns	Preston 1936-37 to 1937-38	Ipswich 1938-39 to 1951-52
David Johnson	Ipswich 1972-73 to 1975-76	Preston 1984-85
Alex Mathie	Ipswich 1994-95 to 1998-99	Preston 1999-00

Dave Johnson is one of only three players to have both played for Ipswich and Preston, ending his illustrious career with the Lilywhites after trying his hand with North American side Tulsa Roughnecks.

v. Queens Park Rangers

Season	League	Date	Result	Home Ipswich	QPR	Date	Result	Away Ipswich	QPR	Final Positions Ipswich	QPR
1938-39	Division 3S	10 April	Won	1	0	7 April	Drew	0	0	7th	6th
1946-47	Division 3S	26 December	Drew	1	1	25 December	Won	3	1	6th	2nd
1947-48	Division 3S	25 October	Won	1	0	13 March	Lost	0	2	4th	1stP
1952-53	Division 3S	18 April	Lost	0	1	29 November	Drew	2	2	16th	20th
1953-54	Division 3S	10 April	Won	2	1	5 December	Lost	1	3	1stP	18th
1955-56	Division 3S	14 January	Won	4	1	10 September	Drew	1	1	3rd	18th
1956-57	Division 3S	3 November	Won	4	0	16 March	Won	2	0	1stP	10th
1967-68	Division 2	27 April	Drew	2	2	1 December	Lost	0	1	1stP	2ndP
1968-69	Division 1	27 August	Won	3	0	8 October	Lost	1	2	12th	22ndR
1973-74	Division 1	15 April	Won	1	0	12 April	Won	1	0	4th	8th
1974-75	Division 1	12 April	Won	2	1	5 October	Lost	0	1	3rd	11th
1975-76	Division 1	15 November	Drew	1	1	21 February	Lost	1	3	6th	2nd
1976-77	Division 1	28 August	Drew	2	2	16 May	Lost	0	1	3rd	14th
1977-78	Division 1	27 December	Won	3	2	25 March	Drew	3	3	18th	19th
1978-79	Division 1	28 October	Won	2	1	11 May	Won	4	0	6th	20thR
1983-84	Division 1	15 October	Lost	0	2	7 April	Lost	0	1	12th	5th
1984-85	Division 1	13 October	Drew	1	1	16 March	Lost	0	3	17th	19th
1985-86	Division 1	14 December	Won	1	0	17 August	Lost	0	1	20thR	13th
1992-93	Premiership	9 February	Drew	1	1	5 September	Drew	0	0	16th	5th
1993-94	Premiership	26 March	Lost	1	3	1 October	Lost	0	3	19th	9th
1994-95	Premiership	11 April	Lost	0	1	27 August	Won	2	1	22ndR	8th
1996-97	Division 1	8 February	Won	2	0	30 October	Won	1	0	4th	9th
1997-98	Division 1	10 January	Drew	0	0	9 August	Drew	0	0	5th	21st
1998-99	Division 1	5 April	Won	3	1	1 December	Drew	1	1	3rd	20th
1999-00	Division 1	16 October	Lost	1	4	22 April	Lost	1	3	3rdP	10th
2004-05	Champ'ship	26 February	Lost	0	2	11 December	Won	4	2	3rd	11th

FA Cup

										Division	
1945-46	Round 2	15 December	Lost	0	2	8 December	Lost	0	4	Div 3S	Div 3S

League Cup

										Division	
1983-84	Round 3	9 November	Won	3	2					Div 1	Div 1
1984-85	Q'ter-Final	23 January	Drew	0	0	28 January	Won	2	1	Div 1	Div 1

Summary	P	W	D	L	F	A
Ipswich's home league record	26	13	7	6	39	28
Ipswich's away league record	26	7	7	12	28	35
Ipswich's cup record	5	2	1	2	5	9
TOTAL	**57**	**22**	**15**	**20**	**72**	**72**

FACT FILE

- Due to the two-legged nature of the 1946 FA Cup, Ipswich lost two matches in the same FA Cup competition for the only time.
- From 1954 to 1978, Ipswich were unbeaten in 11 home games against QPR.

Ipswich's top scorers vs QPR
Tommy Parker 6
Tom Garneys, Ted Phillips, Eric Gates 4
Paul Mariner, John Wark, Matt Holland 3

Ipswich hat-tricks vs QPR
3 November 1956   Ted Phillips

Played for both clubs

George Smith	QPR 1947-48 to 1948-49	Ipswich 1949-50
John Gibbons	QPR 1948-49	Ipswich 1949-50
Frank Clarke	QPR 1967-68 to 1969-70	Ipswich 1969-70 to 1972-73
John O'Rourke	Ipswich 1967-68 to 1969-70	QPR 1971-72 to 1972-73
Phil Parkes	QPR 1970-71 to 1978-79	Ipswich 1990-91
Paul Goddard	QPR 1977-78 to 1979-80	Ipswich 1990-91 to 1993-94
Alan Brazil	Ipswich 1977-78 to 1982-83	QPR 1986-87
David Kerslake	QPR 1984-85 to 1989-90	Ipswich 1997-98
Mark Stein	QPR 1988-89 to 1989-90	Ipswich 1997-98
Chris Kiwomya	Ipswich 1988-89 to 1994-95	QPR 1998-99 to 2000-01
Steve Palmer	Ipswich 1989-90 to 1995-96	QPR 2001-02 to 2003-04
Georges Santos	Ipswich 2003-04	QPR 2004-05

Midfielder Steve Palmer started his career at Ipswich, signing at the start of 1989-90 season. In his six seasons at the club, he failed to achieve 'regular' status, as his 101 appearances show. A move to Watford in 1995 was good for him and he became a first-team regular, notching up almost 250 appearances in a similar timeframe before transferring to QPR on a free transfer in 2001. Palmer is still going strong at the age of 37, in League One with MK Dons.

v. Reading

Season	League	Date	Result	Home Ipswich	Reading	Date	Result	Away Ipswich	Reading	Final Positions Ipswich	Reading
1938-39	Division 3S	3 May	Won	2	1	24 September	Lost	1	2	7th	5th
1946-47	Division 3S	28 September	Won	2	0	1 February	Won	3	1	6th	9th
1947-48	Division 3S	27 September	Won	1	0	14 February	Won	2	1	4th	10th
1948-49	Division 3S	11 September	Won	3	2	22 January	Lost	1	2	7th	2nd
1949-50	Division 3S	14 January	Won	2	0	10 September	Lost	1	3	17th	10th
1950-51	Division 3S	30 December	Lost	0	2	1 September	Lost	0	2	8th	3rd
1951-52	Division 3S	1 September	Won	4	2	29 December	Lost	0	4	17th	2nd
1952-53	Division 3S	30 August	Lost	1	2	3 January	Drew	1	1	16th	11th
1953-54	Division 3S	23 January	Lost	0	1	12 September	Lost	1	3	1stP	8th
1955-56	Division 3S	10 March	Drew	3	3	29 October	Won	5	1	3rd	17th
1956-57	Division 3S	20 October	Won	4	2	1 March	Won	3	1	1stP	13th
1986-87	Division 2	9 May	Drew	1	1	13 December	Won	4	1	5th	13th
1987-88	Division 2	7 November	Won	2	1	1 April	Drew	1	1	8th	22ndR
1995-96	Division 1	6 April	Lost	1	2	28 October	Won	4	1	7th	19th
1996-97	Division 1	24 August	Won	5	2	22 March	Lost	0	1	4th	18th
1997-98	Division 1	28 March	Won	1	0	22 November	Won	4	0	5th	24thR
2002-03	Division 1	18 March	Won	3	1	19 October	Lost	1	3	7th	4th
2003-04	Division 1	9 August	Drew	1	1	10 January	Drew	1	1	5th	9th
2004-05	Champ'ship	28 September	Drew	1	1	22 January	Drew	1	1	3rd	7th

FA Cup

Season	Round	Date	Result	Ipswich	Reading	Division	
1890-91	1st Qual	4 October	Won	2	0	Non L	Non L
1953-54	Round 1	21 November	Won	4	1	Div 3S	Div 3S

Summary

	P	W	D	L	F	A
Ipswich's home league record	19	11	4	4	37	24
Ipswich's away league record	19	7	4	8	34	30
Ipswich's cup record	2	2	0	0	6	1
TOTAL	**40**	**20**	**8**	**12**	**77**	**55**

FACT FILE

- Reading were the opponents for Ipswich's first-ever FA Cup tie. They decided to forgo the Suffolk Senior Cup for a stab at the national competition, and won 2-0 with goals from Sheringham and Turner.
- There has never been a goalless draw between the sides.
- The last four matches have all ended 1-1.

Ipswich's top scorers vs Reading
Tom Garneys 6
Tommy Parker, Ted Phillips 5
Albert Day, Bill Jennings, Wilf Grant,
    Kevin Wilson, David Lowe, James Scowcroft 3

Ipswich hat-tricks vs Reading
29 October 1955   Wilf Grant
2 March 1957   Ted Phillips

Played for both clubs

Ron Blackman	Reading 1946-47 to 1953-54	Ipswich 1955-56 to 1957-58
George McLuckie	Ipswich 1953-54 to 1957-58	Reading 1958-59 to 1960-61
Bobby Hunt	Ipswich 1967-68 to 1970-71	Reading 1972-73 to 1973-74
Ron Fearon	Reading 1980-81 to 1982-83	Ipswich 1987-88 to 1988-89
Irvin Gernon	Ipswich 1981-82 to 1986-87	Reading 1988-89 to 1989-90
Ian Juryeff	Reading 1984-85	Ipswich 1988-89
Andy Bernal	Ipswich 1987-88	Reading 1994-95 to 1999-00
Andrew Legg	Ipswich 1997-98	Reading 1997-98 to 1998-99

Tony Mowbray winning an aerial tussle against Reading's Robert Fleck at Portman Road.

v. Rotherham United

Season	League	Date	Result	**Home** Ipswich Rotherham	Date	Result	**Away** Ipswich Rotherham	**Final Positions** Ipswich Rotherham
1954-55	Division 2	18 December	Drew	2 2	21 August	Lost	2 3	21stR 3rd
1957-58	Division 2	31 August	Lost	1 2	28 December	Won	4 1	8th 18th
1958-59	Division 2	13 December	Won	1 0	23 April	Won	2 1	16th 20th
1959-60	Division 2	17 October	Lost	2 3	5 March	Won	4 1	11th 8th
1960-61	Division 2	4 February	Drew	1 1	17 September	Drew	1 1	1stP 15th
1964-65	Division 2	10 October	Drew	4 4	20 February	Drew	2 2	5th 14th
1965-66	Division 2	4 December	Drew	0 0	30 April	Drew	0 0	15th 7th
1966-67	Division 2	19 November	Won	3 2	15 April	Won	2 0	5th 18th
1967-68	Division 2	13 April	Won	2 0	18 November	Won	3 1	1stP 21stR
2002-03	Division 1	7 December	Lost	1 2	21 April	Lost	1 2	7th 15th
2003-04	Division 1	4 October	Won	2 1	10 April	Won	3 1	5th 17th
2004-05	Champ'ship	5 April	Won	4 3	28 August	Won	2 0	3rd 24thR

Summary	P	W	D	L	F	A
Ipswich's home league record	12	5	4	3	23	20
Ipswich's away league record	12	7	3	2	26	13
TOTAL	**24**	**12**	**7**	**5**	**49**	**33**

Ipswich's top scorers vs Rotherham
Ray Crawford 8
Tom Garneys 5
Danny Hegan 4
John Colrain, Darren Bent, Pablo Counago, Shefki Kuqi 3

Played for both clubs

Roy Stephenson	Rotherham 1956-57 to 1957-58	Ipswich 1960-61 to 1964-65
Billy Houghton	Ipswich 1966-67 to 1968-69	Rotherham 1969-70 to 1973-74
Ron Wigg	Ipswich 1967-68 to 1969-70	Rotherham 1972-73 to 1974-75
Brian Gayle	Ipswich 1989-90 to 1991-92	Rotherham 1996-97
Phil Whelan	Ipswich 1991-92 to 1994-95	Rotherham 1998-99
Chris Swailes	Ipswich 1994-95 to 1997-98	Rotherham 2001-02 to 2004-05
Earl Jean	Ipswich 1996-97	Rotherham 1996-97
Paolo Vernazza	Ipswich 1998-99	Rotherham 2004-05
Mark Burchill	Ipswich 2000-01	Rotherham 2004-05

FACT FILE

- There were six consecutive draws in the series between 1960 and 1966.
- In each of the last eight seasons that Ipswich have met Rotherham, whichever team won the first match also won the second - unless the first match was a draw, in which case the second match was too.

v. Scunthorpe United

				Home				Away	Final Positions	
Season	League	Date	Result	Ipswich	Scunthorpe	Date	Result	Ipswich Scunthorpe	Ipswich	Scunthorpe
1958-59	Division 2	20 December	Won	3	1	23 August	Drew	1 1	16th	18th
1959-60	Division 2	27 February	Won	1	0	10 October	Drew	2 2	11th	15th
1960-61	Division 2	30 August	Won	2	0	25 August	Lost	0 4	1stP	9th

League Cup

									Division	
1986-87	Round 2	7 October	Won	2	0	23 September	Won	2 1	Div 2	Div 4

Summary	P	W	D	L	F	A
Ipswich's home league record	3	3	0	0	6	1
Ipswich's away league record	3	0	2	1	3	7
Ipswich's cup record	2	2	0	0	4	1
TOTAL	**8**	**5**	**2**	**1**	**13**	**9**

Ipswich's top scorers vs Scunthorpe
Ray Crawford 4
Ted Phillips 3

Played for both clubs

Ron Wigg	Ipswich 1967-68 to 1969-70	Scunthorpe 1977-78 to 1978-79
David Hill	Scunthorpe 1983-84 to 1987-88 & 1990-91 to 1992-93	Ipswich 1988-89 to 1990-91
Neil Woods	Ipswich 1987-88 to 1989-90	Scunthorpe 1997-98
Ian Juryeff	Ipswich 1988-89	Scunthorpe 1993-94 to 1994-95
Matt Elliott	Scunthorpe 1991-92 to 1993-94	Ipswich 2003-04
Neil Gregory	Scunthorpe 1994-95	Ipswich 1994-95 to 1997-98
Tony Vaughan	Ipswich 1994-95 to 1996-97	Scunthorpe 2001-02
Lee Hodges	Ipswich 1998-99	Scunthorpe 1999-00 to 2001-02

v. Severalls Athletic

FA Cup	Date	Result	Home Ipswich Severalls	Division Ipswich Severalls
1930-31 1st Qual	4 October	Won	6 1	Non L Non L

Summary	P	W	D	L	F	A
Ipswich's cup record	1	1	0	0	6	1
TOTAL	1	1	0	0	6	1

FACT FILE

- This win took Ipswich's tally in the 1930-31 competition to 16 goals in three games, of which Dammo Green scored nine. In the next round, however they only scored twice against Crittalls Athletic, and lost.

Ipswich's top scorers vs Severalls
Dammo Green 5

Ipswich hat-tricks vs Severalls
4 October 1930 Dammo Green (5) (cup)

v. Sheffield United

Season	League		Home				Away			Final Positions	
		Date	Result	Ipswich	Sheffield U	Date	Result	Ipswich	Sheffield U	Ipswich	Sheffield U
1957-58	Division 2	7 April	Won	1	0	8 April	Drew	1	1	8th	6th
1958-59	Division 2	30 April	Won	1	0	8 November	Lost	0	2	16th	3rd
1959-60	Division 2	26 March	Won	2	0	7 November	Lost	0	1	11th	4th
1960-61	Division 2	15 October	Lost	0	1	7 March	Won	3	1	1stP	2ndP
1961-62	Division 1	3 March	Won	4	0	14 October	Lost	1	2	1st	5th
1962-63	Division 1	21 December	Won	1	0	25 August	Lost	1	2	17th	10th
1963-64	Division 1	29 February	Won	1	0	9 October	Lost	1	3	22ndR	12th
1971-72	Division 1	15 April	Drew	0	0	27 November	Lost	0	7	13th	10th
1972-73	Division 1	28 April	Drew	1	1	29 August	Drew	0	0	4th	14th
1973-74	Division 1	27 April	Lost	0	1	12 March	Won	3	0	4th	13th
1974-75	Division 1	1 March	Lost	0	1	31 August	Lost	1	3	3rd	6th
1975-76	Division 1	29 November	Drew	1	1	20 March	Won	2	1	6th	22ndR
1986-87	Division 2	6 December	Drew	2	2	4 May	Drew	0	0	5th	9th
1987-88	Division 2	24 October	Won	1	0	26 March	Lost	1	4	8th	21stR
1989-90	Division 2	13 January	Drew	1	1	26 August	Lost	0	2	9th	2ndP
1992-93	Premiership	26 September	Drew	0	0	16 January	Lost	0	3	16th	14th
1993-94	Premiership	22 February	Won	3	2	28 August	Drew	1	1	19th	20thR
1995-96	Division 1	16 December	Drew	1	1	30 September	Drew	2	2	7th	9th
1996-97	Division 1	18 March	Won	3	1	14 September	Won	3	1	4th	5th
1997-98	Division 1	9 November	Drew	2	2	3 March	Won	1	0	5th	6th
1998-99	Division 1	9 May	Won	4	1	20 December	Won	2	1	3rd	8th
1999-00	Division 1	29 January	Drew	1	1	28 August	Drew	2	2	3rdP	16th
2002-03	Division 1	8 February	Won	3	2	9 November	Drew	0	0	7th	3rd
2003-04	Division 1	22 November	Won	3	0	30 April	Drew	1	1	5th	8th
2004-05	Champ'ship	1 November	Won	5	1	5 February	Won	2	0	3rd	8th

Division One play-offs

Season	League		Home				Away			Final Positions	
1996-97	Semi-Final	14 May	Drew*	2	2	10 May	Drew	1	1	4th	5th

FA Cup

Season	Round									Division	
1973-74	Round 3	5 January	Won	3	2					Div 1	Div 1
1997-98	Round 4	24 January	Drew	1	1	3 February	Lost	0	1	Div 1	Div 1
2002-03	Round 4					25 January	Lost	3	4	Div 1	Div 1

FACT FILE

- Ipswich have not lost in their last 18 league matches, but have, in this period, lost to the Blades twice in the FA Cup and once in the play-offs (albeit on away goals).
- Sheffield United scored once in their first eight visits to Portman Road, and have never scored more than two in a game there.
- Between 1958 and 1993, Ipswich lost 10 times in 15 visits to Bramall Lane.

Summary

	P	W	D	L	F	A
Ipswich's home league record	25	13	9	3	41	19
Ipswich's away league record	25	7	8	10	28	40
Ipswich's cup record	6	1	3	2	10	11
TOTAL	**56**	**21**	**20**	**15**	**79**	**70**

Ipswich's top scorers vs Sheff U
Ray Crawford 7
James Scowcroft 5
Neil Gregory, Darren Bent, Shefki Kuqi 4

Ipswich hat-tricks vs Sheff U
18 March 1997 Neil Gregory

Played for both clubs

Mick Hill	Sheffield U 1966-67 to 1969-70	Ipswich 1969-70 to 1972-73
Les Tibbott	Ipswich 1975-76 to 1978-79	Sheffield U 1978-79 to 1981-82
David Barnes	Ipswich 1982-83 to 1983-84	Sheffield U 1989-90 to 1993-94
Brian Gayle	Ipswich 1989-90 to 1991-92	Sheffield U 1991-92 to 1995-96
Gus Uhlenbeek	Ipswich 1995-96 to 1997-98	Sheffield U 2000-01 to 2001-02
David Johnson	Ipswich 1997-98 to 2000-01	Sheffield U 2004-05
Jonathan Hunt	Ipswich 1998-99	Sheffield U 1998-99 to 1999-00
Manuel Thetis	Ipswich 1998-99 to 1999-00	Sheffield U 2000-01
Marcus Bent	Sheffield U 1999-00 to 2000-01	Ipswich 2001-02 to 2003-04
Georges Santos	Sheffield U 2000-01 to 2001-02	Ipswich 2003-04
Paul Gerrard	Ipswich 2002-03	Sheffield U 2003-04

Shefki Kuqi soars above Sheffield United captain Phil Jagielka. Kuqi signed for Ipswich from United's neighbours Sheffield Wednesday in November 2003 after a successful loan period. In only four appearances for Ipswich against the Blades, Kuqi has already netted four times, two of which came in the 5-1 demolition of their championship rivals at Portman Road in November 2004. Kuqi transferred to the Premiership with Blackburn Rovers in June 2005.

v. Sheffield Wednesday

Season	League	Date (Home)	Result	Ipswich	Shef W	Date (Away)	Result	Ipswich	Shef W	Ipswich	Shef W
			Home				**Away**			**Final Positions**	
1958-59	Division 2	30 August	Lost	0	2	3 January	Lost	1	3	16th	1stP
1961-62	Division 1	9 March	Won	2	1	30 September	Won	4	1	1st	6th
1962-63	Division 1	1 December	Won	2	0	20 April	Won	3	0	17th	6th
1963-64	Division 1	11 January	Lost	1	4	7 September	Lost	1	3	22ndR	6th
1968-69	Division 1	25 April	Won	2	0	7 September	Lost	1	2	12th	15th
1969-70	Division 1	4 October	Won	1	0	31 January	Drew	2	2	18th	22ndR
1984-85	Division 1	13 April	Lost	1	2	22 September	Drew	2	2	17th	8th
1985-86	Division 1	30 November	Won	2	1	3 May	Lost	0	1	20thR	5th
1990-91	Division 2	25 August	Lost	0	2	15 December	Drew	2	2	14th	3rdP
1992-93	Premiership	10 March	Lost	0	1	21 November	Drew	1	1	16th	7th
1993-94	Premiership	6 November	Lost	1	4	23 April	Lost	0	5	19th	7th
1994-95	Premiership	16 October	Lost	1	2	5 May	Lost	1	4	22ndR	13th
2002-03	Division 1	12 October	Won	2	1	15 March	Won	1	0	7th	22ndR

FA Cup										Division	
1984-85	Round 5	4 March	Won	3	2					Div 1	Div 1

League Cup											
1992-93	Q'ter-Final	19 January	Drew	1	1	3 February	Lost	0	1	Prem	Prem

Summary	P	W	D	L	F	A
Ipswich's home league record	13	6	0	7	15	20
Ipswich's away league record	13	3	4	6	19	26
Ipswich's cup record	3	1	1	1	4	4
TOTAL	**29**	**10**	**5**	**14**	**38**	**50**

Steve Sedgeley wins the ball against Sheffield Wednesday in the 2–1 defeat at Portman Road in October 1994. John Wark scored the Ipswich goal that day. It was not a good season for goals as Sedgeley was joint second top-scorer with Wark, with only four strikes, a mere one behind top-scorer Claus Thomsen.

FACT FILE

- There has never been a goalless draw between the sides.
- Prior to their league double over Wednesday in 2002-03, Ipswich had not won in 11 games in the series.

Ipswich's top scorers vs Wednesday
Ray Crawford 9
Ted Phillips, Mich D'Avray 3
Eric Gates, Pablo Counago 2

Ipswich hat-tricks vs Wednesday
20 April 1963 Ray Crawford

Played for both clubs

Ellis Rimmer	Wednesday 1927-28 to 1937-38	Ipswich 1938-39
John Roy	Wednesday 1936-37 to 1937-38	Ipswich 1946-47
Allenby Driver	Wednesday 1937-38 to 1938-39	Ipswich 1949-50 to 1951-52
Derek Jefferson	Ipswich 1967-68 to 1972-73	Wednesday 1976-77
Steve McCall	Ipswich 1979-80 to 1986-87	Wednesday 1987-88 to 1990-91
Ian Cranson	Ipswich 1983-84 to 1987-88	Wednesday 1987-88 to 1988-89
Lee Chapman	Wednesday 1984-85 to 1987-88	Ipswich 1994-95 to 1995-96
Dalian Atkinson	Ipswich 1985-86 to 1988-89	Wednesday 1989-90
Steve Whitton	Wednesday 1988-89 to 1990-91	Ipswich 1990-91 to 1993-94
Chris Bart-Williams	Wednesday 1991-92 to 1994-95	Ipswich 2003-04
Danny Sonner	Ipswich 1996-97 to 1998-99	Wednesday 1998-99 to 1999-00
Jim Magilton	Wednesday 1997-98 to 1998-99	Ipswich 1998-99 to 2004-05
David Johnson	Ipswich 1997-98 to 2000-01	Wednesday 2001-02
Mark Burchill	Ipswich 2000-01	Wednesday 2003-04
Shefki Kuqi	Wednesday 2001-02 to 2003-04	Ipswich 2003-04 to 2004-05

v. Shrewsbury Town

Season	League	Date	Result	Home Ipswich	S'bury	Date	Result	Away Ipswich	S'bury	Final Positions Ipswich	S'bury
1951-52	Division 3S	5 April	Won	1	0	17 November	Won	2	0	17th	20th
1952-53	Division 3S	24 September	Won	2	1	11 April	Drew	2	2	16th	23rd
1953-54	Division 3S	27 March	Drew	0	0	7 November	Drew	1	1	1stP	21st
1955-56	Division 3S	21 September	Won	2	1	28 April	Drew	1	1	3rd	13th
1956-57	Division 3S	26 January	Won	5	1	28 March	Drew	1	1	1stP	9th
1986-87	Division 2	6 September	Won	1	0	3 January	Lost	1	2	5th	18th
1987-88	Division 2	18 December	Won	2	0	22 August	Drew	0	0	8th	18th
1988-89	Division 2	18 March	Won	2	0	20 September	Won	5	1	8th	22ndR

FA Cup										Division	
1966-67	Round 3	28 January	Won	4	1					Div 2	Div 3
1980-81	Round 4	24 January	Drew	0	0	27 January	Won	3	0	Div 1	Div 2
1981-82	Round 5					13 February	Lost	1	2	Div 1	Div 2
1983-84	Round 4					28 January	Lost	0	2	Div 1	Div 2

League Cup											
1990-91	Round 2	9 October	Won	3	0	25 September	Drew	1	1	Div 2	Div 3

Summary	P	W	D	L	F	A
Ipswich's home league record	8	7	1	0	15	3
Ipswich's away league record	8	2	5	1	13	8
Ipswich's cup record	7	3	2	2	12	6
TOTAL	**23**	**12**	**8**	**3**	**40**	**17**

Hartlepool-born defender David Linighan signed for Ipswich in a £300,000 transfer from Shrewsbury Town in June 1988. Linighan became a mainstay in the Ipswich back-line over the next seven seasons, making 324 appearances and scoring 13 goals. From a footballing family, brother Andy scored the winning goal in the FA Cup final for Arsenal against Sheffield Wednesday in 1993, in the last minute of extra-time.

FACT FILE

- Nine wins and two draws constitute a very successful return from Town's home games against Shrewsbury.
- Shrewsbury have only won one of the sides' 16 league encounters.

Ipswich's top scorers vs S'bury
Simon Milton 4
Tom Garneys, Ted Phillips, Jimmy Leadbetter,
    Mich D'Avray 3

Ipswich hat-tricks vs S'bury
26 January 1957 Ted Phillips
20 September 1988 Simon Milton

Played for both clubs

Frank Clarke	Shrewsbury 1961-62 to 1967-68	Ipswich 1969-70 to 1972-73
Ian Atkins	Shrewsbury 1975-76 to 1981-82	Ipswich 1985-86 to 1987-88
David Geddis	Ipswich 1976-77 to 1978-79	Shrewsbury 1986-87 to 1988-89
David Linighan	Shrewsbury 1986-87 to 1987-88	Ipswich 1988-89 to 1995-96
Louie Donowa	Ipswich 1989-90	Shrewsbury 1993-94
Brian Gayle	Ipswich 1989-90 to 1991-92	Shrewsbury 1997-98 to 1998-99
Darren Currie	Shrewsbury 1994-95 to 1997-98	Ipswich 2004-05
Richard Logan	Ipswich 1998-99 to 1999-00	Shrewsbury 2004-05

Season	League	Date	Result	Home Ipswich	So'ton	Date	Result	Away Ipswich	So'ton	Final Positions Ipswich	So'ton
1953-54	Division 3S	7 April	Won	2	1	17 April	Drew	1	1	1stP	6th
1955-56	Division 3S	24 August	Won	4	2	31 August	Drew	2	2	3rd	14th
1956-57	Division 3S	9 March	Won	2	0	1 May	Won	2	0	1stP	4th
1960-61	Division 2	24 September	Drew	3	3	11 February	Drew	1	1	1stP	8th
1964-65	Division 2	19 April	Won	2	0	21 April	Drew	1	1	5th	4th
1965-66	Division 2	18 December	Won	3	0	16 October	Won	2	1	15th	2ndP
1968-69	Division 1	12 April	Drew	0	0	21 September	Drew	2	2	12th	7th
1969-70	Division 1	4 April	Won	2	0	27 August	Lost	2	4	18th	19th
1970-71	Division 1	3 April	Lost	1	3	29 August	Lost	0	1	19th	7th
1971-72	Division 1	18 March	Drew	1	1	21 August	Drew	0	0	13th	19th
1972-73	Division 1	27 January	Drew	2	2	9 September	Won	2	1	4th	13th
1973-74	Division 1	1 February	Won	7	0	15 December	Lost	0	2	4th	20thR
1978-79	Division 1	10 February	Drew	0	0	30 September	Won	2	1	6th	14th
1979-80	Division 1	24 November	Won	3	1	19 April	Won	1	0	3rd	8th
1980-81	Division 1	13 May	Lost	2	3	8 November	Drew	3	3	2nd	6th
1981-82	Division 1	16 February	Won	5	2	3 October	Lost	3	4	2nd	7th
1982-83	Division 1	1 January	Won	2	1	20 November	Won	1	0	9th	12th
1983-84	Division 1	21 February	Lost	0	3	29 October	Lost	2	3	12th	2nd
1984-85	Division 1	1 December	Lost	0	1	4 May	Lost	0	3	17th	5th
1985-86	Division 1	31 August	Drew	1	1	18 January	Lost	0	1	20thR	14th
1992-93	Premiership	7 November	Drew	0	0	13 March	Lost	3	4	16th	18th
1993-94	Premiership	17 August	Won	1	0	8 December	Won	1	0	19th	18th
1994-95	Premiership	25 February	Won	2	1	1 October	Lost	1	3	22ndR	10th
2000-01	Premiership	16 December	Won	3	1	2 April	Won	3	0	5th	10th
2001-02	Premiership	1 March	Lost	1	3	24 October	Drew	3	3	18thR	11th

FA Cup

Season	Round	Date	Result	Ipswich	So'ton	Date	Result	Ipswich	So'ton	Division Ipswich	So'ton
1960-61	Round 3					7 January	Lost	1	7	Div 2	Div 2
1990-91	Round 3					5 January	Lost	2	3	Div 2	Div 1
1999-00	Round 3	13 December	Lost	0	1					Div 1	Prem

League Cup

Season	Round	Date	Result	Ipswich	So'ton					Division Ipswich	So'ton
1967-68	Round 2	12 September	Won	5	2					Div 2	Div 1
1990-91	Round 3	30 October	Lost	0	2					Div 2	Div 1

Summary	P	W	D	L	F	A
Ipswich's home league record	25	13	7	5	49	29
Ipswich's away league record	25	8	8	9	38	41
Ipswich's cup record	5	1	0	4	8	15
TOTAL	**55**	**22**	**15**	**18**	**95**	**85**

FACT FILE

- Town's heaviest-ever FA Cup defeat came at the hands of Southampton, an inexplicable 7-1 defeat in a season that saw them win the Second Division. Southampton came eighth.
- Three matches in Ipswich history have seen one of their players score five goals. The most recent was Alan Brazil's tally in 1982, when Mich D'Avray made four of the goals for him.
- When Ipswich won with a great performance at the Dell on the final day of the season in 1957, they had to wait for the result to come through from Selhurst Park, where Torquay's failure to beat Palace (they drew 1-1) meant promotion for Ipswich.
- Town were unbeaten in their first 14 games in the series.

Ipswich's top scorers vs So'ton
Paul Mariner, Alan Brazil 7
Ray Crawford, John Wark, Marcus Stewart 5
Tommy Parker, Frank Brogan, Bryan Hamilton 4

Ipswich hat-tricks vs So'ton
12 September 1967 Ray Crawford (4) (cup)
16 February 1982 Alan Brazil (5)
2 April 2001 Marcus Stewart

Played for both clubs

Wilf Grant	Southampton 1946-47 to 1949-50	Ipswich 1954-55 to 1956-57
Mick Mills	Ipswich 1965-66 to 1982-83	Southampton 1982-83 to 1984-85
Russell Osman	Ipswich 1977-78 to 1984-85	Southampton 1988-89 to 1991-92
Ian Juryeff	Southampton 1983-84	Ipswich 1988-89
Jim Magilton	Southampton 1993-94 to 1997-98	Ipswich 1998-99 to 2004-05

Marcus Stewart (partially hidden) turns away to celebrate his goal against the Saints as James Beattie, Paul Jones, Wayne Bridge and Jason Dodd look on in despair.

v. Southend United

Season	League	Date	Result	Home Ipswich	Southend	Date	Result	Away Ipswich	Southend	Final Positions Ipswich	Southend
1938-39	Division 3S	27 August	Won	4	2	19 April	Drew	0	0	7th	12th
1946-47	Division 3S	3 May	Won	1	0	12 September	Drew	1	1	6th	8th
1947-48	Division 3S	3 September	Won	4	0	27 August	Lost	2	3	4th	9th
1948-49	Division 3S	18 April	Lost	1	3	15 April	Drew	1	1	7th	18th
1949-50	Division 3S	10 April	Lost	1	3	7 April	Drew	2	2	17th	3rd
1950-51	Division 3S	9 September	Won	1	0	13 January	Lost	0	1	8th	7th
1951-52	Division 3S	18 August	Won	4	1	29 April	Lost	0	5	17th	9th
1952-53	Division 3S	13 September	Drew	0	0	24 January	Lost	0	2	16th	8th
1953-54	Division 3S	19 September	Drew	1	1	6 February	Lost	1	3	1stP	16th
1955-56	Division 3S	7 April	Won	3	0	26 November	Won	3	2	3rd	4th
1956-57	Division 3S	27 April	Drew	3	3	30 March	Lost	0	2	1stP	7th
1991-92	Division 2	7 September	Won	1	0	4 April	Won	2	1	1stP	12th
1995-96	Division 1	22 November	Drew	1	1	20 April	Lost	1	2	7th	14th
1996-97	Division 1	9 November	Drew	1	1	1 February	Drew	0	0	4th	24thR

League Cup									Division		
1987-88	Round 3	27 October	Won	1	0					Div 2	Div 3

Summary	P	W	D	L	F	A
Ipswich's home league record	14	7	5	2	26	15
Ipswich's away league record	14	2	5	7	13	25
Ipswich's cup record	1	1	0	0	1	0
TOTAL	**29**	**10**	**10**	**9**	**40**	**40**

Ipswich struggled against Southend in their 1953-54 promotion winning campaign, losing the away game and only managing a draw at home. Neil Myles (pictured) scored for Town at Portman Road, one of only three goals he scored in the league that season.

- In the summer of 1938, Ipswich narrowly won a ballot to join the Football League for the first time, just two years after turning professional. They replaced Gillingham, and in their first league match they celebrated with a 4-2 win over Southend. Fred Jones scored Town's first league goal. Incidentally, Southend had travelled to Ipswich by boat!

Ipswich's top scorers vs Southend
Tommy Parker 4
Ron Blackman 3

Played for both clubs

Sam McCrory	Ipswich 1949-50 to 1951-52	Southend 1955-56 to 1959-60
Bobby Kellard	Southend 1959-60 to 1962-63	Ipswich 1965-66
Chris Barnard	Southend 1965-66	Ipswich 1966-67 to 1970-71
Trevor Whymark	Ipswich 1969-70 to 1978-79	Southend 1983-84 to 1984-85
Kevin O'Callaghan	Ipswich 1979-80 to 1984-85	Southend 1991-92 to 1992-93
Kevin Steggles	Ipswich 1980-81 to 1985-86	Southend 1983-84
Glenn Pennyfather	Southend 1980-81 to 1987-88	Ipswich 1989-90 to 1992-93
Scott Houghton	Ipswich 1990-91	Southend 1998-99 to 2000-01
Phil Whelan	Ipswich 1991-92 to 1994-95	Southend 2000-01 to 2002-03
Andrew Petterson	Ipswich 1992-93 & 1995-96	Southend 2003-04
Jonathan Hunt	Southend 1993-94 to 1994-95	Ipswich 1998-99
Lee Chapman	Southend 1994-95	Ipswich 1994-95 to 1995-96
David Whyte	Ipswich 1997-98	Southend 1997-98 to 1998-99
Lee Hodges	Ipswich 1998-99	Southend 1998-99

v. Southport

		Home					Away		Division	
FA Cup	Date	Result	Ipswich Southport	Date	Result	Ipswich Southport			Ipswich	Southport
1965-66 Round 3	25 January	Lost	2 3	22 January	Drew	0 0			Div 2	Div 4

Summary	P	W	D	L	F	A
Ipswich's cup record	2	0	1	1	2	3
TOTAL	2	0	1	1	2	3

FACT FILE

● Goals from Baker and Brogan were not enough to prevent a shock defeat.

Played for both clubs

Matt O'Mahoney   Southport 1934-35   Ipswich 1939-40 to 1948-49

Joe Davin played in the 3-2 defeat at Portman Road, watched by 15,459.

v. Spennymoor United

		Home							Division
FA Cup	*Date*	*Result*	Ipswich Spennymoor						Ipswich Spennymoor
1936-37 Round 2	12 December	Lost	1 2						Non L Non L

Summary	P	W	D	L	F	A
Ipswich's cup record	1	0	0	1	1	2
TOTAL	1	0	0	1	1	2

FACT FILE

- This defeat brought an end to a remarkable cup run. Ipswich scored 34 goals (and conceded two) in the first four rounds of qualifying. They then won 2-1 against Cambridge Town in the last round of qualifying and against Watford in the first round proper. This cup run marked Ipswich's first season as a professional club. As such, they competed in the Southern League (at the time, the most prestigious competition in non-league football) for the first time, and won it. Before long, they would be in the Football League.

Jock Carter (pictured) scored the consolation goal for Ipswich in their only fixture against the side from Durham.

v. Stockport County

Season	League	Date	Result	Home Ipswich	Stockport	Date	Result	Away Ipswich	Stockport	Final Positions Ipswich	Stockport
1997-98	Division 1	4 November	Lost	0	2	14 March	Won	1	0	5th	8th
1998-99	Division 1	20 April	Won	1	0	24 October	Won	1	0	3rd	16th
1999-00	Division 1	28 December	Won	1	0	15 April	Won	1	0	3rdP	17th

League Cup

										Division	
1995-96	Round 2	3 October	Lost*	1	2	19 September	Drew	1	1	Div 1	Div 2

Summary	P	W	D	L	F	A
Ipswich's home league record	3	2	0	1	2	2
Ipswich's away league record	3	3	0	0	3	0
Ipswich's cup record	2	0	1	1	2	3
TOTAL	**8**	**5**	**1**	**2**	**7**	**5**

FACT FILE

● **All five of Ipswich's wins have been achieved by a 1-0 scoreline.**

Ipswich's top scorers vs Stockport
David Johnson (II) 2

Played for both clubs

Jack Connor	Ipswich 1946-47	Stockport 1951-52 to 1956-57
Paul Cooper	Ipswich 1973-74 to 1986-87	Stockport 1990-91
Alun Armstrong	Stockport 1994-95 to 1997-98	Ipswich 2000-01 to 2003-04
Tony Dinning	Stockport 1994-95 to 2000-01	Ipswich 2004-05
Shefki Kuqi	Stockport 2000-01 to 2001-02	Ipswich 2003-04 to 2004-05

David Johnson, seen here with Aston Villa's Gareth Southgate, is the only Ipswich player to have scored more than one goal against the Hatters (or simply 'County' to Stockport fans) in the eight matches between the sides.

v. Stoke City

Season	League	Date	Result	Home Ipswich	Stoke C	Date	Result	Away Ipswich	Stoke C	Final Positions Ipswich	Stoke C
1954-55	Division 2	22 September	Lost	0	1	11 April	Lost	0	3	21stR	5th
1957-58	Division 2	8 March	Lost	1	3	26 October	Lost	1	5	8th	11th
1958-59	Division 2	27 September	Lost	0	2	16 February	Lost	0	1	16th	5th
1959-60	Division 2	3 October	Won	4	0	30 March	Won	2	1	11th	17th
1960-61	Division 2	11 March	Won	2	1	22 October	Won	4	2	1stP	18th
1963-64	Division 1	9 November	Lost	0	2	21 March	Lost	1	9	22ndR	17th
1968-69	Division 1	28 September	Won	3	1	5 April	Lost	1	2	12th	19th
1969-70	Division 1	7 March	Drew	1	1	22 November	Drew	3	3	18th	9th
1970-71	Division 1	17 October	Won	2	0	15 August	Drew	0	0	19th	13th
1971-72	Division 1	23 October	Won	2	1	12 February	Drew	3	3	13th	17th
1972-73	Division 1	16 September	Won	2	0	4 April	Lost	0	1	4th	15th
1973-74	Division 1	12 January	Drew	1	1	15 September	Drew	1	1	4th	5th
1974-75	Division 1	24 September	Won	3	1	18 March	Won	2	1	3rd	5th
1975-76	Division 1	13 March	Drew	1	1	11 October	Won	1	0	6th	12th
1976-77	Division 1	26 February	Lost	0	1	18 September	Lost	1	2	3rd	21stR
1979-80	Division 1	1 September	Won	3	1	12 January	Won	1	0	3rd	18th
1980-81	Division 1	31 January	Won	4	0	23 August	Drew	2	2	2nd	11th
1981-82	Division 1	17 April	Won	2	0	21 November	Lost	0	2	2nd	18th
1982-83	Division 1	18 September	Lost	2	3	22 January	Lost	0	1	9th	13th
1983-84	Division 1	10 September	Won	5	0	11 February	Lost	0	1	12th	18th
1984-85	Division 1	6 May	Won	5	1	8 December	Won	2	0	17th	22ndR
1986-87	Division 2	25 October	Won	2	0	25 March	Drew	0	0	5th	8th
1987-88	Division 2	29 August	Won	2	0	1 January	Won	2	1	8th	11th
1988-89	Division 2	21 January	Won	5	1	27 August	Drew	1	1	8th	13th
1989-90	Division 2	30 September	Drew	2	2	6 March	Drew	0	0	9th	24thR
1995-96	Division 1	30 August	Won	4	1	10 February	Lost	1	3	7th	4th
1996-97	Division 1	21 December	Drew	1	1	8 March	Won	1	0	4th	12th
1997-98	Division 1	20 September	Lost	2	3	7 February	Drew	1	1	5th	23rdR
2002-03	Division 1	8 March	Drew	0	0	22 September	Lost	1	2	7th	21st
2003-04	Division 1	18 October	Won	1	0	1 March	Lost	0	2	5th	11th
2004-05	Champ'ship	28 December	Won	1	0	14 September	Lost	2	3	3rd	12th

FA Cup

Season	Round	Date	Result	Ipswich	Stoke C	Date	Result	Ipswich	Stoke C	Division Ipswich	Stoke C
1958-59	Round 4					24 January	Won	1	0	Div 2	Div 2
1963-64	Round 4	25 January	Drew	1	1	29 January	Lost	0	1	Div 1	Div 1
1970-71	Round 5	16 February	Lost	0	1	13 February	Drew	0	0	Div 1	Div 1

League Cup

Season	Round	Date	Result	Ipswich	Stoke C	Date	Result	Ipswich	Stoke C	Division Ipswich	Stoke C
1967-68	Round 3					11 October	Lost	1	2	Div 2	Div 1
1972-73	Round 3	3 October	Lost	1	2					Div 1	Div 1
1974-75	Round 4	12 November	Won	2	1					Div 1	Div 1

- 1963-64, just two seasons after Ipswich's league title success, was a terrible season. They conceded six or more on seven different occasions. Their 9-1 defeat to Stoke came one match after losing 6-0 to Liverpool. By the end of the season, they had conceded 121 league goals. Remarkably, in over 40 years since no other team has conceded more than 100 in the top flight.
- Stoke have won once in their last 12 meetings at Portman Road.

Summary	P	W	D	L	F	A
Ipswich's away league record	31	8	9	14	34	53
Ipswich's cup record	8	2	2	4	6	8
TOTAL	**70**	**28**	**17**	**25**	**103**	**90**

Ipswich's top scorers vs Stoke City
Ray Crawford, John Wark 6
Alan Brazil, Kevin Wilson 5
Dermot Curtis, Colin Viljoen, Eric Gates,
    Paul Mariner 4

Ipswich hat-tricks vs Stoke City
3 October 1959 Dermot Curtis (4)
6 May 1985 Kevin Wilson

Played for both clubs
Brian Siddall	Stoke 1950-51 to 1953-54	Ipswich 1957-58 to 1960-61
Wilf Hall	Stoke 1954-55 to 1959-60	Ipswich 1960-61 to 1962-63
Mick Mills	Ipswich 1965-66 to 1982-83	Stoke 1985-86 to 1987-88
Jimmy Robertson	Ipswich 1969-70 to 1971-72	Stoke 1972-73 to 1976-77
Brian Talbot	Ipswich 1973-74 to 1978-79	Stoke 1986-87 to 1987-88
Keith Bertschin	Ipswich 1975-76 to 1976-77	Stoke 1984-85 to 1986-87
Lee Chapman	Stoke 1979-80 to 1981-82	Ipswich 1994-95 to 1995-96
Ian Cranson	Ipswich 1983-84 to 1987-88	Stoke 1989-90 to 1996-97
Louie Donowa	Stoke 1985-86	Ipswich 1989-90
Nigel Gleghorn	Ipswich 1985-86 to 1987-88	Stoke 1992-93 to 1995-96
Graham Harbey	Ipswich 1987-88 to 1989-90	Stoke 1992-93 to 1993-94
Mark Stein	Stoke 1991-92 to 1993-94 & 1996-97	Ipswich 1997-98
Tony Dinning	Stoke 2001-02	Ipswich 2004-05

Chesterfield-born left-back Graham Harbey started his career as an apprentice at Derby County before signing for Ipswich in July 1987. A solid but not spectacular player, Harbey made 70 (+7) appearances for Ipswich before returning to the Midlands with WBA in 1992. A move across to Staffordshire beckoned when Stoke City were ordered by a tribunal to pay WBA £80,000 for Harbey in 1994, but his time there also proved a little disappointing and the inevitable move into non-league football followed with Gresley Rovers.

v. Stowmarket

FA Cup	Date	Result	Home Ipswich Stowmarket		Division Ipswich Stowmarket
1936-37 1st Qual	3 October	Won	8	0	Non L Non L

Summary	P	W	D	L	F	A
Ipswich's cup record	1	1	0	0	8	0
TOTAL	**1**	**1**	**0**	**0**	**8**	**0**

Ipswich's top scorers vs Stowmarket
Bobby Bruce, Jock Carter 3

Ipswich hat-tricks vs Stowmarket
3 October 1936 Bobby Bruce (cup)
3 October 1936 Jock Carter (cup)

Although it was Jock Carter and Bobby Bruce who claimed the plaudits with their hat-tricks against Stowmarket, it must not be forgotten that George Perrett and Jackie Little (pictured) also scored. Little played a big part in Town's history, being a member of the first-ever team to play in the Football League against Southend in 1938, and the last player from that era to leave the club at the end of the 1949-50 season. Ironically, his next port of call was as manager-coach of Stowmarket.

v. Street

		Home		Division

FA Cup	Date	Result	Ipswich	Street		Ipswich	Street
1938-39 Round 1	26 November	Won	7	0		Div 3S Non L	

Summary	P	W	D	L	F	A
Ipswich's cup record	1	1	0	0	7	0
TOTAL	1	1	0	0	7	0

FACT FILE

- This is Ipswich's biggest ever win in the FA Cup competition proper.
- Street played only one other match in the competition proper, a 5-0 defeat to Cheltenham in 1947.

Ipswich's top scorers vs Street
Fred Chadwick 4
Bryn Davies 2

Ipswich hat-tricks vs Street
26 November 1938 Fred Chadwick (4) (cup)

Legendary manager A. Scott Duncan took charge of Ipswich Town on 12 November 1937, replacing Mick O'Brien. Just over a year later, Town recorded their biggest ever FA Cup win when they hammered Street 7-0 . Apart from Fred Chadwick with four goals and Bryn Davies's brace, Charlie Fletcher also troubled the scorers.

v. Sunderland

Season	League	Date	Result	Home Ipswich	Sunderland	Date	Result	Away Ipswich	Sunderland	Final Positions Ipswich	Sunderland
1958-59	Division 2	7 February	Lost	0	2	20 September	Won	2	0	16th	15th
1959-60	Division 2	19 September	Won	6	1	6 February	Won	1	0	11th	16th
1960-61	Division 2	22 April	Won	4	0	3 December	Lost	0	2	1stP	6th
1968-69	Division 1	4 April	Won	1	0	14 August	Lost	0	3	12th	17th
1969-70	Division 1	21 March	Won	2	0	6 December	Lost	1	2	18th	21stR
1976-77	Division 1	23 November	Won	3	1	19 March	Lost	0	1	3rd	20thR
1980-81	Division 1	28 March	Won	4	1	25 October	Won	2	0	2nd	17th
1981-82	Division 1	29 August	Drew	3	3	7 April	Drew	1	1	2nd	19th
1982-83	Division 1	23 April	Won	4	1	4 December	Won	3	2	9th	16th
1983-84	Division 1	5 May	Won	1	0	3 December	Drew	1	1	12th	13th
1984-85	Division 1	15 December	Lost	0	2	11 May	Won	2	1	17th	21stR
1986-87	Division 2	20 September	Drew	1	1	28 February	Lost	0	1	5th	20thR
1988-89	Division 2	3 September	Won	2	0	25 March	Lost	0	4	8th	11th
1989-90	Division 2	9 December	Drew	1	1	22 August	Won	4	2	9th	6thP
1991-92	Division 2	5 November	Lost	0	1	14 April	Lost	0	3	1stP	18th
1995-96	Division 1	1 September	Won	3	0	20 February	Lost	0	1	7th	1stP
1997-98	Division 1	28 April	Won	2	0	28 February	Drew	2	2	5th	3rd
1998-99	Division 1	29 August	Lost	0	2	17 January	Lost	1	2	3rd	1stP
2000-01	Premiership	26 August	Won	1	0	1 January	Lost	1	4	5th	7th
2001-02	Premiership	29 December	Won	5	0	18 August	Lost	0	1	18thR	17th
2003-04	Division 1	12 April	Won	1	0	30 September	Lost	2	3	5th	3rd
2004-05	Champ'ship	17 April	Drew	2	2	21 November	Lost	0	2	3rd	1stP

FA Cup

Season	Round	Date	Result	Ipswich	Sunderland	Date	Result	Ipswich	Sunderland	Division Ipswich	Sunderland
2000-01	Round 4					27 January	Lost	0	1	Prem	Prem
2003-04	Round 4	24 January	Lost	1	2					Div 1	Div 1

Summary

	P	W	D	L	F	A
Ipswich's home league record	22	14	4	4	46	18
Ipswich's away league record	22	6	3	13	23	38
Ipswich's cup record	2	0	0	2	1	3
TOTAL	46	20	7	19	70	59

Ipswich's top scorers vs Sunderland
Ted Phillips, Dermot Curtis, Eric Gates,
   John Wark, Alex Mathie 4
Paul Mariner, Alan Brazil 3

Ipswich hat-tricks vs Sunderland
19 September 1959 Dermot Curtis
19 September 1959 Ted Phillips
2 September 1995 Alex Mathie

FACT FILE

- Ipswich's 5-0 win over Sunderland in 2001 is their biggest ever Premiership win. It was a rare bright spot in a disappointing season that saw Sunderland narrowly pip Ipswich to avoiding relegation.
- Their 4-0 win over Sunderland in 1961 ensured promotion to top-flight football for the first time. A year later, Ipswich were champions.
- Ipswich have lost eight and drawn one of their last nine visits to Sunderland.
- There has never been a goalless draw between the sides.

Played for both clubs

Pat Curran	Sunderland 1937-38	Ipswich 1938-39
Danny Hegan	Ipswich 1963-64 to 1968-69	Sunderland 1973-74
Rod Belfitt	Ipswich 1971-72 to 1972-73	Sunderland 1973-74 to 1974-75
Eric Gatea	Ipswich 1973-74 to 1984-85	Sunderland 1985-86 to 1989-90
George Burley	Ipswich 1973-74 to 1985-86	Sunderland 1985-86 to 1986-87
Keith Bertschin	Ipswich 1975-76 to 1976-77	Sunderland 1986-87 to 1987-88
Terry Butcher	Ipswich 1977-78 to 1985-86	Sunderland 1992-93
Ian Atkins	Sunderland 1982-83 to 1983-84	Ipswich 1985-86 to 1987-88
Lee Chapman	Sunderland 1983-84	Ipswich 1994-95 to 1995-96
Chris Makin	Sunderland 1997-98 to 2000-01	Ipswich 2000-01 to 2003-04
Marcus Stewart	Ipswich 1999-00 to 2002-03	Sunderland 2002-03 to 2004-05

Marcus Stewart has been a success at every club that he has appeared for. He is seen here challenging Jody Craddock, a future teammate at Sunderland, the club he joined for £1.25 million in August 2002. It was an emotional season for Stewart in 2004-05 as the Black Cats won the Championship to return to the fabled land that is the Premiership, yet he opted to leave the club and return home to try and improve the fortunes of his first-ever team, Bristol City.

v. Swansea City

Season	League	Date	Result	Home Ipswich	Swansea	Date	Result	Away Ipswich	Swansea	Final Positions Ipswich	Swansea
1947-48	Division 3S	3 January	Won	3	2	30 August	Drew	1	1	4th	5th
1948-49	Division 3S	15 January	Won	2	0	4 September	Lost	0	2	7th	1stP
1954-55	Division 2	23 April	Drew	1	1	4 December	Lost	1	6	21stR	10th
1957-58	Division 2	5 October	Lost	0	1	15 February	Drew	0	0	8th	19th
1958-59	Division 2	21 February	Won	3	2	4 October	Lost	2	4	16th	11th
1959-60	Division 2	26 August	Won	4	1	3 September	Lost	1	2	11th	12th
1960-61	Division 2	29 October	Lost	0	3	29 April	Lost	1	2	1stP	7th
1964-65	Division 2	27 February	Won	3	0	17 October	Drew	1	1	5th	22ndR
1981-82	Division 1	7 November	Lost	2	3	27 March	Won	2	1	2nd	6th
1982-83	Division 1	27 November	Won	3	1	30 April	Drew	1	1	9th	21stR

League Cup

Season	Round	Date	Result			Date	Result			Division	
1961-62	Round 2	24 October	Won	3	2	3 October	Drew	3	3	Div 1	Div 2

Summary

	P	W	D	L	F	A
Ipswich's home league record	10	6	1	3	21	14
Ipswich's away league record	10	1	4	5	10	20
Ipswich's cup record	2	1	1	0	6	5
TOTAL	**22**	**8**	**6**	**8**	**37**	**39**

Ipswich's top scorers vs Swansea
Ray Crawford 7
Ted Phillips 6
George Rumbold, Roy Stephenson, Paul Mariner 2

Ipswich hat-tricks vs Swansea
21 February 1959 Ray Crawford
26 August 1959 Ted Phillips

Played for both clubs
Tom Lang	Swansea 1937-38	Ipswich 1946-47
Sam McCrory	Swansea 1946-47 to 1949-50	Ipswich 1949-50 to 1951-52
Jim Feeney	Swansea 1946-47 to 1949-50	Ipswich 1949-50 to 1955-56
Jack Parry	Swansea 1946-47 to 1950-51	Ipswich 1951-52 to 1954-55
Ken Wookey	Swansea 1948-49 to 1949-50	Ipswich 1950-51
Billy Reed	Ipswich 1953-54 to 1957-58	Swansea 1957-58
Robin Turner	Ipswich 1975-76 to 1983-84	Swansea 1984-85 to 1985-86
Andrew Legg	Swansea 1988-89 to 1992-93	Ipswich 1997-98
Lee Chapman	Ipswich 1994-95 to 1995-96	Swansea 1995-96
Richard Appleby	Ipswich 1995-96	Swansea 1996-97 to 2001-02

- **Ipswich have won once in 11 visits to the Vetch Field.**

v. Swindon Town

Season	League	Date	Result			Date	Result			Final Positions	
			Home	Ipswich	Swindon T		**Away**	Ipswich	Swindon T	Ipswich	Swindon T
1938-39	Division 3S	11 March	Won	3	1	5 November	Drew	1	1	7th	9th
1946-47	Division 3S	7 December	Won	3	1	12 April	Lost	1	2	6th	4th
1947-48	Division 3S	8 November	Lost	0	1	27 March	Won	1	0	4th	16th
1948-49	Division 3S	1 April	Won	4	2	6 November	Lost	0	4	7th	4th
1949-50	Division 3S	28 January	Won	3	1	15 April	Won	3	0	17th	14th
1950-51	Division 3S	28 October	Won	4	1	17 March	Lost	0	2	8th	17th
1951-52	Division 3S	27 October	Lost	1	5	15 March	Won	2	1	17th	16th
1952-53	Division 3S	15 April	Drew	1	1	25 April	Lost	0	2	16th	18th
1953-54	Division 3S	24 April	Won	2	0	24 October	Won	2	1	1stP	19th=
1955-56	Division 3S	3 September	Won	6	2	31 December	Won	1	0	3rd	24th
1956-57	Division 3S	19 January	Won	4	1	15 September	Lost	1	3	1stP	23rd
1964-65	Division 2	13 March	Drew	0	0	31 October	Lost	1	3	5th	21stR
1987-88	Division 2	19 September	Won	3	2	28 December	Lost	2	4	8th	12th
1988-89	Division 2	4 March	Lost	1	2	12 November	Won	3	2	8th	6th
1989-90	Division 2	20 March	Won	1	0	14 October	Lost	0	3	9th	4th
1990-91	Division 2	8 December	Drew	1	1	28 August	Lost	0	1	14th	21st
1991-92	Division 2	3 September	Lost	1	4	20 December	Drew	0	0	1stP	8th
1993-94	Premiership	16 April	Drew	1	1	20 November	Drew	2	2	19th	22ndR
1996-97	Division 1	19 November	Won	3	2	12 April	Won	4	0	4th	19th
1997-98	Division 1	1 September	Won	2	1	28 December	Won	2	0	5th	18th
1998-99	Division 1	17 October	Won	1	0	3 April	Won	6	0	3rd	17th
1999-00	Division 1	15 January	Won	3	0	15 August	Won	4	1	3rdP	24thR

FA Cup

										Division	
1947-48	Round 1					29 November	Lost	2	4	Div 3S	Div 3S
1964-65	Round 3					9 January	Won	2	1	Div 2	Div 2
1993-94	Round 3	18 January	Won*	2	1	8 January	Drew	1	1	Prem	Prem

League Cup

										Division	
1985-86	Round 4	26 November	Won	6	1					Div 1	Div 4

FACT FILE

- Ipswich's only League Cup match against Swindon provided their biggest win in the competition to date.
- In April 1999, Ipswich matched their highest away win of all time in the league. Their previous 6-0 success was against Notts County in 1982.
- Ipswich have won the last eight matches between the sides.

Summary	P	W	D	L	F	A
Ipswich's home league record	22	14	4	4	48	29
Ipswich's away league record	22	10	3	9	36	32
Ipswich's cup record	5	3	1	1	13	8
TOTAL	**49**	**27**	**8**	**14**	**97**	**69**

Ipswich's top scorers vs Swindon
Tommy Parker 6
Stan Parker, Sam McCrory 5
Richard Naylor, David Johnson (II) 4

Ipswich hat-tricks vs Swindon
3 September 1955 Tommy Parker

Played for both clubs

Geoff Fox	Ipswich 1946-47	Swindon 1955-56 to 1956-57
Dave Harper	Ipswich 1964-65 to 1966-67	Swindon 1967-68
Bryan Hamilton	Ipswich 1971-72 to 1975-76	Swindon 1978-79 to 1980-81
David Geddis	Ipswich 1976-77 to 1978-79	Swindon 1988-89
David Kerslake	Swindon 1989-90 to 1992-93	Ipswich 1997-98
	& 1996-97 to 1998-99	
John Moncur	Ipswich 1991-92	Swindon 1991-92 to 1993-94
Kevin Horlock	Swindon 1992-93 to 1996-97	Ipswich 2004-05
Robert Howe	Ipswich 1996-97	Swindon 1997-98 to 2001-02

Ipswich Town's biggest home league win against Swindon came on 3 September 1955, as over 13,000 spectators saw Town run out 6-2 winners. The scorers that day were Tommy Parker (3), Tom Garneys, Wilf Grant and Billy Reed (pictured).

Season	League	Date	Result	Home Ipswich	Home Torquay	Date	Result	Away Ipswich	Away Torquay	Final Positions Ipswich	Final Positions Torquay
1938-39	Division 3S	29 October	Won	1	0	4 March	Drew	1	1	7th	19th
1946-47	Division 3S	12 October	Drew	1	1	15 February	Drew	0	0	6th	11th
1947-48	Division 3S	3 April	Won	2	1	15 November	Lost	0	3	4th	18th
1948-49	Division 3S	25 August	Won	5	1	1 September	Drew	1	1	7th	9th
1949-50	Division 3S	22 April	Won	3	1	3 December	Drew	2	2	17th	5th
1950-51	Division 3S	14 October	Won	3	1	3 March	Won	1	0	8th	20th
1951-52	Division 3S	30 January	Won	2	0	3 May	Lost	0	2	17th	11th
1952-53	Division 3S	14 January	Drew	2	2	31 January	Lost	1	4	16th	12th
1953-54	Division 3S	26 August	Won	2	1	1 September	Drew	1	1	1stP	13th
1955-56	Division 3S	20 August	Lost	0	2	17 December	Drew	2	2	3rd	5th
1956-57	Division 3S	15 December	Won	6	0	18 August	Lost	1	4	1stP	2nd

FA Cup

Season	Round	Date	Result	Ipswich	Torquay					Division	
1938-39	Round 2	10 December	Won	4	1					Div 3S	Div 3S
1946-47	Round 1	30 November	Won	2	0					Div 3S	Div 3S

League Cup

Season	Round	Date	Result	Ipswich	Torquay	Date	Result	Ipswich	Torquay	Division	
1997-98	Round 2	16 September	Drew	1	1	23 September	Won	3	0	Div 1	Div 3

Summary

	P	W	D	L	F	A
Ipswich's home league record	11	8	2	1	27	10
Ipswich's away league record	11	1	6	4	10	20
Ipswich's cup record	4	3	1	0	10	2
TOTAL	**26**	**12**	**9**	**5**	**47**	**32**

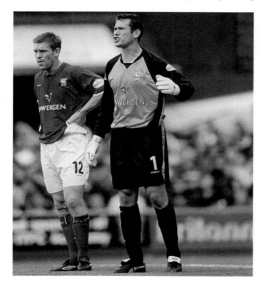

Ipswich's first-choice 'keeper in both seasons following his transfer from Wimbledon in July 2003, Kelvin Davis had a spell on loan at Torquay while learning his trade at Luton Town, the team he joined as a trainee in 1994. Bedford-born Davies made his debut against Reading in the 1-1 draw at Portman Road on 9 August 2003. His final game ended in despair as Town missed out once again in the play-offs, losing to West Ham United in the semi-finals in May 2005. Eager to play at the highest level, Davis followed Tommy Miller to Sunderland in a £1.25 million move in June 2005.

Ipswich's top scorers vs Torquay
Tom Garneys 6
Bill Jennings 5
Jackie Little, Stan Parker 4
Tommy Parker 3

Played for both clubs

Dernot Curtis	Ipswich 1958-59 to 1962-63	Torquay 1966-67
Bobby Kellard	Ipswich 1965-66	Torquay 1975-76
Chris Barnard	Ipswich 1966-67 to 1970-71	Torquay 1970-71 to 1971-72
Steve McCall	Ipswich 1979-80 to 1986-87	Torquay 1996-97 to 1997-98
Simon Milton	Ipswich 1987-88	Torquay 1987-88
Matt Elliott	Torquay 1988-89 to 1991-92	Ipswich 2003-04
Andrew Petterson	Ipswich 1992-93 & 1995-96	Torquay 2000-01
Kelvin Davis	Torquay 1994-95	Ipswich 2003-04 to 2004-05
Neil Gregory	Ipswich 1994-95 to 1997-98	Torquay 1996-97
Richard Logan	Ipswich 1998-99 to 1999-00	Torquay 2001-02

v. Tottenham Hotspur

		Home				Away				Final Positions	
Season	League	Date	Result	Ipswich	Tottenham	Date	Result	Ipswich	Tottenham	Ipswich	Tottenham
1961-62	Division 1	21 October	Won	3	2	14 March	Won	3	1	1st	3rd
1962-63	Division 1	16 March	Lost	2	4	26 December	Lost	0	5	17th	2nd
1963-64	Division 1	23 November	Lost	2	3	4 April	Lost	3	6	22ndR	4th
1968-69	Division 1	26 October	Lost	0	1	18 March	Drew	2	2	12th	6th
1969-70	Division 1	27 December	Won	2	0	30 August	Lost	2	3	18th	11th
1970-71	Division 1	23 March	Lost	1	2	10 April	Lost	0	2	19th	3rd
1971-72	Division 1	3 April	Won	2	1	1 October	Lost	1	2	13th	6th
1972-73	Division 1	1 September	Drew	1	1	20 January	Won	1	0	4th	8th
1973-74	Division 1	6 October	Drew	0	0	23 February	Drew	1	1	4th	11th
1974-75	Division 1	14 December	Won	4	0	17 August	Won	1	0	3rd	19th
1975-76	Division 1	31 January	Lost	1	2	20 August	Drew	1	1	6th	9th
1976-77	Division 1	21 August	Won	3	1	22 January	Lost	0	1	3rd	22ndR
1978-79	Division 1	28 April	Won	2	1	9 December	Lost	0	1	6th	11th
1979-80	Division 1	21 December	Won	3	1	1 April	Won	2	0	3rd	14th
1980-81	Division 1	14 March	Won	3	0	17 December	Lost	3	5	2nd	10th
1981-82	Division 1	17 May	Won	2	1	10 April	Lost	0	1	2nd	4th
1982-83	Division 1	31 August	Lost	1	2	16 April	Lost	1	3	9th	4th
1983-84	Division 1	27 August	Won	3	1	14 January	Lost	0	2	12th	8th
1984-85	Division 1	17 November	Lost	0	3	20 April	Won	3	2	17th	3rd
1985-86	Division 1	24 August	Won	1	0	21 December	Lost	0	2	20thR	10th
1992-93	Premiership	30 August	Drew	1	1	27 January	Won	2	0	16th	8th
1993-94	Premiership	26 September	Drew	2	2	19 March	Drew	1	1	19th	15th
1994-95	Premiership	30 August	Lost	1	3	8 March	Lost	0	3	22ndR	7th
2000-01	Premiership	30 December	Won	3	0	19 August	Lost	1	3	5th	12th
2001-02	Premiership	12 January	Won	2	1	22 December	Won	2	1	18thR	9th

FA Cup										Division	
1964-65	Round 4					30 January	Lost	0	5	Div 2	Div 1
1993-94	Round 4	29 January	Won	3	0					Prem	Prem

FACT FILE

- Ipswich did the double over Spurs in 2001-02 but still got relegated. Their only other double that season was against Derby, who were also relegated.
- Ipswich won five in a row at home (1976-82), while Spurs won four in a row at home (1982-85).
- In 1961-62, Ipswich won the second and first division trophies in consecutive years, replacing Spurs as league champions, and at the same time emulating Spurs' own feat of 1950-51. It has not been achieved since.

Summary

	P	W	D	L	F	A
Ipswich's home league record	25	13	4	8	45	33
Ipswich's away league record	25	7	4	14	30	48
Ipswich's cup record	2	1	0	1	3	5
TOTAL	**52**	**21**	**8**	**23**	**78**	**86**

Ipswich's top scorers vs Tottenham
Eric Gates, Paul Mariner 6
Ted Phillips, Ray Crawford, Colin Viljoen,
   Alan Brazil 4
Gerry Baker, Mick Lambert 3

Ipswich hat-tricks vs Tottenham
4 April 1964 Gerry Baker

Played for both clubs

Aled Owen	Tottenham 1953-54	Ipswich 1958-59 to 1961-62
Jimmy Robertson	Tottenham 1963-64 to 1968-69	Ipswich 1969-70 to 1971-72
Ken Hancock	Ipswich 1964-65 to 1968-69	Tottenham 1969-70 to 1970-71
Alan Brazil	Ipswich 1977-78 to 1982-83	Tottenham 1982-83 to 1983-84
Jason Dozzell	Ipswich 1983-84 to 1992-93}	Tottenham 1993-94 to 1996-97 1997-98
John Moncur	Tottenham 1986-87 to 1990-91	Ipswich 1991-92
Steve Sedgley	Tottenham 1989-90 to 1993-94	Ipswich 1994-95 to 1996-97
Scott Houghton	Ipswich 1990-91	Tottenham 1991-92
Jason Cundy	Tottenham 1991-92 to 1995-96	Ipswich 1996-97 to 1998-99
David Kerslake	Tottenham 1993-94 to 1995-96	Ipswich 1997-98
Mauricio Taricco	Ipswich 1995-96 to 1998-99	Tottenham 1998-99 to 2003-04
Jamie Clapham	Tottenham 1996-97	Ipswich 1997-98 to 2002-03
John Scales	Tottenham 1996-97 to 1999-00	Ipswich 2000-01

Sir Alf Ramsey is lauded as England's all time greatest manager after he led the 1966 team to their only World Cup win. Like Bobby Robson, it is often overlooked that Ramsey was a good player too, winning the league title while with Spurs in 1951 after only one season in the top flight following the second division title the previous year. Ramsey was also capped 32 times for England. Like Robson again though, it is his management that he is best remembered for and he was ultimately rewarded by becoming a knight of the realm in 1967. When Ramsey was appointed Ipswich manager in 1955, Town fans didn't really know what was about to hit them. Within two years they had been promoted as champions from Division Three South. A further four years of solid progress and Ipswich won the Division Two Championship, exactly 10 years after Ramsey's achievement at Spurs as a player. Remarkably, also like Spurs, Ipswich went on to win the First Division title the following year, but unlike Spurs, this was their first-ever attempt at the top honour. Sir Alf Ramsey died in Ipswich at the age of 79 in 1999, a true legend both in Ipswich and across the footballing world.

v. Tranmere Rovers

				Home				Away		Final Positions	
Season	League	Date	Result	Ipswich	Tranmere	Date	Result	Ipswich	Tranmere	Ipswich	Tranmere
1991-92	Division 2	30 November	Won	4	0	21 February	Won	1	0	1stP	14th
1995-96	Division 1	16 March	Lost	1	2	17 April	Lost	2	5	7th	13th
1996-97	Division 1	26 October	Lost	0	2	30 November	Lost	0	3	4th	11th
1997-98	Division 1	11 April	Drew	0	0	6 December	Drew	1	1	5th	14th
1998-99	Division 1	6 March	Won	1	0	29 September	Won	2	0	3rd	15th
1999-00	Division 1	12 November	Drew	0	0	22 March	Won	2	0	3rdP	13th

FA Cup										Division	
1992-93	Round 4					23 January	Won	2	1	Prem	Div 1
1998-99	Round 3					1 January	Won	1	0	Div 1	Div 1

League Cup											
1989-90	Round 2	19 September	Lost	0	1	3 October	Lost	0	1	Div 2	Div 3

Summary	P	W	D	L	F	A
Ipswich's home league record	6	2	2	2	6	4
Ipswich's away league record	6	3	1	2	8	9
Ipswich's cup record	4	2	0	2	3	3
TOTAL	**16**	**7**	**3**	**6**	**17**	**16**

FACT FILE

● **Tranmere have not scored in their last six matches against Ipswich.**

Ipswich's top scorers vs Tranmere
Simon Milton, Ian Marshall, David Johnson (II) 2

Played for both clubs

Ellis Rimmer	Tranmere 1924-25 to 1927-28	Ipswich 1938-39
John Roy	Tranmere 1938-39	Ipswich 1946-47
Bryan Hamilton	Ipswich 1971-72 to 1975-76	Tranmere 1980-81 to 1984-85
John McGreal	Tranmere 1991-92 to 1998-99	Ipswich 1999-00 to 2003-04
Alan Mahon	Tranmere 1996-97 to 1999-00	Ipswich 2003-04
Georges Santos	Tranmere 1998-99 to 1999-00	Ipswich 2003-04

v. Walsall

Season	League	Date	Result	Ipswich	Walsall	Date	Result	Ipswich	Walsall	Ipswich	Walsall
			Home				**Away**			**Final Positions**	
1938-39	Division 3S	29 April	Won	1	0	29 August	Won	1	0	7th	21st
1946-47	Division 3S	25 January	Won	2	1	21 September	Lost	2	4	6th	5th
1947-48	Division 3S	21 February	Won	3	1	4 October	Won	2	1	4th	3rd
1948-49	Division 3S	27 December	Won	3	2	25 December	Lost	1	2	7th	14th
1949-50	Division 3S	12 November	Lost	1	5	1 April	Won	3	1	17th	19th
1950-51	Division 3S	6 January	Won	3	1	27 January	Lost	0	2	8th	15th
1951-52	Division 3S	10 November	Lost	0	1	29 March	Won	3	1	17th	24th
1952-53	Division 3S	4 April	Won	5	0	15 November	Won	3	1	16th	24th
1953-54	Division 3S	31 October	Won	3	0	19 August	Won	2	0	1stP	24th
1955-56	Division 3S	7 September	Won	5	2	15 September	Won	3	1	3rd	20th
1956-57	Division 3S	12 September	Drew	2	2	6 September	Lost	0	2	1stP	15th
1988-89	Division 2	8 November	Won	3	1	14 January	Won	4	2	8th	24thR
1999-00	Division 1	7 May	Won	2	0	23 October	Won	1	0	3rdP	22ndR
2002-03	Division 1	28 December	Won	3	2	10 August	Won	2	0	7th	17th
2003-04	Division 1	16 September	Won	2	1	16 March	Won	3	1	5th	22ndR

FA Cup

										Division	
1946-47	Round 2	18 December	Lost	0	1	14 December	Drew	0	0	Div 3S	Div 3S
1995-96	Round 4	13 February	Won	1	0					Div 1	Div 2

League Cup

1963-64	Round 2	25 September	Drew	0	0	3 October	Lost	0	1	Div 1	Div 3

Summary

	P	W	D	L	F	A
Ipswich's home league record	15	12	1	2	38	19
Ipswich's away league record	15	11	0	4	30	18
Ipswich's cup record	5	1	2	2	1	2
TOTAL	**35**	**24**	**3**	**8**	**69**	**39**

FACT FILE

- The win in October 1953 was Ipswich's eighth league win in a row, a club record.
- Ipswich have won just once in five cup games, but have 23 wins in 30 league games.
- The sides have averaged 3.5 goals per game in the league, but just 0.6 goals per game in the cups.

Ipswich's top scorers vs Walsall
Tommy Parker 6
Albert Day, Tom Garneys 5
Billy Reed, Darren Bent 4

Ipswich hat-tricks vs Walsall
7 September 1955 Billy Reed
16 March 2004 Darren Bent

Played for both clubs

Gilbert Alsop	Walsall 1931-32 to 1935-36 & 1938-39 to 1946-47	Ipswich 1938-39
Allenby Driver	Ipswich 1949-50 to 1951-52	Walsall 1952-53
Thomas Brown	Ipswich 1952-53 to 1955-56	Walsall 1956-57 to 1957-58
Phil Parkes	Walsall 1968-69 to 1969-70	Ipswich 1990-91
Jimmy Robertson	Ipswich 1969-70 to 1971-72	Walsall 1977-78
Keith Bertschin	Ipswich 1975-76 to 1976-77	Walsall 1988-89 to 1989-90
Kevin Wilson	Ipswich 1984-85 to 1986-87	Walsall 1994-95 to 1996-97
Frederick Barber	Walsall 1986-87 to 1990-91	Ipswich 1995-96
Ron Fearon	Ipswich 1987-88 to 1988-89	Walsall 1992-93
Louie Donowa	Ipswich 1989-90	Walsall 1996-97 to 1997-98
Scott Houghton	Ipswich 1990-91	Walsall 1994-95 to 1995-96
Andrew Petterson	Ipswich 1992-93 & 1995-96	Walsall 2003-04
Gus Uhlenbeek	Ipswich 1995-96 to 1997-98	Walsall 2001-02
Danny Sonner	Ipswich 1996-97 to 1998-99	Walsall 2002-03
Samassi Abou	Ipswich 1998-99	Walsall 1999-00
Tony Dinning	Walsall 2003-04	Ipswich 2004-05

Danny Sonner has played for 10 clubs in a varied career since he began as a trainee at home-town club Wigan Athletic in August 1990. Never staying at a club for more than three seasons (in fact Ipswich's 28-month service was his second longest spell at any club), midfielder Sonner was sold to Sheffield Wednesday by George Burley in 1998 for £75,000, his only transfer to involve a fee. Sonner's spell at Walsall lasted a single season, 2002-03, when he made 24 (+4) appearances and scored five goals.

v. Walthamstow Avenue

FA Cup		Date	Result	Home Ipswich	W'stow	Date	Result	Away Ipswich	W'stow	Division Ipswich	W'stow
1953-54	Round 2	12 December	Drew	2	2	16 December	Won	1	0	Div 3S	Non L

Summary	P	W	D	L	F	A
Ipswich's cup record	2	1	1	0	3	2
TOTAL	2	1	1	0	3	2

FACT FILE

- The amateurs from Walthamstow led 2-0 against the leaders of Division Three South, but a comeback, followed by an 86th-minute winner from Alex Crowe in the replay, settled the issue.

Neil Myles and Tom Brown saved Ipswich's blushes with the goals at home in front of 18,403 fans after being 2-0 down at half-time. At Walthamstow, 11,000 home supporters packed in to witness a potential upset, but Alex Crowe's goal, which secured the Ipswich win, just nine days before Christmas, left them wondering what might have been. Pictured here are the goalscorers, from left: Alex Crowe, Tommy Parker (unusually not on the scoresheet), Neil Myles and Tommy Brown.

v. Watford

Season	League	Date	Result	Ipswich	Watford	Date	Result	Ipswich	Watford	Ipswich	Watford
				Home				**Away**		**Final Positions**	
1938-39	Division 3S	25 March	Won	5	1	19 November	Drew	0	0	7th	4th
1946-47	Division 3S	14 September	Won	2	0	18 January	Lost	0	2	6th	16th
1947-48	Division 3S	6 March	Lost	1	3	18 October	Won	3	2	4th	15th
1948-49	Division 3S	25 September	Lost	1	2	19 February	Won	2	1	7th	17th
1949-50	Division 3S	3 September	Drew	1	1	31 December	Lost	0	6	17th	6th
1950-51	Division 3S	26 March	Won	2	1	23 March	Won	2	0	8th	23rd
1951-52	Division 3S	19 April	Won	3	0	1 December	Drew	1	1	17th	21st
1952-53	Division 3S	7 February	Drew	1	1	20 September	Lost	0	1	16th	10th
1953-54	Division 3S	3 October	Won	1	0	3 March	Lost	0	1	1stP	4th
1955-56	Division 3S	5 November	Drew	0	0	17 March	Won	2	0	3rd	21st
1956-57	Division 3S	26 December	Won	4	1	25 December	Lost	1	2	1stP	11th
1982-83	Division 1	7 May	Won	3	1	18 December	Lost	1	2	9th	2nd
1983-84	Division 1	14 March	Drew	0	0	30 August	Drew	2	2	12th	11th
1984-85	Division 1	3 November	Drew	3	3	16 April	Lost	1	3	17th	11th
1985-86	Division 1	1 January	Drew	0	0	29 March	Drew	0	0	20thR	12th
1988-89	Division 2	17 September	Won	3	2	1 April	Lost	2	3	8th	4th
1989-90	Division 2	31 October	Won	1	0	7 April	Drew	3	3	9th	15th
1990-91	Division 2	29 September	Drew	1	1	16 March	Drew	1	1	14th	20th
1991-92	Division 2	17 March	Lost	1	2	7 March	Won	1	0	1stP	10th
1995-96	Division 1	16 September	Won	4	2	24 February	Won	3	2	7th	23rdR
1998-99	Division 1	1 March	Won	3	2	26 September	Lost	0	1	3rd	5thP
2002-03	Division 1	14 February	Won	4	2	17 November	Won	2	0	7th	13th
2003-04	Division 1	20 March	Won	4	1	27 September	Won	2	1	5th	16th
2004-05	Champ'ship	22 February	Lost	1	2	23 October	Drew	2	2	3rd	18th

FA Cup

										Division	
1936-37	Round 1	28 November	Won	2	1					Non L	Div 3S
1956-57	Round 2					8 December	Won	3	1	Div 3S	Div 3S

League Cup

1981-82	Q'ter-Final	18 January	Won	2	1					Div 1	Div 2

Summary	P	W	D	L	F	A
Ipswich's home league record	24	13	7	4	49	28
Ipswich's away league record	24	8	7	9	31	36
Ipswich's cup record	3	3	0	0	7	3
TOTAL	**51**	**24**	**14**	**13**	**87**	**67**

FACT FILE

- Ipswich were unbeaten in 15 home games from 1949 to 1990.
- Ipswich have scored in all but one of their last 18 meetings with the Hornets.

Ipswich's top scorers vs Watford

Ted Phillips, John Wark 5
Tom Garneys 4
Stan Parker, Sam McCrory, John Elsworthy,
  Dean Bowditch 3

Ipswich hat-tricks vs Watford

26 December 1956 Ted Phillips
20 March 2004 Dean Bowditch

Played for both clubs

Pat Curran	Ipswich 1938-39	Watford 1939-40
Albert Day	Ipswich 1946-47 to 1948-49	Watford 1949-50
Billy Baxter	Ipswich 1960-61 to 1970-71	Watford 1971-72
Billy Houghton	Watford 1964-65 to 1965-66	Ipswich 1966-67 to 1968-69
Charlie Woods	Ipswich 1966-67 to 1969-70	Watford 1970-71 to 1971-72
Ron Wigg	Ipswich 1967-68 to 1969-70	Watford 1970-71 to 1972-73
Brian Talbot	Ipswich 1973-74 to 1978-79	Watford 1985-86 to 1986-87
John Stirk	Ipswich 1977-78	Watford 1978-79
David Barnes	Ipswich 1982-83 to 1983-84	Watford 1993-94 to 1995-96
Trevor Putney	Ipswich 1982-83 to 1985-86	Watford 1991-92 to 1992-93
Steve Palmer	Ipswich 1989-90 to 1995-96	Watford 1995-96 to 2000-01
Stuart Slater	Ipswich 1993-94 to 1995-96	Watford 1996-97 to 1997-98
Paolo Vernazza	Ipswich 1998-99	Watford 2000-01 to 2003-04

Steve Sedgeley seems to be providing assistance to Ian Marshall in his attempt to win the ball at home to Watford on 16 September 1995. It was a good day for Ipswich as goals from Gus Uhlenbeek, Claus Thomsen and Neil Gregory (2) secured a 4-2 win. Watford's season never got any better, and by May they were relegated to Division Two.

v. West Bromwich Albion

			Home				Away		Final Positions	
Season	League	Date	Result	Ipswich	WBA	Date	Result	Ipswich	WBA	Ipswich	WBA
---	---	---	---	---	---	---	---	---	---	---	---
1961-62	Division 1	13 January	Won	3	0	1 September	Won	3	1	1st	9th
1962-63	Division 1	20 October	Drew	1	1	9 March	Lost	1	6	17th	14th
1963-64	Division 1	28 September	Lost	1	2	8 February	Lost	1	2	22ndR	10th
1968-69	Division 1	7 December	Won	4	1	23 April	Drew	2	2	12th	10th
1969-70	Division 1	13 December	Lost	0	1	13 September	Drew	2	2	18th	16th
1970-71	Division 1	3 October	Drew	2	2	12 April	Won	1	0	19th	17th
1971-72	Division 1	1 January	Lost	2	3	18 September	Won	2	1	13th	16th
1972-73	Division 1	17 March	Won	2	0	23 December	Lost	0	2	4th	22ndR
1976-77	Division 1	6 November	Won	7	0	16 March	Lost	0	4	3rd	7th
1977-78	Division 1	4 March	Drew	2	2	8 October	Lost	0	1	18th	6th
1978-79	Division 1	11 November	Lost	0	1	19 August	Lost	1	2	6th	3rd
1979-80	Division 1	1 January	Won	4	0	7 April	Drew	0	0	3rd	10th
1980-81	Division 1	1 November	Drew	0	0	4 April	Lost	1	3	2nd	4th
1981-82	Division 1	22 September	Won	1	0	5 May	Won	2	1	2nd	17th
1982-83	Division 1	30 October	Won	6	1	12 March	Lost	1	4	9th	11th
1983-84	Division 1	24 September	Lost	3	4	1 January	Lost	1	2	12th	17th
1984-85	Division 1	20 October	Won	2	0	3 April	Won	2	1	17th	12th
1985-86	Division 1	22 March	Won	1	0	7 September	Won	2	1	20thR	22ndR
1986-87	Division 2	3 March	Won	1	0	13 September	Won	4	3	5th	15th
1987-88	Division 2	4 April	Drew	1	1	14 November	Drew	2	2	8th	20th
1988-89	Division 2	22 April	Won	2	1	1 October	Won	2	1	8th	9th
1989-90	Division 2	4 November	Won	3	1	5 May	Won	3	1	9th	20th
1990-91	Division 2	12 January	Won	1	0	1 September	Won	2	1	14th	23rdR
1995-96	Division 1	3 February	Won	2	1	26 August	Drew	0	0	7th	11th
1996-97	Division 1	25 January	Won	5	0	28 September	Drew	0	0	4th	16th
1997-98	Division 1	30 August	Drew	1	1	27 January	Won	3	2	5th	10th
1998-99	Division 1	31 October	Won	2	0	20 March	Won	1	0	3rd	12th
1999-00	Division 1	18 December	Won	3	1	4 April	Drew	1	1	3rdP	21st
2003-04	Division 1	4 April	Lost	2	3	13 September	Lost	1	4	5th	2ndP

FA Cup

										Division	
1970-71	Round 4	26 January	Won	3	0	23 January	Drew	1	1	Div 1	Div 1
1977-78	Semi-Final	8 April		Highbury			Won	3	1	Div 1	Div 1

League Cup

1969-70	Round 3	24 September	Drew	1	1	1 October	Lost	0	2	Div 1	Div 1

Summary	P	W	D	L	F	A
Ipswich's home league record	29	17	6	6	64	27
Ipswich's away league record	29	12	7	10	41	50
Ipswich's cup record	5	2	2	1	8	5
TOTAL	**63**	**31**	**15**	**17**	**113**	**82**

FACT FILE

- Victory over the Baggies at Highbury in 1978 got Ipswich into their first-ever FA Cup final. It was a comfortable win after Ipswich had scored twice in the opening 20 minutes. A later header from John Wark sealed the win, and Ipswich were now off to Wembley to face Arsenal, the team on whose ground they'd booked their ticket.
- No Town player has scored four in a game since John Wark did so in 1982 in a 6-1 win against West Brom.
- Ipswich's biggest league victory is 7-0, achieved three times, but most recently against West Brom in 1976.
- Between 1984 and 2000, Ipswich were unbeaten in 24 games in the series.

Ipswich's top scorers vs WBA
John Wark 11
Eric Gates 5
Doug Moran, Colin Viljoen, Frank Clarke,
  Trevor Whymark, David Lowe 4

Ipswich hat-tricks vs WBA
6 November 1976 Trevor Whymark (4)
30 October 1982 John Wark (4)
13 September 1986 John Deehan

Played for both clubs

Gilbert Alsop	West Brom 1935-36	Ipswich 1938-39
Ray Crawford	Ipswich 1958-59 to 1963-64 & 1965-66 to 1968-69	West Brom 1964-65 to 1965-66
Danny Hegan	Ipswich 1963-64 to 1968-69	West Brom 1969-70
Ian Collard	West Brom 1964-65 to 1968-69	Ipswich 1969-70 to 1974-75
Brian Talbot	Ipswich 1973-74 to 1978-79	West Brom 1987-88 to 1989-90
John Deehan	West Brom 1979-80 to 1981-82	Ipswich 1986-87 to 1987-88
Kevin Steggles	Ipswich 1980-81 to 1985-86	West Brom 1986-87 to 1987-88
Mark Grew	West Brom 1981-82 to 1982-83 & 1985-86	Ipswich 1984-85
Romeo Zondervan	West Brom 1981-82 to 1983-84	Ipswich 1983-84 to 1991-92
Graham Harbey	Ipswich 1987-88 to 1989-90	West Brom 1989-90 to 1991-92
Georges Santos	West Brom 1999-00	Ipswich 2003-04
Thomas Gaardsoe	Ipswich 2001-02 to 2002-03	West Brom 2003-04 to 2004-05

Neil Rimmer is pictured firing in a shot against WBA, under the close attention of ex-Ipswich player Kevin Steggles on 14 November 1987 at the Hawthorns. It was a mixed day for Rimmer as he scored the first goal to give Ipswich a 1-0 half-time lead, but a fightback from the Baggies resulted in a 2-2 draw. David Lowe was the other Ipswich scorer.

v. West Ham United

			Home				**Away**		*Final Positions*	
Season	*League*	*Date*	*Result*	Ipswich West Ham	*Date*	*Result*	Ipswich West Ham	Ipswich	West Ham
1954-55	Division 2	13 November	Lost	0 3	1 April	Lost	0 4	21stR	8th
1957-58	Division 2	26 December	Won	2 1	25 December	Drew	1 1	8th	1stP
1961-62	Division 1	7 October	Won	4 2	24 February	Drew	2 2	1st	8th
1962-63	Division 1	15 April	Lost	2 3	12 April	Won	3 1	17th	12th
1963-64	Division 1	20 December	Won	3 2	30 August	Drew	2 2	22ndR	14th
1968-69	Division 1	23 November	Drew	2 2	21 March	Won	3 1	12th	8th
1969-70	Division 1	29 November	Won	1 0	14 March	Drew	0 0	18th	17th
1970-71	Division 1	7 November	Won	2 1	20 March	Drew	2 2	19th	20th
1971-72	Division 1	29 January	Won	1 0	23 August	Drew	0 0	13th	14th
1972-73	Division 1	7 October	Drew	1 1	1 March	Won	1 0	4th	6th
1973-74	Division 1	5 February	Lost	1 3	27 August	Drew	3 3	4th	18th
1974-75	Division 1	26 April	Won	4 1	19 October	Lost	0 1	3rd	13th
1975-76	Division 1	19 April	Won	4 0	27 December	Won	2 1	6th	18th
1976-77	Division 1	22 March	Won	4 1	16 October	Won	2 0	3rd	17th
1977-78	Division 1	29 October	Lost	0 2	24 March	Lost	0 3	18th	20thR
1981-82	Division 1	13 April	Won	3 2	1 March	Lost	0 2	2nd	9th
1982-83	Division 1	3 May	Lost	1 2	7 September	Drew	1 1	9th	8th
1983-84	Division 1	3 March	Lost	0 3	5 November	Lost	1 2	12th	9th
1984-85	Division 1	17 May	Lost	0 1	25 August	Drew	0 0	17th	16th
1985-86	Division 1	26 October	Lost	0 1	30 April	Lost	1 2	20thR	3rd
1989-90	Division 2	26 December	Won	1 0	17 April	Lost	0 2	9th	7th
1990-91	Division 2	17 April	Lost	0 1	19 September	Lost	1 3	14th	2ndP
1993-94	Premiership	27 December	Drew	1 1	1 April	Lost	1 2	19th	13th
1994-95	Premiership	17 April	Drew	1 1	26 December	Drew	1 1	22ndR	14th
2000-01	Premiership	14 October	Drew	1 1	17 March	Won	1 0	5th	15th
2001-02	Premiership	28 October	Lost	2 3	30 March	Lost	1 3	18thR	7th
2003-04	Division 1	30 August	Lost	1 2	26 December	Won	2 1	5th	4th
2004-05	Champ'ship	1 January	Lost	0 2	18 September	Drew	1 1	3rd	6thP

Division One play-offs

2003-04	Semi-Final	15 May	Won	1 0	18 May	Lost	0 2	5th	4th
2004-05	Semi-Final	18 May	Lost	0 2	14 May	Drew	2 2	3rd	6thP

FA Cup

									Division	
1949-50	Round 3				7 January	Lost	1 5	Div 3S Div 2	
1974-75	Semi-Final	5 April		Villa Park		Drew	0 0	Div 1 Div 1	
		9 April		Stamford Bridge (replay)		Lost	1 3		
1985-86	Round 4	4 February	Drew*	1 1	25 January	Drew	0 0	Div 1 Div 1	
		6 February	Lost*	0 1 (2nd replay)					

Summary

	P	W	D	L	F	A
Ipswich's home league record	28	11	5	12	42	42
Ipswich's away league record	28	7	11	10	32	41
Ipswich's cup record	9	1	4	4	6	13
TOTAL	**65**	**19**	**20**	**26**	**80**	**96**

FACT FILE

- Following the Hammers' two successive play-off semi-final successes, Ipswich have now lost six out of seven play-off semi-finals. They gained more league points than their opponents in all but one of these seasons.
- Town beat West Ham in late December back in '63. It would have been a good night for Ipswich fans, celebrating their first victory in 22 league games, a club record. The joy did not last long, however, as their next game – against Fulham – went badly wrong.
- The Blues reached their first FA Cup semi-final in 1975, but referee Clive Thomas disallowed two Ipswich goals in the replay and the Hammers won through.
- Ipswich's last Christmas Day fixture ended in a 1-1 draw against West Ham in 1957. Derek Rees scored the Blues' goal.
- Ipswich were unbeaten in 13 games from 1963 to 1973.

Ipswich's top scorers vs West Ham
Ted Phillips 5
Ray Crawford 4
Trevor Whymark, David Johnson (I), Paul Mariner,
  Pablo Counago 3

Ipswich hat-tricks vs West Ham
22 March 1977 Paul Mariner

Played for both clubs

Bobby Johnstone	West Ham 1956-57	Ipswich 1957-58 to 1958-59
Andy Nelson	West Ham 1957-58 to 1958-59	Ipswich 1959-60 to 1964-65
Phil Parkes	West Ham 1978-79 to 1989-90	Ipswich 1990-91
Paul Goddard	West Ham 1980-81 to 1986-87	Ipswich 1990-91 to 1993-94
Steve Whitton	West Ham 1983-84 to 1984-85	Ipswich 1990-91 to 1993-94
Stuart Slater	West Ham 1987-88 to 1991-92	Ipswich 1993-94 to 1995-96
Craig Forrest	Ipswich 1988-89 to 1996-97	West Ham 1997-98 to 2000-01
John Moncur	Ipswich 1991-92	West Ham 1994-95 to 2002-03
Lee Chapman	West Ham 1993-94 to 1994-95	Ipswich 1994-95 to 1995-96
Mauricio Taricco	Ipswich 1995-96 to 1998-99	West Ham 2004-05
David Unsworth	West Ham 1997-98	Ipswich 2004-05
Samassi Abou	West Ham 1997-98 to 1998-99	Ipswich 1998-99
Lee Hodges	West Ham 1997-98 to 1998-99	Ipswich 1998-99
Marlon Harewood	Ipswich 1998-99	West Ham 2003-04 to 2004-05
Kevin Horlock	West Ham 2003-04	Ipswich 2004-05

v. Wigan Athletic

Season	League	Date	Result	Ipswich	Wigan A	Date	Result	Ipswich	Wigan A	Ipswich	Wigan A
				Home				**Away**		*Final Positions*	
2003-04	Division 1	7 February	Lost	1	3	26 August	Lost	0	1	5th	7th
2004-05	Champ'ship	21 December	Won	2	1	5 March	Lost	0	1	3rd	2ndP

League Cup

											Division
1992-93	Round 2	6 October	Won	4	0	22 September	Drew	2	2	Prem	Div 2

Summary

	P	W	D	L	F	A
Ipswich's home league record	2	1	0	1	3	4
Ipswich's away league record	2	0	0	2	0	2
Ipswich's cup record	2	1	1	0	6	2
TOTAL	6	2	1	3	9	8

Ipswich's top scorers vs Wigan
Chris Kiwomya 3
Gavin Johnson 2

Ipswich hat-tricks vs Wigan
6 October 1992 Chris Kiwomya (cup)

Played for both clubs

Mark Grew	Wigan 1978-79	Ipswich 1984-85
David Lowe	Wigan 1982-83 to 1986-87 & 1995-96 to 1998-99	Ipswich 1987-88 to 1991-92
Neil Rimmer	Ipswich 1985-86 to 1987-88	Wigan 1988-89 to 1995-96
Neil Woods	Ipswich 1987-88 to 1989-90	Wigan 1997-98
Gavin Johnson	Ipswich 1988-89 to 1994-95	Wigan 1995-96 to 1997-98
Chris Makin	Wigan 1992-93	Ipswich 2000-01 to 2003-04
Michael Clegg	Ipswich 1999-00	Wigan 1999-00
Gary Croft	Ipswich 1999-00 to 2000-01	Wigan 2001-02
Mark Burchill	Ipswich 2000-01	Wigan 2003-04
Jason De Vos	Wigan 2001-02 to 2003-04	Ipswich 2004-05
Tony Dinning	Wigan 2001-02 to 2003-04	Ipswich 2004-05
Alan Mahon	Ipswich 2003-04	Wigan 2003-04 to 2004-05

Alan Mahon, seen here against Derby's Richard Jackson, played just 8 (+4) games for Ipswich while on loan from Blackburn Rovers in 2003. Mahon later became part of the Wigan team that was involved in the three-way dogfight for the two promotion places back to the Premiership in 2005.

v. Wimbledon

				Home			Away		Final Positions	
Season	League	Date	Result	Ipswich Wimbledon	Date	Result	Ipswich Wimbledon		Ipswich	Wimbledon
1992-93	Premiership	12 September	Won	2 1	18 August	Won	1 0		16th	12th
1993-94	Premiership	22 January	Drew	0 0	25 October	Won	2 0		19th	6th
1994-95	Premiership	16 December	Drew	2 2	23 August	Drew	1 1		22ndR	9th
2002-03	Division 1	26 April	Lost	1 5	6 October	Won	1 0		7th	10th
2003-04	Division 1	20 September	Won	4 1	27 March	Won	2 1		5th	24thR

Summary	P	W	D	L	F	A
Ipswich's home league record	5	2	2	1	9	9
Ipswich's away league record	5	4	1	0	7	2
TOTAL	**10**	**6**	**3**	**1**	**16**	**11**

FACT FILE

● Of all the teams to have played Ipswich 10 or more times, nobody has had less success than Wimbledon, who have of course since relocated to Milton Keynes. The consolation for the Dons was that their one success over Ipswich was a big one.

Ipswich's top scorers vs Wimbledon
Micky Stockwell, Darren Bent 3
Simon Milton 2

Played for both clubs
Brian Gayle	Wimbledon 1984-85 to 1987-88	Ipswich 1989-90 to 1991-92
John Scales	Wimbledon 1987-88 to 1994-95	Ipswich 2000-01
Steve Palmer	Ipswich 1989-90 to 1995-96	MK Dons 2004-05
Jonathan Hunt	Ipswich 1998-99	Wimbledon 2000-01
Hermann Hreidarsson	Wimbledon 1999-00	Ipswich 2000-01 to 2002-03
Kelvin Davis	Wimbledon 2000-01 to 2002-03	Ipswich 2003-04 to 2004-05

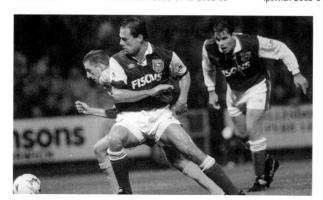

Veteran Steve Palmer, seen pictured against Norwich, became part of the MK Dons set-up in 2004. The move from Wimbledon to Milton Keynes is the first move cross country for a major football club and caused anger among Wimbledon's traditional fan base.

v. Wisbech Town

FA Cup		Home				Away		Division	
	Date	Result	Ipswich	Wisbech	Date	Result	Ipswich	Wisbech	Ipswich Wisbech
1945-46 Round 1	24 November	Won	5	0	17 November	Won	3	0	Div 3S Non L

Summary	P	W	D	L	F	A
Ipswich's cup record	2	2	0	0	8	0
TOTAL	**2**	**2**	**0**	**0**	**8**	**0**

FACT FILE

● **Wisbech and Morecambe are the only teams Ipswich have played twice against without conceding a goal.**

Ipswich's top scorers vs Wisbech
Tommy Parker 3
Jackie Little, George Price 2

Ipswich hat-tricks vs Wisbech
24 November 1945 Tommy Parker (cup)

v. Wolverhampton Wanderers

Season	League	Date	Result	Home Ipswich	Wolves	Date	Result	Away Ipswich	Wolves	Final Positions Ipswich	Wolves
1961-62	Division 1	31 March	Won	3	2	11 November	Lost	0	2	1st	18th
1962-63	Division 1	22 September	Lost	2	3	4 May	Drew	0	0	17th	5th
1963-64	Division 1	14 April	Won	1	0	16 November	Lost	1	2	22ndR	16th
1965-66	Division 2	7 May	Won	5	2	11 December	Lost	1	4	15th	6th
1966-67	Division 2	27 August	Won	3	1	31 December	Drew	0	0	5th	2ndP
1968-69	Division 1	10 August	Won	1	0	1 March	Drew	1	1	12th	16th
1969-70	Division 1	16 September	Drew	1	1	24 January	Lost	0	2	18th	13th
1970-71	Division 1	1 September	Lost	2	3	28 April	Drew	0	0	19th	4th
1971-72	Division 1	6 November	Won	2	1	26 February	Drew	2	2	13th	9th
1972-73	Division 1	21 April	Won	2	1	18 November	Won	1	0	4th	5th
1973-74	Division 1	27 October	Won	2	0	9 March	Lost	1	3	4th	12th
1974-75	Division 1	1 February	Won	2	0	9 November	Lost	1	2	3rd	12th
1975-76	Division 1	17 February	Won	3	0	8 November	Lost	0	1	6th	20thR
1977-78	Division 1	9 May	Lost	1	2	26 November	Drew	0	0	18th	15th
1978-79	Division 1	20 January	Won	3	1	16 September	Won	3	1	6th	18th
1979-80	Division 1	29 December	Won	1	0	25 August	Lost	0	3	3rd	6th
1980-81	Division 1	21 February	Won	3	1	27 September	Won	2	0	2nd	18th
1981-82	Division 1	10 October	Won	1	0	27 February	Lost	1	2	2nd	21stR
1983-84	Division 1	26 December	Won	3	1	21 April	Won	3	0	12th	22ndR
1989-90	Division 2	16 September	Lost	1	3	10 February	Lost	1	2	9th	10th
1990-91	Division 2	1 March	Drew	0	0	1 December	Drew	2	2	14th	12th
1991-92	Division 2	7 April	Won	2	1	23 November	Won	2	1	1stP	11th
1995-96	Division 1	7 October	Lost	1	2	3 December	Drew	2	2	7th	20th
1996-97	Division 1	7 December	Drew	0	0	1 March	Drew	0	0	4th	3rd
1997-98	Division 1	21 March	Won	3	0	15 November	Drew	1	1	5th	9th
1998-99	Division 1	3 November	Won	2	0	28 December	Lost	0	1	3rd	7th
1999-00	Division 1	24 November	Won	1	0	11 March	Lost	1	2	3rdP	7th
2002-03	Division 1	19 February	Lost	2	4	5 March	Drew	1	1	7th	5thP
2004-05	Champ'ship	30 August	Won	2	1	11 April	Lost	0	2	3rd	9th

FA Cup

Season	Round	Date	Result	Ipswich	Wolves	Date	Result	Ipswich	Wolves	Division Ipswich	Wolves
1974-75	Round 3					4 January	Won	2	1	Div 1	Div 1
1975-76	Round 4	24 January	Drew	0	0	27 January	Lost	0	1	Div 1	Div 1
1976-77	Round 4	29 January	Drew	2	2	1 February	Lost	0	1	Div 1	Div 2
1993-94	Round 5	1 March	Lost	1	2	19 February	Drew	1	1	Prem	Div 1

Summary

	P	W	D	L	F	A
Ipswich's home league record	29	20	3	6	55	30
Ipswich's away league record	29	5	11	13	27	39
Ipswich's cup record	7	1	3	3	6	8
TOTAL	**65**	**26**	**17**	**22**	**88**	**77**

- Ipswich won 10 out of 11 home games in the league from 1971 to 1983.
- Ipswich have not won in their first nine, or last eight, visits to Molineux.
- Ipswich have failed to score at home only three times. On each occasion, the match finished 0-0.

Ipswich's top scorers vs Wolves

Colin Viljoen, Paul Mariner, John Wark 5
Ray Crawford, Danny Hegan, Trevor Whymark, Kevin Beattie, James Scowcroft 4

Played for both clubs

Jackie Brown	Wolves 1934-35 to 1936-37	Ipswich 1948-49 to 1950-51
Ray Crawford	Ipswich 1958-59 to 1963-64} & 1965-66 to 1968-69	Wolves 1963-64 to 1964-65
Danny Hegan	Ipswich 1963-64 to 1968-69	Wolves 1970-71 to 1973-74
Derek Jefferson	Ipswich 1967-68 to 1972-73	Wolves 1972-73 to 1975-76
Alan Sunderland	Wolves 1971-72 to 1977-78	Ipswich 1983-84 to 1985-86
David Barnes	Ipswich 1982-83 to 1983-84	Wolves 1984-85 to 1987-88
Steve Sedgley	Ipswich 1994-95 to 1996-97	Wolves 1997-98 to 2000-01
Jermaine Wright	Wolves 1994-95 to 1997-98	Ipswich 1999-00 to 2003-04
Tony Dinning	Wolves 2000-01 to 2001-02	Ipswich 2004-05
Andy Marshall	Ipswich 2001-02 to 2002-03	Wolves 2003-04

Steve Sedgeley is seen here challenging the Wolves 'keeper for the ball, watched by Dean Richards. Sedgeley later transferred to Wolves in 1997.

v. Workington

League Cup		Date	Result	Home Ipswich	W'ton	Date	Result	Away Ipswich	W'ton	Division Ipswich	W'ton
1965-66	Round 3	20 October	Won	3	1	13 October	Drew	1	1	Div 2	Div 3

Summary	P	W	D	L	F	A
Ipswich's cup record	2	1	1	0	4	2
TOTAL	2	1	1	0	4	2

FACT FILE

- A penalty in each leg, converted by John Colrain, helped Town through.

Ipswich's top scorers vs Workington
John Colrain 2

Scottish striker John Colrain (pictured) scored a penalty in each leg. Colrain had only a short spell at Ipswich, making just 61 (+1) appearances in three years before moving to Glentoran in June 1966. The other scorers in the replay on 20 November 1965 were Joe Broadfoot and Frank Brogan.

v. Wrexham

		Home					Away		Division	
FA Cup	Date	Result	Ipswich Wrexham	Date	Result	Ipswich Wrexham		Ipswich	Wrexham	
1994-95 Round 3				7 January	Lost	1	2	Prem	Div 2

Summary	P	W	D	L	F	A
Ipswich's cup record	1	0	0	1	1	2
TOTAL	**1**	**0**	**0**	**1**	**1**	**2**

Played for both clubs

Jackie Williams	Ipswich 1938-39	Wrexham 1938-39 to 1939-40
Francis McGinn	Wrexham 1946-47	Ipswich 1948-49
Aled Owen	Ipswich 1958-59 to 1961-62	Wrexham 1963-64
Steve Stacey	Wrexham 1965-66 to 1968-69	Ipswich 1968-69
Tony Humes	Ipswich 1986-87 to 1991-92	Wrexham 1991-92 to 1997-98
David Lowe	Ipswich 1987-88 to 1991-92	Wrexham 1999-00
Eddie Youds	Wrexham 1989-90	Ipswich 1991-92 to 1994-95

FACT FILE

- Another low point in an infamous season. Such was Ipswich's plight at the time that few people were surprised by this result.

George Burley's reign as manager following Paul Goddard and John Wark's caretaker managership started badly with three defeats in the first four matches. The most embarrassing of these came at the hands of Second Division side Wrexham at the Racecourse Ground in the FA Cup third round. David Linghan (pictured) scored the only Ipswich goal in the 2–1 defeat.

v. Yarmouth Town

FA Cup		Date	Result	Home Ipswich	Yarmouth	Date	Result	Away Ipswich	Yarmouth	Division Ipswich	Yarmouth
1935-36	1st Qual	5 October	Drew	0	0	10 October	Lost	1	4	Non L	Non L

Summary	P	W	D	L	F	A
Ipswich's cup record	2	0	1	1	1	4
TOTAL	2	0	1	1	1	4

FACT FILE

- This was Ipswich's last FA Cup match as an amateur team.

v. Yeovil & Petters United

	Home					Away		Division	
FA Cup	*Date*	*Result*	Ipswich	Yeovil	*Date*	*Result*	Ipswich	Yeovil	Ipswich	Yeovil
1937-38 Round 1					27 November	Lost	1	2	Non L	Non L

Summary	P	W	D	L	F	A
Ipswich's cup record	1	0	0	1	1	2
TOTAL	**1**	**0**	**0**	**1**	**1**	**2**

FACT FILE

- The Somerset team changed their name to Yeovil Town in 1946.

Yeovil & Petters United beat Ipswich 2-1, watched by 6,446 spectators. Len Asthill (pictured) scored Town's goal.

Ipswich in Europe

Ipswich in Europe vs Austrian clubs

Year	Competition	versus	Date	Home Ipswich	Date	Away Ipswich	Aggregate
1978-79	Cup-Winners R/16	Wacker Innsbruck	18 October	Won 1 0	1 November	Drew* 1 1	Won 2 1

Ipswich in Europe vs Belgian clubs

Year	Competition	versus	Date	Home Ipswich	Date	Away Ipswich	Aggregate
1975-76	UEFA Cup R/32	Club Bruges	22 October	Won 3 0	5 November	Lost 0 4	Lost 3 4

Ipswich in Europe vs Czech Republic clubs

Year	Competition	versus	Date	Home Ipswich	Date	Away Ipswich	Aggregate
1980-81	UEFA Cup R/32	Bohemians Prague	22 October	Won 3 0	5 November	Lost 0 2	Won 3 2
2002-03	UEFA Cup R/64	Slovan Liberec	31 October	Won 1 0	14 November	Lost* 0 1	Lost 1 1
							2-4 pens

Ipswich in Europe vs East German clubs

Year	Competition	versus	Date	Home Ipswich	Date	Away Ipswich	Aggregate
1973-74	UEFA Cup QF	Lokomotiv Leipzig	6 March	Won 1 0	20 March	Lost* 0 1	Lost 1 1
							3-4 pens

Ipswich in Europe vs French clubs

Year	Competition	versus	Date	Home Ipswich	Date	Away Ipswich	Aggregate
1980-81	UEFA Cup QF	St Etienne	18 March	Won 3 1	4 March	Won 4 1	Won 7 2

Ipswich in Europe vs West German clubs

Year	Competition	versus	Date	Home Ipswich	Date	Away Ipswich	Aggregate
1980-81	UEFA Cup S F	Cologne	8 April	Won 1 0	22 April	Won 1 0	Won 2 0

Ipswich in Europe vs Greek clubs

Year	Competition	versus	Date	Home Ipswich	Date	Away Ipswich	Aggregate
1980-81	UEFA Cup R1	Aris Salonica	17 September	Won 5 1	1 October	Lost 1 3	Won 6 4

Ipswich in Europe vs Dutch clubs

Year	Competition	versus	Date	Home (Ipswich)	Date	Away (Ipswich)	Aggregate
1973-74	UEFA Cup R/16	Twente Enschede	28 November	Won 1 0	1 December	Won 2 1	Won 3 1
1974-75	UEFA Cup R/64	Twente Enschede	18 September	Drew 2 2	1 October	Drew 1 1	Lost 3 3 away goals
1975-76	UEFA Cup R/64	Feyenoord	1 October	Won 2 0	17 September	Won 2 1	Won 4 1
1978-79	Cup-Winners R/32	AZ67 Alkmaar	27 September	Won 2 0	13 September	Drew 0 0	Won 2 0
1980-81	UEFA Cup Final	AZ67 Alkmaar	6 May	Won 3 0	20 May	Lost 2 4	Won 5 4

Ipswich in Europe vs Italian clubs

Year	Competition	versus	Date	Home (Ipswich)	Date	Away (Ipswich)	Aggregate
1962-63	Euro Cup R/16	AC Milan	28 November	Won 2 1	14 November	Lost 0 3	Lost 2 4
1973-74	UEFA Cup R/32	Lazio	24 October	Won 4 0	7 November	Lost 2 4	Won 6 4
1982-83	UEFA Cup R/64	Roma	29 September	Won 3 1	15 September	Lost 0 3	Lost 3 4
2001-02	UEFA Cup R/32	Inter Milan	22 November	Won 1 0	6 December	Lost 1 4	Lost 2 4

Ipswich in Europe vs Luxembourg clubs

Year	Competition	versus	Date	Home (Ipswich)	Date	Away (Ipswich)	Aggregate
2002-03	UEFA Cup Qual	Avenir Beggen	29 August	Won 8 1	15 August	Won 1 0	Won 9 1

Ipswich in Europe vs Maltese clubs

Year	Competition	versus	Date	Home (Ipswich)	Date	Away (Ipswich)	Aggregate
1962-63	Euro Cup R/32	Floriana	25 September	Won 10 0	28 September	Won 4 1	Won 14 1

Ipswich in Europe vs Norwegian clubs

Year	Competition	versus	Date	Home (Ipswich)	Date	Away (Ipswich)	Aggregate
1979-80	UEFA Cup R/64	Skeid Oslo	3 October	Won 7 0	19 September	Won 3 1	Won 10 1

Ipswich in Europe vs Polish clubs

Year	Competition	versus	Date	Home (Ipswich)	Date	Away (Ipswich)	Aggregate
1980-81	UEFA Cup R/16	Widzew Lodz	26 November	Won 5 0	10 December	Lost 0 1	Won 5 1

Ipswich in Europe vs Russian clubs

Year	Competition	versus	Date	Home (Ipswich)	Date	Away (Ipswich)	Aggregate
2001-02	UEFA Cup R/96	Torpedo Moscow	20 September	Drew 1 1	27 September	Won 2 1	Won 3 2

Ipswich in Europe vs Scottish clubs

				Home			Away		
Year	Competition	versus	Date	Ipswich		Date	Ipswich		Aggregate
1981-82	UEFA Cup R/64	Aberdeen	16 September Drew	1	1	30 September Lost	1	3	Lost 2 4

Ipswich in Europe vs Spanish clubs

				Home			Away		
Year	Competition	versus	Date	Ipswich		Date	Ipswich		Aggregate
1973-74	UEFA Cup R/64	Real Madrid	19 September Won	1	0	3 October Drew	0	0	Won 1 0
1977-78	UEFA Cup R/32	Las Palmas	19 October Won	1	0	1 November Drew	3	3	Won 4 3
1977-78	UEFA Cup R/16	Barcelona	23 November Won	3	0	7 December Lost*	0	3	Lost 3 3
									1-3 pens
1978-79	Cup-Winners QF	Barcelona	7 March Won	2	1	21 March Lost	0	1	Lost 2 2
									away goals

Ipswich in Europe vs Swedish clubs

				Home			Away		
Year	Competition	versus	Date	Ipswich		Date	Ipswich		Aggregate
1977-78	UEFA Cup R/64	Landskrona	28 September Won	5	0	14 September Won	1	0	Won 6 0
2001-02	UEFA Cup R/64	Helsingborgs	18 October Drew	0	0	1 November Won	3	1	Won 3 1

Ipswich in Europe vs Swiss clubs

				Home			Away		
Year	Competition	versus	Date	Ipswich		Date	Ipswich		Aggregate
1979-80	UEFA Cup R/32	Grasshoppers	7 November Drew	1	1	24 October Drew	0	0	Lost 1 1
									away goals

Ipswich in Europe vs Yugoslavian clubs

				Home			Away		
Year	Competition	versus	Date	Ipswich		Date	Ipswich		Aggregate
2002-03	UEFA Cup R/96	FK Sartid	19 September Drew	1	1	3 October Won	1	0	Won 2 1

	P	W	D	L	F	A
TOTAL	62	36	12	14	120	61

(+ three penalty shoot-out defeats)

- European nights at Portman Road in the late 70s and early 80s provided great memories for a generation of Ipswich fans. They qualified for Europe nine times in 10 years from 1973-74 to 1982-83, and to this day have not lost any of their 31 European matches at home.

- Town's first adventure was in the European Cup itself in 1962-63. Having walloped Floriana in the first round, they came up against the mighty AC Milan. Although they trailed 3-0 from the first leg, Town made a great fight of it in the second. They hit the woodwork four times and had a shot cleared off the line before Milan took the lead. Two late goals were never going to be enough, but Ipswich could be content that they'd just won a match against the team that would go on to lift the trophy.

- Ipswich had to wait 10 years for their next crack at Continental opposition. When it came, however, they faced none other than Real Madrid, and beat them. The goal itself was a fortunate own goal, but Town deserved to progress for their willingness to attack against such a negatively minded team.

- They eventually fell in the quarter-finals to Lokomotiv Leipzig on penalties. This started an unbelievable record of bad luck for Ipswich. They have had three ties decided on away goals, and three ties decided on penalties – and Ipswich have lost all six.

- Twice in two years they were eliminated from Europe by Barcelona after winning the first leg. The first of these saw Ipswich triumph 3-0 at Portman Road with one of the best performances in their history. All the good work, sadly, was undone in the second leg.

- Two years earlier, Ipswich had also lost to Bruges, having led 3-0 from the first leg. Only six times have English sides been eliminated from Europe after a three-goal first-leg victory, and yet it happened to Ipswich twice in three years.

- Of course the real highlight of Ipswich's European efforts came in 1981. In the UEFA Cup quarter-finals, they produced an unbelievable 7-2 aggregate victory over a St Etienne team feared throughout Europe, and containing players such as Johnny Rep and Michel Platini. After beating Cologne home and away, they then faced AZ67 Alkmaar in the final. Alkmaar had won the Dutch league three days earlier by beating Feyenoord 5-1, but they were no match for Ipswich, who won 3-0 in the first leg. After scoring an away goal just three minutes into the second leg, Ipswich seemed to have put the tie beyond doubt, as Alkmaar needed five. They nearly got them as well, but a goal from

Jon Wark (partly obscured) scores from the penalty spot against St Etienne on 18 March 1981 in the UEFA Cup quarter-final. Paul Mariner and Terry Butcher scored the other two as Ipswich scored a famous victory against a Michel Platini-inspired side. Ipswich went on to win the trophy after further victories over FC Cologne and AZ67 Alkmaar. John Wark scored in both legs of the final, taking his total to 14 in the competition.

John Wark secured the trophy for Ipswich. It was Wark's 14th goal of the competition, a record that stood until beaten by Jurgen Klinsmann in 1996. The trophy was consolation for having narrowly lost out on the league title earlier in the month.

● After a 19-year absence, Town returned to Europe having finished fifth in the Premiership in 2001. They managed a first-leg win over Inter Milan, but could not recreate the glories of years gone by. The following season, despite having been relegated, they returned by virtue of their fair play record, and, against Avenir Beggen, produced their biggest win in Europe for 40 years.

Action from Ipswich's match against Helsingborg IF in the 2001 UEFA Cup.